CU00746105

POLITICAL IDENTITY AND CONFLICT
IN CENTRAL ANGOLA, 1975–2002

This book examines the internal politics of the war that divided Angola for more than a quarter-century after independence. In contrast to earlier studies, its emphasis is on Angolan people's relationship to the rival political forces that prevented the development of a united nation. Justin Pearce's argument is based on original interviews with farmers and town dwellers, soldiers and politicians in Central Angola. He uses these to examine the ideologies about nation and state that elites deployed in pursuit of hegemony, and traces how people responded to these efforts at politicisation. The material presented here demonstrates the power of the ideas of state and nation in shaping perceptions of self-interest and determining political loyalty. Yet the book also shows how political allegiances could and did change in response to the experience of military force. In so doing, it brings the Angolan case to the centre of debates on conflict in post-colonial Africa.

Justin Pearce is a Leverhulme Early Career Fellow in Politics and International Studies at the University of Cambridge and an associate of St John's College. He has published in journals including *African Affairs* and the *Journal of Southern African Studies*.

AFRICAN STUDIES

The African Studies series, founded in 1968, publishes research monographs by emerging and senior scholars that feature innovative analyses in the fields of history, political science, anthropology, economics and environmental studies. The series also produces mature, paradigm-shifting syntheses that seek to reinterpret and revitalise the scholarly literature in these fields.

Editorial Board

David Anderson, *University of Warwick*
Catherine Boone, *London School of Economics*
Carolyn Brown, *Rutgers University*
Christopher Clapham, *University of Cambridge*
Michael Gomez, *New York University*
Nancy J. Jacobs, *Brown University*
Richard Roberts, *Stanford University*
David Robinson, *Michigan State University*
Leonardo A. Villalón, *University of Florida*

A list of books in this series can be found at the end of this volume.

Political Identity and Conflict in Central Angola, 1975–2002

JUSTIN PEARCE

University of Cambridge

CAMBRIDGE
UNIVERSITY PRESS

CAMBRIDGE
UNIVERSITY PRESS

University Printing House, Cambridge CB2 8BS, United Kingdom

One Liberty Plaza, 20th Floor, New York, NY 10006, USA

477 Williamstown Road, Port Melbourne, VIC 3207, Australia

314-321, 3rd Floor, Plot 3, Splendor Forum, Jasola District Centre, New Delhi - 110025, India

79 Anson Road, #06-04/06, Singapore 079906

Cambridge University Press is part of the University of Cambridge.

It furthers the University's mission by disseminating knowledge in the pursuit of
education, learning and research at the highest international levels of excellence.

www.cambridge.org
Information on this title: www.cambridge.org/9781108468862

© Justin Pearce 2015

This publication is in copyright. Subject to statutory exception
and to the provisions of relevant collective licensing agreements,
no reproduction of any part may take place without the written
permission of Cambridge University Press.

First published 2015
First paperback edition 2018

A catalogue record for this publication is available from the British Library

Library of Congress Cataloging in Publication data
Pearce, Justin, author.
Political identity and conflict in central Angola, 1975–2002 / Justin Pearce.
pages   cm. – (African studies series)
ISBN 978-1-107-07964-9
1. Angola – History – Civil War, 1975–2002.   2. Angola – Politics and government – 1975–
3. Political participation – Angola.   4. União Nacional para a Independência Total de
Angola.   I. Title.   II. Series: African studies series (Cambridge, England)
DT1428.P425   2015
967.304′2–dc23   2015002804

ISBN 978-1-107-07964-9 Hardback
ISBN 978-1-108-46886-2 Paperback

Cambridge University Press has no responsibility for the persistence or
accuracy of URLs for external or third-party internet websites referred to in
this publication, and does not guarantee that any content on such websites is,
or will remain, accurate or appropriate.

For Rafael, Fern and Okidi

Contents

A Note on Anonymous Sources

The past is a politically sensitive subject in Angola. With the exception of my interviews with elite public figures, all interviews quoted in this book were conducted on the understanding of anonymity so as to allow interviewees to speak freely without fear of the possible consequences. I have assigned a single pseudonym to each interviewee so as to indicate to the reader when the same interviewee is quoted more than once.

Acknowledgements

This book is the product of an acquaintanceship with Angola that grew and deepened over the course of a decade. It would not have been possible without a large amount of goodwill from people and munificence from institutions. The bulk of the research was done in the course of my doctoral studies at St Antony's College, University of Oxford, between 2007 and 2011. Oxford Research in the Scholarship and Humanities of Africa (ORISHA) funded my doctoral studies and living expenses, supplemented by an award from the Warden's Bursary Fund at St Antony's. My field research was made possible by grants from St Antony's College and the Norman Chester fund at Oxford. The award of a Postdoctoral Fellowship from the Economic and Social Research Council (grant reference ES/I031456/1), held at the School of Oriental and African Studies (SOAS), University of London, in 2011–2012, made it possible to rework my doctoral research material into the manuscript of this book. In 2011 I was hosted by the National History Center at the annual Seminar on Decolonization in Washington, DC, and the research I did there helped shape Chapter 1. The final stages of editing the book have been completed at the start of my tenure as a Leverhulme Early Career Fellow (research grant number 74978) at the University of Cambridge. While acknowledging how I have benefitted from time spent in three great universities, I also take the opportunity to express my dismay at the policies of the Conservative–Liberal Democrat coalition government in the United Kingdom that have undermined a higher education system built over centuries.

No less important than the funding has been the moral and material support that I have received from many individuals in Angola and elsewhere. Here my first thanks are to Father Daniel Nogueira Chimbulungunjo and the Benedictine Community of Huambo for providing me with a home over many months during my field research. Without their help, this project would never even have started, and it could not have continued without the help of many others. I gratefully acknowledge the accommodation and help offered to me by the Trappist Community of Soke, Father Alberto Sambundo, Father David Sandambongo, Father Nito Tchatalika, Father Nicolau Costa and Archbishop José de Queirós Alves. Also in Huambo, I enjoyed valuable assistance from the staff of Development Workshop and Acção para o Desenvolvimento Rural e Ambiente (ADRA).

My special gratitude goes to the many people I interviewed, some of whom overcame initial misgivings in order to speak to me, and others who were generous with sharing their memories and reflections from the start. I particularly would like to thank General Peregrino Isidro Wambu Chindondo, Marcolino Moco and Penina Paulino for the amount of time they were prepared to spend talking to me, and for helping me to meet others. Mary Daly shared insights born of long experience in Angola and introduced me to other interviewees whose thoughts and recollections formed a great contribution to my research. Paula Cristina Roque also provided valuable contacts and has been a valued sharer of ideas over the years that we have both studied Angola, as has Lara Pawson.

In developing the ideas presented in this book I have benefitted hugely from the advice, intellectual rigour and friendship of my doctoral supervisors, Jocelyn Alexander and Ricardo Soares de Oliveira. My thesis examiners David Anderson and Christopher Cramer, as well as William Beinart and Gavin Williams, have also been valued sources of support and inspiration over the years during which this book has had its gestation. Gerald Bender and an anonymous reviewer made valuable comments on the manuscript and Nakul Krishna's keen editorial eye greatly improved the quality of the final text. I take this opportunity to honour the memory of Terence Ranger, who died as this book was going to press, and whose work on Zimbabwe made me aware of the kind of questions that could and needed to be asked on Angola.

Others who have helped to shape my thinking are too numerous to name, but you know who you are: my colleagues and students at Oxford, SOAS and Cambridge, and the friendly international network of Angola scholars that has developed over the last few years. Many friends and relations in South Africa and in the United Kingdom were a source of support and stability during a few years when research rendered irrelevant the idea of a fixed abode. Again, more than I can mention by name, but particular thanks are due to Lesley and Lucas Cowling, Stephen Garratt, Ryan Meyer, Devon Curtis, Adam Higazi, Richard Naxton, Pauline and Malcolm Pearce, Anthony Philbrick, Ros Taylor and David Turnbull, as well Lorraine Pratt RSCJ, Ana Margarida Santos and the rest of the community at Norham Gardens in Oxford. Finally, special gratitude to Fern Teodoro for her extraordinary generosity and hospitality and to Rafael Marques for his steadfast support over the years since I first arrived in Angola.

Introduction

'I used to be a member of UNITA. But now I'm a member of the government.'
'Why are you a member of the government?'
'Because I am here with the government.'

These words were spoken by a young woman in Mavinga in 2002, a few months after the Angolan government signed a peace accord with the *União Nacional para a Independência Total de Angola* (UNITA), its adversary in a war that had lasted since before independence in 1975. What she said disrupted a lot of what I thought I knew both about Angola and about the politics of civil conflict. A thousand kilometres from Luanda, Mavinga and its surrounds had always had a peculiar relationship with successive attempts to govern Angola. The Mavinga that I saw in 2002 comprised the neatly aligned ruins of brick and concrete buildings that marked out a single broad street through the dust, bordered with the dry stumps of what had once been orange trees. This urban planning was the legacy of a Portuguese administration that had viewed the south-east as '*as terras ao fim do mundo*', the lands at the end of the earth. For UNITA, which had dominated this region throughout the 1980s and 1990s, Mavinga had been part of '*as terras livres de Angola*', the free lands of Angola, despite being a long way from the Central Highlands that are generally regarded as UNITA's political heartland. Even now, the slogan '*Viva o Doutor Savimbi*' remained daubed on the wall of a roofless hospital building. For the ruling party, the *Movimento Popular de Libertação de Angola* (MPLA), Mavinga had been one of the last places where the state established a presence, in 2001, a quarter of a century after the MPLA had officially taken control of an independent Angola. A year later, that state was visible in Mavinga in the figure of a single policeman and a poster of President José Eduardo dos Santos plastered alongside the UNITA graffiti on the shrapnel-spattered hospital wall.

1

Even when the state had planted its flag in Mavinga, the town became no more than an outpost in enemy lands. The UNITA detail had fled ahead of the advancing government forces, taking the civilian population with it. In the ensuing months, the Angolan Armed Forces (FAA) went forth from their new base, rounding up anyone who was living in the bush and who might therefore be suspected of supplying food or labour to UNITA. Among them was the woman who was now telling me her story. She spoke of having spent most of her life with UNITA, whose soldiers had 'caught' her from her home village in Moxico province further north. Then in the last month of the war, the government troops had 'caught' her and brought her to Mavinga. The meaning of her words was more complex, and more puzzling, than her casual tone suggested. We think of a 'member' of a rebel movement as someone who bears arms. Membership of a movement whose reputation, by 2002, was as unpleasant as that of UNITA was hard to attribute to this gently spoken woman who smiled at my naive questions. Even more puzzlingly, to switch one's allegiance between two movements whose mutual enmity had defined twenty-seven years of war was never supposed to sound as effortless and as unproblematic as she suggested. When she described herself as a 'member' of the government, of course, she was not suggesting that she was a member of the executive. What was clear was that she now considered herself in some sense to belong to the government and that this belonging was of the same nature as the sense of belonging that she had previously felt to UNITA. What is more, her sense of being a 'member' of the two movements in succession seemed, in her reckoning, to be consistent with being 'caught' by UNITA many years ago, and 'caught' by the government more recently.

These questions about political and national identities among the people of the Angolan Central Highlands and their relationship to political power are the central concern of this book. The implications of what my interviewee in Mavinga said did not so much challenge existing writings on the Angolan conflict as suggest new directions that had been ignored by scholarly research and by journalism alike. While a reasonable historical literature exists on colonial Angola and the foundations of Angolan nationalism from the 1950s onwards, serious studies of the decades after independence are rare. The themes that writers explored in relation to colonial-era Angola – the agency of rival Angolan elites and the formation of national, sub-national and political identities among the population at large – disappear abruptly from the literature from the moment of Angolan independence.[1] The literature that exists

---

[1]   A welcome recent exception to this silence, though not directly concerned with the conflict in the Central Highlands, is the emerging literature on the previously suppressed subject of the divisions within the MPLA that led to the uprising of 27 May 1977 and

concerning this period is preoccupied with the relationship between Angola and the wider world and has largely overlooked the question of people's participation in the war and their relationship to the dominant political movements, a question that I address in the central chapters of this book.

Many accounts of the conflict after 1975 portray it as the enactment on a southern African stage of the global rivalry between the Cold War superpowers or as a manifestation of apartheid South Africa's efforts to defend white rule. This interpretation is based on the fact of the South African invasion as the Portuguese withdrew from Angola in 1975, the military and technical assistance that Cuba provided to the MPLA state from 1975 onwards, and the renewed South African intervention in support of UNITA in the 1980s alongside military assistance from the Reagan administration in Washington. Wright emphasises US support for UNITA as part of a strategy aimed at blocking Soviet influence in Africa and ultimately at securing global hegemony for a US-led capitalist system.[2] Wright draws conclusions about the MPLA and UNITA on the basis of their international connections but says little about their engagement with Angolan society. Minter's study, emphasising the South African role, is more even-handed. He concludes that although external intervention did not cause the conflict in Angola, it lengthened and deepened it. He notes that while UNITA used both persuasion and force in gathering support, research difficulties had hindered the examination of questions of mobilisation.[3] Cold War involvement in Angola received fresh attention in the early 2000s as newly available materials from both Western- and Eastern-bloc archives stimulated historical research into the impact of the superpower rivalry on state formation and political contestation in developing countries.[4] While this generation of literature provides important information

---

subsequent killing of thousands of government opponents. Dalina Cabrita Mateus and Álvaro Mateus, *Purga em Angola: Nito Alves, Sita Valles, Zé Van Dunem, o 27 de Maio de 1977* (Lisbon, 2007); Lara Pawson, *In the Name of the People: Angola's Forgotten Massacre* (London, 2014).

[2] George Wright, *The Destruction of a Nation: United States' Policy Toward Angola since 1945* (London, 1997).

[3] William Minter, *Apartheid's Contras: An Inquiry into the Roots of War in Angola and Mozambique* (London, 1994), 217.

[4] Piero Gleijeses, *Conflicting Missions: Havana, Washington and Africa 1959–1976* (Chapel Hill NC, 2002); Odd Arne Westad, *The Global Cold War: Third World Interventions and the Making of Our Times* (New York, 2007); Stephen Ellis, *External Mission: The ANC in Exile, 1960–1990* (London, 2012); Jamie Miller, 'Things Fall Apart: South Africa and the Collapse of the Portuguese Empire, 1973–74', *Cold War History* 12.2 (2012), 183–204; Jamie Miller, 'Yes, Minister: Reassessing South Africa's Intervention in the Angolan Civil War, 1975–1976', *Journal of Cold War Studies* 15.3 (2013), 4–33; Piero Gleijeses, *Visions of Freedom: Havana, Washington, Pretoria and the Struggle for Southern Africa 1976–1991* (Chapel Hill, NC, 2013).

about the motivations and strategies both of the superpowers and of smaller international players such as Cuba and South Africa, it is less concerned with political visions and agency in the countries that were on the receiving end of intervention.

Some writers have acknowledged the limitations of focussing on external intervention. Guimarães notes that political cleavages in Angola were formed before the Cold War rivals arrived.[5] Heywood, while mindful of foreign intervention, argues that to see the Cold War as the main driver of conflict in Angola 'misses the more dynamic domestic perspective' (186) and ignores the agency of Angolan actors, notably the choice by UNITA's leader, Jonas Savimbi, to accept American and South African assistance in order to advance an agenda that she sees as having Ovimbundu nationalism at its heart: 'The war became both a civil war between Angolan nationalists and a proxy war between Cold War enemies' (200).[6] Nevertheless, the internal dynamics of the conflict between 1975 and 1991, in particular the question of the relationship between elites and the broader Angolan population, remain relatively neglected by researchers, and this is one of the lacunae that this book sets out to address.

The understanding of the Angolan conflict as a product of the Cold War paralleled the diplomatic orthodoxy of the period. That same orthodoxy was the premise of the Bicesse peace accord in 1991 and the elections of 1992: an arrangement that arose not from any initiative from Angolan society but as a response by political actors outside Angola to a complex series of changes in the international balance of military and political power. By 1993, the Angolan war had resumed in a more destructive form than ever before. In line with a broader turn in the scholarship on warfare after 1990, writers on Angola turned their attention away from political considerations and towards the economic activity that provided the material conditions for conflict, above all, UNITA's domination of diamond mining. Malaquias views this period as confirming UNITA's transformation from a guerrilla movement into a 'criminal insurgency'.[7] This is not to say that accounts of the period reduce the war simply to looting. Le Billon, for example, recognises the need to consider politics as well as the effects of resource endowment in determining the course of

---

[5]   Fernando Andresen Guimarães, *The Origins of the Angolan Civil War: Foreign Intervention and Domestic Political Conflict* (Basingstoke, 2001).

[6]   Linda Heywood, *Contested Power in Angola: 1840s to the Present* (Rochester, NY, 2002). The Ovimbundu are the ethnolinguistic group associated with the Central Highlands.

[7]   Assis Malaquias, *Rebels and Robbers: Violence in Post-Colonial Angola* (Uppsala, 2007). See also Jakkie Cilliers and Christian Dietrich (eds.), *Angola's War Economy: The Role of Oil and Diamonds* (Pretoria, 2000).

the war.[8] Nevertheless, not only did the sudden shift in perspective serve to obscure the longer history of the Angolan conflict, but the 'resource war' paradigm also helped ensure that questions about political mobilisation remained largely absent from research on Angola as the end of the century approached, a fact that was compounded by researchers' difficulties in gaining access to the Angolan interior before the end of the war in 2002. My treatment of the 1990s in this book involves addressing the same questions about political mobilisation in Angola that I raise first with respect to the Cold War period. I also investigate the continuities in ideologies and identities between the two periods, which the existing literature deals with, in essence, as two separate episodes of conflict.

THE ANGOLAN CASE IN CONTEXT

Having sketched the main trends in the existing literature on Angola's recent history, I turn now to developments in the theoretical and comparative literature on conflict that have informed my perspectives on the Angolan war. Any study of late-twentieth-century Angola needs to take into account the burgeoning of conflict studies as a sub-field within a number of social science disciplines since 1990, as scholars sought to explain the persistence of violence in developing countries in the post–Cold War world. Kaldor's influential concept of the 'new war' links an emphasis on the role of commodities in sustaining warfare to forms of supranational and sub-national solidarity that served to weaken the nation state 'from above and from below'.[9] Clapham and Reno, among others, have used the concept of the 'warlord', a military leader who controls territory by force of arms not for political ends but in order to extract tribute from economic activity, typically mining, logging or narcotics.[10] For Clapham, a warlord insurgency 'is directed towards a change of leadership which does not entail the creation of a state any different from that which it seeks to overthrow, and which may involve the creation of a personal territorial fiefdom separate from existing state structures and boundaries'.[11] Reno links the warlord phenomenon to the loss of state security guarantees since the end of the Cold War; he observes how the rulers of weak states privatise security

[8] Philippe le Billon, 'Angola's Political Economy of War: The Role of Oil and Diamonds, 1975–2000', *African Affairs* 100.398 (2001), 55–80.
[9] Mary Kaldor, *New and Old Wars: Organized Violence in a Global Era* (Cambridge, 1998), 5.
[10] Christopher Clapham (ed.), *African Guerrillas* (Oxford, 1998); William Reno, *Warlord Politics and African States* (Boulder, CO, 1998).
[11] Clapham, *African Guerrillas*, 7.

and turn state resources to their own material benefit, to the point where the line between weak state ruler and warlord becomes indistinct.

The link between natural resource endowment and conflict has also become the principal theme in a body of econometrically based research, of which the work of Collier and Hoeffler is best known.[12] The questions addressed by these quantitative studies have been framed in terms of the material conditions that create an incentive for taking up arms and guarantee the viability of a rebel military force. This body of literature views politics as epiphenomenal and sees desire for material gain as the main driver of conflict. Literature within this tradition has nevertheless more recently taken a 'political turn' and analysed independent variables concerning the character of the state and other institutions. This later wave of research still assumes a causal relationship between mineral endowment and conflict but seeks more sophisticated ways of articulating it.[13]

A further body of literature on civil war that emerged after 1990 addresses questions concerning the human motivation for becoming involved in conflict. Much of this literature frames itself explicitly against what it sees as the economic determinism of the quantitative studies of civil war. Sociological and anthropological studies of conflict have looked for forms of social solidarity outside of the state, on the assumption that the state was in retreat. They examine the construction of new identities and loyalties at the sub-national or supra-national level, including, for example, those framed in terms of messianic religious adherence in the case of Uganda or economic marginalisation and globalised youth culture breaking down older patterns of social order in the case of Sierra Leone.[14]

---

[12]   Paul Collier and Anke Hoeffler, 'On Economic Causes of Civil War', *Oxford Economic Papers* 50.4 (1998) 563–573; Paul Collier and Anke Hoeffler, 'Greed and Grievance in Civil War', *The Centre for the Study of African Economies Working Paper Series* (Oxford, 2000); Paul Collier and Anke Hoeffler et al., 'On the Duration of Civil War', *Journal of Peace Research* 41.3 (2004) 253–273.

[13]   Pierre Englebert and James Ron, 'Primary Commodities and War: Congo-Brazzaville's Ambivalent Resource Curse', *Comparative Politics* 37.1 (2004), 61–81; James Ron, 'Paradigm in Distress? Primary Commodities and Civil War', *Journal of Conflict Resolution* 49.4 (2005), 443–450; Jeremy Weinstein, 'Resources and the Information Problem in Rebel Recruitment', *Journal of Conflict Resolution* 49.4 (2005), 443–450; Richard Snyder, 'Does Lootable Wealth Breed Disorder? A Political Economy of Extraction Framework', *Comparative Political Studies* 39.8 (2006), 943–968; Edward Aspinall, 'The Construction of Grievance: Natural Resources and Identity in a Separatist Conflict', *Journal of Conflict Resolution* 51.6 (2007), 950–972.

[14]   On Uganda, Heike Behrend, *Alice Lakwena and the Holy Spirits: War in Northern Uganda 1986–87* (Oxford, 1999); Ruddy Doom and Koen Vlassenroot, 'Kony's Message: A New Koine? The Lord's Resistance Army in Northern Uganda', *African Affairs* 98 (1999), 5–36; on Sierra Leone, Paul Richards, *Fighting for the Rain Forest: War, Youth and Resources in Sierra Leone* (Oxford, 1996); David Keen, *Conflict and Collusion in Sierra Leone* (Oxford, 2005); Krijn Peters, *War and the Crisis of Youth in Sierra Leone* (Cambridge, 2011).

Despite the profound differences in intention and methodology across the range of research on civil war that has been done since 1990, two common shortcomings become apparent when the Angolan case is brought into consideration. I will consider these in turn here in order to demonstrate the changes in perspective that are required by a study of wartime Angola. First among these shortcomings is a tendency to overlook questions of state making and nation building. The concern with the post–Cold War present has confined researchers to a common narrative about the erosion of the state and its associated national identities. Yet at an early stage of my research in Angola, it became clear that the idea of nation building was central to how people understood their affiliation to the MPLA, to UNITA or their lack of affiliation to either movement, from the 1970s until the new century. Ideas about nation building may have been articulated originally by elites associated with one or other political movement but became part of the framework of ideas through which people in towns and villages understood their relationship to a wider Angolan nation. The idea of Angola and their relationship to it, the building of an Angolan nation through processes of elite-led modernisation and their relation to this process were the pivot of how people constructed their own identity. Nationalism (or conflicting nationalisms) was a political tool for elites in making hegemonic the rule of a political movement. The elites' success in doing this was measured in the extent to which preferred ideas about the nation and the position of the political movement in the nation became part of the everyday currency of ideas among a population. Questions about political identity at a sub-national level proved thus to be inseparable from conflicting ideas about nation building. Several years into the twenty-first century, Angolans continued to express their political identity in terms of antagonisms that originated during anti-colonial struggles more than thirty years earlier. A perspective that emphasised state failure and the erosion of national identity would blind us to the fact that both for the MPLA and for UNITA, the conflict was about consolidating an Angolan national identity through a project of state building.

With this in mind, my perspective has been influenced by a turn taken by African historiography since the start of the present century quite separate from the literature that I have already discussed on civil war. I refer here to literature that has revisited African nationalism, finding its source material both in newly opened archives and in interviews with people old enough to remember liberation struggles and decolonisation.[15] After an earlier generation

---

[15] To give a few examples from a wide array of scholarship: Jocelyn Alexander, JoAnn McGregor and Terence Ranger, *Violence and Memory: One Hundred Years in the 'Dark Forests' of*

of nationalist historiography had become tainted as a result of its uncritical stance towards post-independence governments, the newer wave of research has examined currents of nationalist thought and mobilisation that did not contribute to the preferred genealogical narratives of ruling parties and which was consequently neglected or suppressed in earlier accounts. I do not intend to make value judgements about different nationalisms or to explore counter-factuals in which a party other than the MPLA controlled the Angolan state after independence but rather to acknowledge the existence and the political potency of multiple discourses of nationhood irrespective of their relationship to the state.

The second shortcoming that I identify with the post-1990 literature on conflict, whether quantitative or qualitative in method, is a tendency to see state and rebels as two things of a different nature. This is related to the first shortcoming, since 'state' and 'rebels' are defined in terms of the narrative of state decay and state destruction that I have noted. Explanations of civil war are sought through asking questions about the factors (be these economic, ideological or institutional) that facilitate rebel organisation or that weaken the state. Implicit in this is the idea that rule by a state, the unchallenged monopoly of violence in a bounded territory, is a normal condition.[16] Studies of civil war start from the premise that a rebellion is a phenomenon of exception that needs to be accounted for.[17] The inadequacies of such an approach should be evident as soon as the origins of the MPLA and UNITA and the history of people's association with them are taken into account. When UNITA mobilised people, there was no ready-made historic grievance against the MPLA for UNITA to invoke. UNITA's mobilisation efforts began before the MPLA had assumed power in Luanda. Even after the MPLA took control of the Angolan state, most of the people to whom UNITA addressed itself had

---

Matabeleland (Oxford, 2000); Heywood, *Contested Power*; David M. Anderson, '"Yours in Struggle for Majimbo". Nationalism and the Party Politics of Decolonization in Kenya, 1955–64', *Journal of Contemporary History* 40.3 (July 2005), 547–564; Daniel Branch, *Defeating Mau Mau, Creating Kenya: Counterinsurgency, Civil War and Decolonization* (Cambridge, 2009); Timothy Gibbs, *Mandela's Kinsmen: Nationalist Elites and Apartheid's First Bantustan* (Oxford, 2014).

[16] 'While Weber's ideal type of the modern state has become hegemonic in the global system – when political elites speak, virtually everyone appears to assume, particularly after the end of the Cold War, that Weber's kind of state is what the state should be – we have to realize that this ideal type describes political reality nowhere, not even in the developed "West".' Donald L. Donham, 'Staring at Suffering', in Edna Bay and Donald Donham, *States of Violence: Politics, Youth, and Memory in Contemporary Africa* (Charlottesville, NC, 2006), 20–21.

[17] See Roland Marchal and Christine Messiant, 'Une lecture symptomale de quelques théorisations récentes des guerres civiles', *Revue Lusotopie* XIII.2 (2006), 3–46.

never lived under the rule of the MPLA. In short, from the point of view of most of the people who were attached to UNITA, UNITA had been part of the political landscape for at least as long as the MPLA, and UNITA was the norm against which other possibilities would be evaluated; later I will examine how UNITA's own belief in its state-like status would be the cornerstone of the ideology on which it based its claims to legitimacy. Similarly, if we seek to explain the Angolan conflict in terms of a rebellion provoked by the presence of mineral resources, we have still to explain why UNITA was already well established as a political and military force long before the diamond trade became its main source of revenue in the 1990s. To try to account for the Angolan war by asking why UNITA rose up in rebellion against the MPLA, therefore, would involve several questionable assumptions. As Richards has suggested, we may learn more about conflict by concentrating on 'aspects of social process, rather than focusing exclusively on causes'. Richards emphasises the need to 'comprehend the practices of war and peace: how people mobilise and organise for war, and the role played by ideational factors in such mobilisation and organisation'.[18]

ANGOLA AND THE NATURE OF POLITICAL BELONGING

The relationship between people and political movements in the Angolan civil war – the relationship idiosyncratically referred to as 'membership' by the woman in Mavinga – is the central concern of this book. She was not alone in implying that being a 'member' of UNITA and being a 'member' of the government involved essentially the same kind of belonging. Among the people I interviewed who had experienced the control of both UNITA and the Angolan government at different times during the war, many voiced opinions about the relative effectiveness of the MPLA and of UNITA as governing organisations or about the relative conditions of life under the control of one or the other. Yet contrary to the assumption by some scholars of a value-laden categorical distinction between state and rebels, most people in the Central Highlands saw the MPLA and UNITA as two entities of the same nature that had competed for popular allegiance. Neither one was, a priori, more worthy than the other. Some people had experienced UNITA above all as a violent, predatory movement, but others had suffered violence perpetrated by government soldiers or by both armies. At the same time, the positive qualities that typically reinforce the contract between states and citizens were not the

[18] Paul Richards, 'New War: An Ethnographic Approach', in Paul Richards (ed.), *No Peace, No War: An Anthropology of Contemporary Conflict* (Oxford, 1996), 13.

exclusive prerogative of the MPLA state. People in the towns of the Central Highlands had experienced the political control of UNITA for a brief period, followed by a much longer period of control and a more sustained project of state building by the MPLA. Yet for many rural people, UNITA was the only political movement that they encountered for at least fifteen years after independence. The nearest thing to a state that they knew consisted in UNITA's efforts at state building, and their sense of being part of a larger Angolan nation was constituted through ideas of a nation and its history as UNITA wished to see them.

If the categorisation of 'state' and 'rebels' poses one obstruction to understanding the political dynamics of the Angolan conflict, the binary of 'greed' and 'grievance' assumed by Collier and Hoeffler – the notion that conflict can best be explained either as an expression of grievance or as the pursuit of material gain – has created a further false dichotomy that has persisted even among scholars whose approach is more nuanced than Collier and Hoeffler's original treatment.[19] My approach here is that how a war is paid for and the ideologies and politics that shape people's allegiances are two different sets of questions, and my focus is on the latter. Some more recent studies have allowed that political grievance and material gain are both potential drivers of civil conflict but see them as mutually exclusive.[20] Yet the research presented in this book shows that external backing or resource endowment does not necessarily erode ideological commitment. The ideas about national liberation that UNITA used to command loyalty in the last years of colonial rule were no less significant to UNITA's followers after UNITA came to command support from the South African and United States governments and to make profits from international trade.

Other debates have revolved around the agency of people who participate in civil conflict or in whose name the conflict is waged. One debate concerns whether people join or support rebel movements because they recognise a common political interest with the rebels or because they are compelled to do so.[21] Kriger has noted a related debate within scholarship on peasants' participation in civil war, which she sees as being divided between 'voluntarist' accounts that emphasise the agency of participants and 'structuralist'

---

[19]   See the critiques offered by Christopher Cramer, *Civil War Is Not a Stupid Thing: Accounting for Violence in Developing Countries* (London, 2006) and Stathis Kalyvas, 'The Ontology of "Political Violence": Action and Identity in Civil Wars', *Perspectives on Politics* 1.3 (2003), 475–494.

[20]   William Reno, *Warfare in Independent Africa* (Cambridge, 2006).

[21]   Christopher Clapham, 'Introduction: Analysing African Insurgencies', in Christopher Clapham (ed.), *African Guerrillas* (Oxford, 1998), 14.

explanations in which class imperatives leave no room for individual choice.[22] Recent scholarship has begun to move beyond questions of coercion versus choice or, as Mitchell would have it, 'the opposition between a physical and mental form of power'. As Mitchell argues:

> Many forms of exploitation and control cannot be reduced to this binary form. The attempts to make them fit seem to arise from a desire to present certain political groups as self-formed political subjects, meaning subjects who preserve against an essentially physical coercion a space of mental autonomy.[23]

An influential development in conflict studies has been Kalyvas's conclusion that military control of an area has a strong influence on the political identities that people express.[24] An approach of this kind offers a way out of the debates about voluntarism and coercion by allowing the possibility that political identities and even subjective perceptions of self-interest may be profoundly influenced by the political control of a dominant movement.[25] Conflict in this view is less an expression of pre-existing grievances and identity differences than a mechanism that produces grievances and differences.

My concern in this book is to examine the mechanics of this relationship between political or military power and expressions of political identity – how the creation and sustenance of ideas of grievance and identity became politically functional and to what extent people were able to articulate ideas that challenged those of the dominant political movement. Two immediate possibilities suggest themselves. One is that political control is based above all on fear and that people know to say whatever the dominant movement requires them to say. The other is that propaganda has the effect of shaping people's understandings and opinions. There is a danger, however, that seeing either of these hypothetical processes working in a deterministic manner would leave no room for the possibility of political choice. I show here how people's reaction to political education was not uniform but was influenced by factors that included people's occupation, location, experience of events and whether they had previously come into contact with different political ideas. On the other hand, the reality of the Angolan conflict was that for a

---

[22] Norma Kriger, *Zimbabwe's Guerrilla War: Peasant Voices* (Cambridge, 1992), 168.

[23] Timothy Mitchell, 'Everyday Metaphors of Power', *Theory and Society*, 19.5 (October 1990), 545–577. Mitchell's contrasting of 'physical' and 'mental' power echoes Hannah Arendt's distinction between 'violence' and 'power': 'A Special Supplement: Reflections on Violence', *The New York Review of Books* (February 27, 1969).

[24] Stathis Kalyvas, *The Logic of Violence in Civil War* (Cambridge, 2006).

[25] Branch, *Defeating Mau Mau* also shows how the experience of the war had a strong determining influence on people's choices.

great many people, their understanding of politics had been shaped by their exposure to the narratives of only one political movement, and neither movement tolerated the expression of dissent. In understanding the complementary roles of consent and violent force in maintaining domination, I use Gramsci's notion of hegemony: '[t]he "spontaneous" consent given by the great masses of the population to the general direction imposed on social life by the dominant fundamental group'.[26] Even if the idea of hegemony has typically been deployed to understand how states perpetuate their power, close studies of non-state armed groups have shown how they seek to shape public discourse and thereby mould group and individual identities in order to secure legitimacy.[27] UNITA, as much as the MPLA, sought hegemonic control over people in the parts of Angola that it dominated: that is, it sought to make its power legitimate in the eyes of those over whom it ruled. This book's main focus is on the two movements' mutually exclusive projects of securing hegemony and the relationship, on each side, between this political task and the military objective of establishing a monopoly of force.

A large part of my source material comprises interviews, with both political elites and non-elite people, about their understandings of politics and how these had developed over time. Through studying these different accounts by people who were more or less closely involved with the political movements, it became possible to discern the preferred narratives of the MPLA and of UNITA, as well as the ways in which they were understood and interpreted by people who were not actively involved in either movement, but whose views had been influenced by either or by both.[28] Interviews made clear that each side of the conflict was associated with a distinct set of narratives about Angolan history, about the role of the two political movements within this history and the relationship of the movements to the Angolan people. Only a minority of interviewees had ever been in a position to listen to both sides and to make a choice about which best represented their interests. For most, their earliest

---

[26] Antonio Gramsci, *Selections from the Prison Notebooks of Antonio Gramsci* (New York, 1971), 12.

[27] Zachariah Mampilly, *Rebel Rulers: Insurgent Governance and Civilian Life during War* (Ithaca, NY, 2011).

[28] In considering how the meanings and identities constituted in individual Angolans' narratives are constrained by the workings of political power, my thinking is influenced by Bourdieu's notion of habitus, 'the durably installed generative principle of regulated improvisations'. While on the one hand, '[e]ach agent, wittingly or unwittingly, willy nilly, is a producer and reproducer of objective meaning', political power works through imposing limits on this process of production and reproduction: 'the specifically symbolic power to impose the principles of the construction of reality – in particular, social reality – is a major dimension of political power'. Pierre Bourdieu, *Outline of a Theory of Practice* (Cambridge, 1977), 78–79, 165.

consciousness of politics – indeed, their earliest awareness of themselves as being part of a wider nation – was constituted within the narratives of one or other political movement. People who lived in the government-controlled towns for the most part believed that the MPLA's army, FAPLA, was defending their security. People in the parts of the countryside controlled by UNITA believed that UNITA was defending them against government forces that were a threat to their security. Such views were the consequence of the efforts at political education conducted by both political movements, but this did not make them any less deeply felt. Partisan views about politics had taken on the status of common sense in the parties' respective areas of control: in Bourdieu's terms, part of the habitus 'produced and reproduced' by individual actors but constrained by the dominant power.

IMAGINING THE STATE

Central to the narratives propagated by the movements and accepted to a greater or lesser degree by people on both sides was the idea of national liberation. UNITA and the MPLA both originated as anti-colonial movements, and echoes of anti-colonialism remained in the ideologies of both sides for decades after the Portuguese had left. With the real coloniser gone, the anti-colonial movements turned anti-colonialism against each other. To the MPLA, UNITA was the puppet of apartheid South Africa and the imperialist West. To UNITA, the MPLA was led by the mixed-race offspring of the erstwhile colonisers and had become the tool of godless Cuban invaders. More obviously ideological appeals were present as well: the MPLA's ideas of socialist internationalism and UNITA's eclectic invocation of African tradition, Maoist peasant revolution, Christianity, conservative anticommunism and liberal democracy. But the idea of the political movement as the defender of the nation against an alien enemy was the dominant strand in the ideologies of legitimacy on both sides.

Words alone, however, were not enough for either movement to assert its authority. On both sides, narratives were intertwined with practices. When people spoke about the worth either of the MPLA or of UNITA, they did not recite theoretical tracts; they recounted things that one or the other organisation had done, and it was in their interpretation of events and of practices that the ideology of the parties could be discerned. What was remarkable in this was the similarity between the ideologies that defined the self-image of each party and the attitude of each towards the opposite party. To both, the idea of the state was central. UNITA followers would talk about UNITA as a state. Even when no explicit reference was made to the state, the performance of the functions of statehood was invoked by UNITA adherents as much as by MPLA adherents as a reason for the superiority of their movement. The state-like functions of which people spoke were both developmental and defensive. On both sides, people who had been most active as politicians, cadres or military officers were the ones who presented the most enthusiastic and most ideologically coherent picture of their movement's undertakings. Civil servants and party activists who had been in the MPLA during the war years spoke of a modernising programme of state building that involved schools and hospitals. UNITA cadres and officers recalled fondly the systems of social care that they claimed to have established and maintained at UNITA's bases in the bush and at its showcase headquarters, Jamba. MPLA devotees saw their party both as the only true liberator of Angola from colonial oppression and as the guardian of the Angolan nation against an imperialist onslaught of which UNITA was the local instrument. Equally, for UNITA's followers, their movement drew credibility from its opposition to the Portuguese colonial regime in the past and in defending an authentic, black African and Christian Angola that was under assault from an atheist Creole-dominated state in Luanda that was also the tool of Soviet imperialism.

This logic of state building, which dominated elite accounts of the politics of the war, was discernible to lesser degrees in the recollections of people who had not been actively involved in the work of the MPLA or of UNITA but who had come into contact with it and received some benefit from it. Still others who had a yet more distant relationship with either movement, living within its domain without ever receiving any active benefit from it, spoke of that movement above all as a provider or guarantor of security. This role as security guarantor was the minimal condition for hegemonic acceptance. For both movements, defining security was an ideological task, coterminous with the political task of making violence legitimate. Making violence legitimate depended in turn upon the movement's ability to convince people that it was bearing arms in the defence of a community. As Tilly has it, the ideological work of mobilising people for conflict is a process of hardening group boundaries, of creating perceptions of 'us' and 'them' that serve both to cement the identity of 'us' and to engender fear of 'them'.[29] In Angola, the community of 'us' was defined within the discourse of each movement as the Angolan nation. The construction of an ideology that equated the interests of the movement with those of the nation in turn required the propagation of ideas about the alien, anti-Angolan character of the enemy. The politics of the conflict

---

[29] Charles Tilly, *The Politics of Collective Violence* (Cambridge, 2003), 75.

became constitutive of two different and mutually exclusive versions of the Angolan nation.

THE PROBLEM OF IDENTITY

The MPLA and UNITA, then, each achieved at least a degree of hegemonic control over the people in the territory that they dominated by spreading the idea that they were acting for the common good. The extent to which their control was hegemonic is difficult to determine precisely, a difficulty that arises from the problems inherent in conducting oral research in political circumstances that have changed in the years that have passed since the events in question. Those people who had lived under the control of different political movements at different times knew that their own survival depended on expressing loyalty to whichever movement was in power at the time. As Branch has noted with respect to many rural Kenyans during the conflict of the 1950s, they 'dealt in the currency of survival rather than ideology'.[30] For the woman in Mavinga quoted at the beginning of this chapter, political identity appeared to be defined above all in terms of the political movement that ruled over the territory where she happened to be at a particular time. Her account of her changing political identity was not couched in terms of changing beliefs; the labels that she attached to herself were rather an expression of who was in charge. In this respect, her characterisation was not unusual. Peasant farmers, and more particularly those farmers who had suffered violence from both armies at different times, commonly recalled having cooperated with whichever was dominant in order to ensure they were not punished.

The question of political identity was further complicated by the fact that military and civilian officials on both sides habitually assigned identity to people simply on the basis of where the people were. Throughout the 1980s, when the state was confined to the coast and to isolated urban outposts in the interior, soldiers would regard anyone living beyond the security perimeter of the towns as '*povo da UNITA*': UNITA people. UNITA, similarly, was suspicious of anyone who had lived under the control of the government and saw such people as potentially treacherous '*povo do governo*' or '*povo do MPLA*': government or MPLA people. This top-down assignation of political identity went together with a strategy, used by both armies, of forcibly relocating people. UNITA, at least in its guerrilla incarnation in the Central Highlands in the 1980s, depended on the support of the farming population. The MPLA state's response to this was counterinsurgency based on the

---

[30] Branch, *Defeating Mau Mau*, 14.

evacuation of the countryside, a strategy that had already been practised by the Portuguese state against the liberation movements in the 1960s and early 1970s. The post-independence MPLA government did not have the military capacity to depopulate the countryside completely. Instead, the strategy was to evacuate people from the bush within a certain radius around each town. UNITA's response was also to force people to move so that they would remain beyond the reach of government soldiers.

Yet while some people accepted the labels of *'povo da UNITA'* or *'povo do governo'*, political identity was not always a crude function of political control. On the one hand, people could secretly maintain allegiances to a political movement other than the one that was in control where they lived: the clearest example of this is the existence of clandestine groups of UNITA supporters who lived in government-controlled towns and provided information and goods to UNITA and sometimes plotted violence. On the other hand, political education was often, if not always, effective. This meant that while many people's political identities did indeed change as the consequence of living under the control of a particular movement, this was more than just a calculated strategy to avoid punishment; it involved a real shifting of belief in favour of the movement that was in charge at the time. For those interviewees whose earliest contact with a political movement had been with UNITA, their views about the character and history of the Angolan nation and their own place within it had been conditioned by UNITA's version of events in the absence of alternative perspectives. As later chapters will illustrate, some people who had spent most of their lives under the control of UNITA and later found themselves under government control changed their minds about UNITA as a result of hearing and eventually internalising the government narratives about the war. Crucially, however, this process seems to have been reinforced by their experience of events. Disillusionment with the hardships of life in UNITA-controlled areas, the realisation that the government was not necessarily as hostile to their interests as UNITA's ideologues had led them to believe, and the experience of life in a government-controlled town as better than life in the bush with UNITA, in many cases trumped whatever ideological claims had previously bound people to UNITA. The nature of political identity was not the same in all cases, and what was said did not always correspond with what was felt. For one person, talking about being 'a UNITA person' or 'a government person' could signal the acceptance of an ideology, but for another person it might simply be said in necessary homage to the fact that UNITA or the government was in control of the area where the person lived. Such ambiguity was politically useful: it allowed elites on both sides to claim as willing and voluntary supporters those whose relationship with the movement was in fact the consequence of circumstance rather than of choice.

SOURCES AND METHOD

The slippery question of what it meant to be 'a UNITA person' or 'a government person' presented particular challenges when it came to researching questions of political loyalty and identity and how they changed over the course of the war. Written sources on the conflict are few and are the work of political elites or of non-Angolans. Of necessity, this study relies on interviews conducted several years after the end of the war. Such a method is nevertheless appropriate for the book's central concerns, which are political legitimation and the relationship between political movements and people. These questions are constituted in discourse, and talking to people about how their relationship to politics had been shaped was therefore an apt way in which to study them. Much of the qualitative research on internal conflict in post-colonial Africa has used a similar method, although a large part of this literature has drawn additionally on written sources to a greater extent than was possible in the Angolan case.

The question was complicated further by the fact that most of my research was conducted in 2008 and 2009, at a time when the government and the MPLA were taking steps to consolidate the FAA's 2002 military victory by tightening their political control over parts of the country that had once been under the influence of UNITA. Research was most difficult in rural villages, where chiefs had been incorporated into an administrative system that was indistinguishable from the local MPLA hierarchy. In most of the villages where I conducted research, the *soba* (chief) had declared allegiance to the MPLA. If I tried to arrange interviews in private with individuals other than the chief, the response was invariably that social norms did not allow this. I was permitted to talk to the *soba* or to participate in a group discussion in which the *soba* was present. The result was that in such situations, people who had lived in UNITA areas during the war were fearful of talking about their past affiliation with UNITA. As Kriger has observed, researchers' access to rural populations in a war or post-conflict situation 'is invariably contingent on demonstrable political allegiance to the incumbent regime or to the revolutionary organization'.[31] The situation in Angola in 2008 and 2009 was not as restrictive as that which Kriger describes, but there were limits on my access to rural people and on their ability to speak freely to me.

---

[31] Kriger, *Zimbabwe's Guerrilla War*, 7.

Yet despite this unfavourable climate, there were spaces in which some people were willing to speak about having worked for UNITA in the past. People who had moved from villages to towns were able to talk of the past without the interference of traditional authorities. I also encountered communities of people, mostly living in peri-urban areas, who had remained with UNITA until the very end of the war and were bound together by their continued deep loyalty to the movement. In such settings, people would talk about having worked for UNITA during the war, though the factual reliability of these accounts was compromised by the fact that such communities had their own authority figures who ensured that junior members of the community would say nothing to challenge the dominant pro-UNITA discourse.

Scepticism regarding sources is nowhere more necessary than when dealing with oral accounts that are subject to the vicissitudes of selective memory and communal political influence. Indeed, whether people spoke of their work for UNITA as reluctant cooperation or as active and willing support was closely connected with their political views at the time of the interview: those who continued to identify with UNITA after the war spoke positively of their work with UNITA in earlier years. Far from being a transparent record of events, the discourse of the people I interviewed itself embodied the processes that were the object of my investigation: the processes whereby ideologies are made, unmade and remade in the interplay between language and political power. The complicating consequences of present-day political affiliations and pressures made it impossible to be certain about how any given individual's affiliation changed over time. What does become evident from people's own accounts is that some of them continued to believe in the superiority of one political movement no matter what happened, while others revised their beliefs. It was possible to trace how people's political identities and sometimes their beliefs changed as a result of their experience of events combined with their exposure to different political narratives. In this way, I document how ideologies of state and nation developed on both sides of the Angolan conflict and how these came to define the relationship between political movements and people.

Where I refer to written sources, these serve above all to frame the interview accounts by providing a systematic and chronological record that is seldom present in oral recollections, as well as to offer an understanding of the viewpoints of political elites. Journalistic accounts are often tainted by the writer's preference for UNITA or for the MPLA, a shortcoming that seems inevitable given that foreigners' access to the country before 1990 was possible only as a guest of one of the movements. However, read in context and with necessary scepticism, journalism is useful as a solid record of dates and events.[32] I also draw upon political memoirs, in which the bias is evident but which offer insight into elite thinking and strategy. Improved access for researchers in the last decade of the war gave rise to a number of human rights-focused reports produced by international organisations, which make some attempt to address the relationship between combatants and society. These reports, however, aimed as they are at denouncing human rights violations, concentrate on those moments when the conflict was most violent rather than on those periods when UNITA and the MPLA interacted with people on a consensual and peaceful basis.[33]

WHERE, WHAT AND WHEN

Angola is diverse in terms of geography, demographics and historical experience. The region on which I focus, the Central Highlands, is one whose people witnessed and were participants in a particularly intense and prolonged contestation of political and military power that began soon after the Portuguese revolution of 1974 opened the way to independence for Angola and continued until the last days of the war in 2002. It was in the Central Highlands that UNITA made its strongest identity-based claims and concentrated its efforts of mobilisation as independence approached. Huambo, the principal city of the Central Highlands, was the most significant urban centre ever to fall under UNITA control, for three months from late 1975 to early 1976 and again for more than a year between 1993 and 1994. Moreover, the Central Highlands constituted one of the most developed parts of the colonial state and, as such, was of symbolic and economic importance to the MPLA as well as to UNITA. The region therefore offers a case study that illuminates the political strategies of the two movements in urban and in rural areas and the ways in which people responded to them. Notwithstanding this regional focus, I recognise that Angolan history played out on a national (and indeed an international) stage as ideas flowed and people moved or were forcibly moved from one part of the country to another. When people from the Central Highlands spoke of their understandings of their region's politics, it was clear that for many of

[32] The reports in the *Washington Post* by Leon Dash, who spent several months with UNITA in 1973 and 1977, are particularly useful. Dash's reports retain a critical voice, and he avoids making unsubstantiated claims.

[33] Anna Richardson, *Children Living with UNITA: A Report for UNICEF Angola* (UNICEF, Luanda, 2001); Human Rights Watch, *Angola Unravels: The Rise and Fall of the Lusaka Peace Process* (New York, 1999); International Research Network on Children and Armed Conflict, *Angola Report* (2005).

them, their perceptions had been shaped by events in Luanda in 1975 and for others by their experience of living at UNITA's base at Jamba in south-eastern Angola. In investigating the evolution of the politics of the people of the Central Highlands, this book's scope extends beyond the physical confines of the region where appropriate.

The interview-based research made it possible to draw conclusions about broad political processes over the decades of the war. This method did not, however, provide a basis on which to provide detailed accounts of events. The most obvious omission concerns the matter of violence. There are two reasons for the lack of useful oral accounts of violence. First, the political pressures that stood in the way of obtaining testimony of any kind were intensified when it came to a subject as morally and as emotionally burdened as violence. Second, the field of enquiry covered a period of several decades, during which memories had faded. In this respect, the interviews were most useful not as records of fact but rather as evidence that people were inclined to speak about violence according to a preferred political script. They provided ample illustration of how the remembering, narrating or denial of violence was politically functional. People who had once been in the middle ranks of UNITA's army often denied that UNITA had perpetrated any sort of violence – clearly an implausible assertion. The educated people at the top of UNITA's command sought not to deny violence but to minimise it and to justify it in terms of political necessity, often by claiming state-like prerogatives of violence for UNITA. Long-time sympathisers of the MPLA, if they spoke of violence, similarly justified it as the prerogative of a state faced with an external enemy. People who had experienced violence and predation from both sides would speak about this but only in the most general terms. Such testimony was insufficient to support credible conclusions either about specific practices of violence or about the frequency of violent incidents. I do not seek to downplay the violence that occurred during the war and certainly not to exonerate the perpetrators. But given the lack of reliable data about violence, my focus is elsewhere.

This approach may seem peculiar, given that a large part of the literature on war is concerned above all with explaining occurrences of violence or assessing the political consequences of violence. But the war that framed the political identities that form the object of this study lasted from the 1960s until the early twenty-first century. In speaking of the Angolan war, I am not referring to decades of unremitting combat but rather to a period in which the legitimacy of the state remained contested and no single entity maintained a monopoly of violence over the legally recognised territory of Angola. A paradigm that envisaged war only as a series of violent acts would scarcely be appropriate for the study of Angola. Hobbes characterised war as consisting 'not in Battell onely, or the act of fighting; but in a tract of time, wherein the Will to contend by Battell is sufficiently known ... not in actuall fighting, but in the known disposition thereto during all the time there is no assurance to the contrary.'[34] The situation of war described in this book is one in which violence occurred at the boundaries of the control of the two main political movements and occurred at times when one movement or the other was seeking to extend its influence over people or territory that were under the dominance of the opposing movement.[35] I say 'people or territory' because territorial warfare was not the predominant mode of conflict for much of the period under consideration in Angola. At least as important as battles for territory were both armies' efforts, outlined earlier in this introduction, to displace people physically. This was often, though not always, a violent process. When soldiers used violence, its victims were those who were unable to convince the perpetrators that they were not collaborating with the other side. Away from these zones of contestation, it was in the areas that were securely under the control of one or other political movement that the dominant movement was able to engage with the people of that area and attempt to make its control hegemonic. The experience of violence, by contrast, undermined political relationships.

Equally, this book makes no claims to being a comprehensive study of Angolan nationalism. My intention is to study political identity and political legitimation, and as such, my interest in nationalism consists in the ways in which nationalism was deployed as a political tool by UNITA and the MPLA and in the extent to which these politicised nationalisms moulded people's national and political consciousness. The questions posed during the course of research were about politics, and the book takes its direction from how people responded to these questions. I do not delve into those aspects of nationalism in the sense of a developing national consciousness that took place independently of the ideologies put forward by the rival nationalist movements.[36]

In terms of temporal remit, my primary concern is with the years after the departure of the Portuguese from Angola, during which the MPLA commanded an internationally recognised state and UNITA controlled varying portions of Angolan territory. This period is crucial to an understanding of

[34] Thomas Hobbes, *Leviathan* (Cambridge, 2005), 88–89.

[35] As Arendt has it, 'loss of power tempts men to substitute violence for power'. Arendt, 'Reflections on Violence', 16.

[36] In contrast to my own narrow approach to politically functional nationalism, Marissa Moorman, *Intonations: A Social History of Music and Nation in Luanda, Angola, from 1945 to Recent Times* (Athens OH, 2008), has broken new ground in the study of Angolan nationalism by identifying cultural nationalist tendencies that developed independently of the three political movements usually associated with Angolan nationalism.

the making of the Angolan state, yet as already noted, little research has been done on the internal dimension of militarised politics during this period. However, there would be little point in trying to understand this period without considering the events that led up to independence. Chapter 1, therefore, shows how the nature of colonial rule in Angola and the circumstances of decolonisation contributed to particular understandings of political authority that were to persist throughout the civil war after independence. It shows how the repressive character of the colonial state restricted the possibilities of anti-colonial mobilisation and how this in turn determined the weak and class-differentiated penetration of the anti-colonial movements into Central Highlands society. The Portuguese revolution of April 1974 prompted a hasty decolonisation process in which the rival independence movements competed by force to take control of territory and to assume the prerogatives of statehood, while the experience of violence ensured that people who previously had had no interest in the conflict had no option but to take sides.

The chapters that follow deal with the period from independence in 1975 until the peace initiatives of the late 1980s. Chapter 2 examines UNITA's attempts at instituting government in the Central Highlands cities that it briefly controlled at the end of 1975. Chapter 3 is concerned with urban politics after the arrival of the MPLA in the cities and analyses the relationship among state, party and people that was established under MPLA control: mass organisations shaped political consciousness and blurred the boundaries between party and state. Chapter 4 introduces the complex relationship among territorial control and political identity, politicisation and the forced movement of people. These themes are continued in Chapters 5 and 6, which deal with UNITA's efforts to establish a political and economic relationship with peasant communities in the Central Highlands and with its attempts at creating a state-like entity at Jamba in south-eastern Angola during the 1980s. While the practical importance of Jamba was self-evident, more relevant in terms of my arguments is Jamba's symbolic importance as an emblem of UNITA's aspirations to statehood. Chapters 7 and 8 concentrate on the consequences of the changed political and military situation after 1992, when UNITA found itself on the defensive in a war of attrition and lost the material resources that it needed to sustain its legitimacy in the eyes of its followers. Chapter 9 examines how the end of the war in 2002 was managed in such a way that political legitimacy in post-war Angola continues to rest on understandings of authority that were established in wartime but which now, thanks to the post-war dispensation, benefit the MPLA alone.

1

Anti-Colonial Mobilisation and the Portuguese Exodus

Any attempt to write about the civil war in Angola faces the problem of where to begin. Independence Day, 11 November 1975, might appear to mark the date when the Angolan conflict ceased to be an anti-colonial struggle and began to be a 'civil' war by conventional definition: a conflict between an Angolan state and Angolan opponents of the state, notwithstanding the substantial external support enjoyed by both parties. Yet when seen from the perspective of the Angolan Central Highlands, Independence Day marked no decisive turning point. As early as September, UNITA was the dominant military force in Huambo, while the MPLA was effectively in control of much of Luanda and Portuguese forces had already vacated most of Angola. The last Portuguese left Huambo early in October, and until the arrival of the MPLA four months later, UNITA was the only political movement active in the Central Highlands. These events were accompanied by violence and uncertainty that were as much part of daily life in the months before November 1975 as they were in the months that followed.

If older people in the Central Highlands remember the second half of 1975 as a period of turmoil, they also remember a time barely a year earlier when the political movements competed peacefully for popular support. But that period too was brief. Some could remember a time before the nationalist movements were present at all. Villagers talked of how 'the movements arrived' in 1974, and recalled no kind of political mobilisation in the countryside before that. Many town dwellers had become familiar with nationalist ideas and had known of the existence of nationalist movements during the 1960s, but they too did not recall any systematic political organisation in the region before 1974. The anti-colonial uprisings of the early 1960s had little impact on the Central Highlands, and the 'liberated zones' established by the MPLA, UNITA and the *Frente Nacional de Libertação de Angola* (FNLA) were far away on Angola's northern and eastern margins. People recognised that the Portuguese coup d'état of 25 April 1974 was a significant turning point. But how they responded to the coup and to the events that unfolded after it depended on the ideas about politics that they had encountered over the previous decade or so. Access to currents of political thought was determined by where people were.

This chapter starts, therefore, by considering the origins of Angolan nationalism and sets nationalist politics in the context of late colonial rule so as to account for the limited and socially differentiated reach of nationalist ideas, particularly in the Central Highlands. I then examine the 1974 coup and the rupture that it represented for Portuguese politics, not least for the relationship between Portugal and its colonies. This consideration of interlinked developments in Portugal and in Angola forms a basis on which we can understand how people in Angola responded to the political changes that followed the coup. The period between the coup and independence defined the terms in which the rival movements would stake their claims to power and the logic of political exclusivity that combined with international interests to deepen the antagonism between the Angolan rivals. The same period defined the terms in which Angolans would understand the conflict in later years. I trace how the events of this period were crucial to the gestation of ideas about political legitimacy, authority and responsibility that developed during the years of war that followed: more specifically, how people understood political authority and their relationship to it, and the relationship between military power and popular perceptions of political legitimacy.

COLONIAL RULE, NATIONALISM AND RESISTANCE

Accounts of anti-colonial mobilisation in Angola have documented how the emergence of separate strands of nationalism, associated with regionally based elites, hindered the possibility of a common vision of nationhood. The fragmented character of Angolan nationalism is in turn the product of the differentiated colonial presence across Angola and the political and economic changes that were imposed by the Portuguese *Estado Novo* (new state) in the late colonial period. Marcum's account of 'three major streams of Angolan nationalism' has formed the basis for most scholarly writing about late-colonial Angola.[1] These 'streams' of nationalism are associated with educated elites that came into being at different times as the result of different experiences of

---

[1] John Marcum, *The Angolan Revolution, Volume II (Exile Politics and Guerrilla Warfare, 1962–1976)* (Cambridge, MA, 1978), 13.

colonial rule.[2] One stream of nationalism emerged in Luanda, a city that had grown as a slave-trading post following the gradual Portuguese conquest of its hinterland from 1575 onwards. In the absence of a large settler population in Luanda before the twentieth century, educated elites emerged from the *mestiço* (mixed-race) and *assimilado* (culturally assimilated black) people of the region. It was among these communities, as well as among a small number of whites with a long genealogy in the colony, that anti-colonial ideas began to be discussed.[3]

The second nationalist stream identified by Marcum emerged in the former Kongo kingdom, which had extended from north-western Angola into the present-day Democratic Republic of Congo but which by the nineteenth century was in decline with its titular monarch largely dependent on Portuguese patronage. A common nationalist discourse with irredentist elements developed throughout the former kingdom in areas under Belgian as well as Portuguese rule. This nationalism is associated in particular with the communities surrounding the Protestant missions that were established in the region from the mid-nineteenth century. The third strand of nationalism, in the Central Highlands, was also associated with the mission schools, at Protestant missions in particular. Since this region had been brought under colonial domination only in 1902, nationalism in its modern form is generally recognised as having appeared in the Central Highlands only later in the twentieth century.[4]

Debates continue as to whether the three strands of nationalism were phenomena worthy of comparison on the same terms. Wheeler and Pélissier distinguish the 'modernist' Luanda nationalism from the 'ethno-nationalisms' of the Bakongo north-west and of the Central Highlands. 'Modernist' nationalism 'with its pretensions to be pan-Angolan – that is, anti-tribalist – remained in most cases an elite and urban phenomenon, lacking the support of the great rural masses without which any national uprising in Angola was doomed to failure'.[5] For Messiant, the forms and identities of

---

[2] Christine Messiant, *1961: L'Angola Coloniale, Histoire et Société. Les Premises du Mouvement Nationaliste* (Basel, 2006); Linda Heywood, *Contested Power in Angola: 1840s to the Present* (Rochester, NY, 2002), 124.

[3] Marissa Moorman has written of the role of music in the creation of a nonpolitical nationalism in Luanda. *Intonations: A Social History of Music and Nation in Luanda, Angola, from 1945 to Recent Times* (Athens, OH, 2008).

[4] Heywood recognises continuities between pre-colonial ideologies of rule and the ideologies employed by Jonas Savimbi. Linda Heywood, 'Towards an Understanding of Modern Political Ideology in Africa: The Case of the Ovimbundu of Angola', *Journal of Modern African Studies* 36.1 (1998), 139–167.

[5] Douglas Wheeler and René Pélissier, *Angola* (London, 1971), 162.

political mobilisation were determined by not so much by pre-existing ethnic categories as by the relationship with colonialism of elites and people in different regions of Angola: the Luanda hinterland, the Bakongo north-west and the Central Highlands. Messiant and Péclard, among other writers, have also challenged Pélissier's distinction between 'modernising nationalism' and 'ethno-nationalism' and pointed to the importance of ideas of modernity in the Central Highlands strand of nationalism, an observation that is supported by the evidence presented in this book.[6]

These three currents of nationalist thought, based in Luanda, the Bakongo north and the Central Highlands, gave rise in the 1950s and 1960s to the MPLA, the FNLA and UNITA respectively. The channelling of nationalism into political activity and the emergence of these movements as political entities need to be understood in the context of the political changes that took place in Angola as a result of the overthrow of the Portuguese Republic by António Salazar in 1926 and the creation of the authoritarian regime known as the *Estado Novo* (new state). Even as the other European powers withdrew from Africa after the Second World War, the *Estado Novo* was built on an ideology that envisaged Portugal as the centre of a reconfigured empire with control centralised in Lisbon over colonies which, through state-led economic modernisation, were to become a site for Portuguese capital investment. This vision was given substance by the commodity boom that followed the Second World War, in which Portugal had remained neutral. Investment was accompanied by a rapid increase in white settlement.[7] In 1951, Portugal changed the status of its colonies to overseas provinces in an effort to pre-empt international pressure for decolonisation.[8] In 1954, the *Estatuto dos Indígenas* (Native Statute) codified a two-tier system of citizenship that conceded rights to a tiny number of *assimilados* while excluding the *indígena* (native) majority.[9]

The *Estado Novo's* plans for the Central Highlands ensured that colonial dispossession in the region was at its height in the mid-twentieth century. Land reform measures saw more than three million hectares transferred to Portuguese ownership by the 1940s, with what Heywood describes as 'disastrous' consequences for the people of the region. At the same time, the Highland towns received a large proportion of the post-1940 wave of white

---

[6] Didier Péclard, 'Religion and Politics in Angola: The Church, the Colonial State and the Emergence of Angolan Nationalism 1940–1961'. *Journal of Religion in Africa* 28.2 (May 1998), 180.

[7] Gerald Bender, *Angola Under the Portuguese: The Myth and the Reality* (Trenton, NJ, 2004).

[8] Norrie Macqueen, *The Decolonization of Portuguese Africa: Metropolitan Revolution and the Dissolution of Empire* (London, 1997), 11.

[9] Heywood, *Contested Power*, 63–91.

settlement, and these newcomers occupied positions in the administrative, trade and service sectors that would otherwise have provided employment for Africans. Plantation agriculture and other capitalist ventures depended on state-enforced labour. Tax liability was widened, and the onus was placed on traditional authorities to enforce taxation or to render men for labour when tax obligations were not met, to the point where by the late 1950s, 'nearly four of every five Ovimbundu males did migrant labour'.[10]

The grievance caused by the political, social and economic changes of the *Estado Novo* was potentially fertile ground for mobilisation. Yet at the same time, the state's repressive nature and the absence of political structures in which Africans could participate hindered the development of popular nationalisms and cemented the elite character of anti-colonial thought and action in Angola. The events of 1961 that are generally regarded as the start of anti-colonial resistance in Angola, namely the riots on cotton plantations in Malange in January and the Luanda prison break on 4 February, were not the initiative of any organised movement.[11] The insurrection that followed in the coffee-growing areas of the north was also in large part spontaneous, although the *União das Populações de Angola* (UPA), the antecedent of the FNLA, did have some role in organising violence.[12] Following the uprising on the coffee plantations, the UPA began more systematically to mobilise a guerrilla army from bases in Zaire (today's Democratic Republic of Congo). The MPLA was initially restricted for want of an ally among Angola's neighbouring states, but by 1964, it had established bases in Congo-Brazzaville from which it was able to carry out raids into the Angolan Cabinda exclave.[13] Later, after gaining the sympathy of the Zambian government, it established 'liberated zones' in eastern Angola.

The Portuguese response to the resistance of the early 1960s came in the form both of reform and of further repression. Reforms included the abolition of forced labour and the repeal of the Native Statute.[14] At the same time, the government introduced further measures to promote white settlement. It also stepped up its military campaign against the guerrillas, including psychosocial counterinsurgency measures, while PIDE (*Polícia Internacional e de Defesa*

---

[10] Heywood, *Contested Power*, 66–86.
[11] Christine Messiant, 'Chez Nous, Même le Passé Est Imprévisible' in Christine Messiant, *L'Angola Postcolonial: 2. Sociologie Politique d'une Oléocratie* (Paris, 2008), 153–202. Originally published in Lusotopie V (1998), 157–197.
[12] Marcum, *Angolan Revolution II*, 125–140.
[13] Cabinda, formerly a Portuguese protectorate separate from Angola, was administered as part of Angola from 1956.
[14] Marcum, *Angolan Revolution II*, 191–192; Bender, *Angola*, 158.

do Estado, the secret police) continued to monitor the civilian population.[15] Two aspects of Portuguese colonial thinking remained unshakeable. One was an insistence on the integrity of the empire and hence a refusal to countenance nationalist activity in the colonies. The other was a vision of empire as a modernising project, tied to increasing white settlement. The Central Highlands remained a focal point of this project.

Though the 1961 uprisings had little direct impact on the Central Highlands, the generation that reached adulthood in the early 1960s in the region recognised that the post-1961 reforms had allowed them to grow up under a system less oppressive than the one their parents had endured.[16] They saw forced labour as a thing of the past, and the remaining grievance was primarily political rather than material. Colonial rule in the 1960s was still far from just, yet beyond a general wish for 'freedom', there is little suggestion that specific grievances had become politically charged in the Central Highlands. This we can attribute in part to the relative improvement of the 1960s over the 1950s, but also to the limited reach of the political movements in the Central Highlands before 1974.[17] UNITA, the movement most closely identified with the Central Highlands, did not emerge until 1966, two years after Jonas Savimbi, previously an official in the FNLA, broke from that movement on the grounds that the Bakongo-led FNLA neglected the interests of migrant workers from the Central Highlands on the northern coffee plantations. Savimbi himself was a product of the Central Highlands strand of nationalism that had developed in the Protestant missions in the first half of the twentieth century. Yet between its foundation in 1966 and the Portuguese coup in 1974, UNITA remained a movement *of* the Central Highlands rather than a movement *in* the Central Highlands, operating in the bush of Moxico hundreds of kilometres from its political heartland.

This late development of political activity in the Central Highlands has ensured that a recurring theme in the literature on Angolan nationalism is the ambiguous position of the Central Highlands and its people in the creation of

---

[15] Marcum, *Angolan Revolution II*, 268–284.

[16] As I conducted interviews in 2008 and 2009, very few interviewees were old enough to have had adult memories of the 1950s.

[17] Compare Moorman's suggestion (*Intonations*, 167) that the arrival of organised politics in Luanda disrupted national unity that had coalesced around a common desire for independence. In eastern Angola, by contrast, guerrillas had had some success in making the nationalist movements known to people during the anti-colonial war: on the MPLA, see Basil Davidson, *In the Eye of the Storm: Angola's People* (London, 1972) and Inge Brinkman, *A War for People: Civilians, Mobility, and Legitimacy in South-East Angola during MPLA's war for Independence* (Cologne, 2005); on UNITA, see Fred Bridgland, *Jonas Savimbi: A Key to Africa.* (Edinburgh, 1986); Samuel Chiwale, *Cruzei-me com a História* (Lisbon, 2006).

Angolan national identity. Pélissier observed in the Central Highlands 'a great blank spot … on the Angolan geopolitical map because ethno-nationalism there was structured much later than elsewhere in the country'.[18] Nearly forty years after Pélissier was writing, we also need to recognise, as Heywood does, that the politicised nationalism of the Central Highlands has in retrospect been tainted by UNITA's subsequent cooperation with the apartheid South African military.[19] The work of Heywood, Péclard and other scholars who trace the ideological roots of a nationalism based in the Central Highlands never-theless points to the need to distinguish between the intellectual nationalism that existed in the region and the political activation and expression of nation-alism that was prevented by a repressive state.[20]

In the absence of organised opposition in the Central Highlands through out the 1960s, nationalist ideas spread through channels that reached only a relatively privileged layer of society. Most important among these was the MPLA radio station, *Rádio Angola Combatente*, broadcast from Brazzaville. The first to hear the MPLA's message were therefore those who had access to a radio, who mostly lived in the towns or were connected with the missions. The broadcasts ensured that the MPLA was known in the Central Highlands several years before UNITA was founded in 1966. A lawyer who had been a young man at the time spoke of a 'great anxiety among intellectuals for inde-pendence', fuelled by the 'intellectuals'' access to the MPLA broadcasts while the war continued in more remote regions of the country.[21] In the villages, by contrast, a typical answer to questions about anti-colonial mobilisation was: 'In this region we knew nothing. We first heard of independence in 1975.'[22]

The vigilance of the PIDE ensured that listening to the MPLA broadcasts and discussing nationalist ideas were dangerous pursuits.[23] However, religious institutions provided a space in which new ideas could be received and dis-cussed.[24] Marcolino Moco, later a provincial governor and, for a while in the

---

[18] René Pélissier, *La Colonie du Minotaure, Nationalismes et Revoltes en Angola (1926–1961)* (Orgeval, 1978), 291, quoted and translated in Didier Péclard, 'UNITA and the Moral Economy of Exclusion in Angola', in Eric Morier-Genoud (ed.), *Sure Road? Nationalisms in Angola, Guinea-Bissau and Mozambique* (Leiden, 2012), 156.

[19] Linda Heywood, 'Unita and Ethnic Nationalism in Angola', *The Journal of Modern African Studies* 27.1 (1989), 47–66.

[20] Didier Péclard, *État Colonial, Missions Chrétiennes et Nationalisme en Angola, 1920–1975: Aux Racines Sociales de l'UNITA* (Paris, 2005).

[21] Interviewee 3, Huambo, 10 May 2008.

[22] Interviewee 42, Huambo, 6 June 2008.

[23] In this respect, the accounts of people I interviewed are similar to those quoted by Moorman, *Intonations*, 149–154.

[24] Heywood, 'Ethnic Nationalism'. Péclard, *État Colonial*.

1990s, Angolan prime minister, said that it was his time at the seminary that had allowed him to challenge the notion that 'God made ... the white man to dominate the world, and the black man to be subjected' and to discover 'that there were independent African states in which blacks controlled their territory, and that Angola also had independence movements'.[25] Service in the colonial army also served, paradoxically perhaps, to spread anti-colonial ideas.[26] Interviewees said they had become aware of the nationalist movements because the war had demonstrated the existence of armed opposition to the colonial regime and through talking to fellow soldiers who had come from different parts of Angola. Similarly, repression by the authorities aroused curiosity about the enemy that the Portuguese were trying to eliminate. According to Horácio Junjuvili, later a UNITA official, 'If you heard that someone had been captured and taken to PIDE and interrogated about being in contact with the bush, one would ask, "who is in the bush?" [and the response would be] "It's Jonas Savimbi who's fighting to drive out the Portuguese." The word was passed around, not through UNITA's own initiative but because people were curious to hear.'[27]

Awareness of organised politics remained the preserve of a limited number of people, whether information came through the radio, through the missions, through military service or through family members. While these urban or mission-educated people were not all particularly privileged in material terms, they enjoyed access to information that farmers lacked. In the words of one Catholic priest, 'The people didn't know who would govern well or badly ... Politics was a bit elevated. The people didn't understand anything.'[28] This assessment reflects the condescending viewpoint of an educated stratum. But the early lack of awareness was acknowledged even by people who later became involved in political movements, such as a farmer who joined UNITA: 'The most educated men discussed things: that Africans must liberate themselves, that the black man must become independent. Blacks who had studied abroad discovered these things – or those who had friends who came from other countries. But the Angolan people themselves didn't know.'[29]

---

[25] Interview, Marcolino Moco, Huambo, 22 August 2009.
[26] According to Gervaise Clarence-Smith, *The Third Portuguese Empire 1825–1975: A Study in Economic Imperialism* (Manchester, 1985), 217, some two-thirds of Portugal's fighting forces in the colonies were black. Heywood, *Contested Power*, 86 notes that a disproportionate number of these were from the Highlands and rural areas.
[27] Interview, Horácio Junjuvili, Luanda, 15 July 2009.
[28] Interview, Huambo, 17 June 2008.
[29] Interview, Huambo, 26 June 2008.

Change, when it happened, was precipitated by events in Portugal rather than in Angola.

THE PORTUGUESE COUP

The events and processes that surrounded the end of the Portuguese empire, starting with the April 1974 coup, were to have a profound impact on the understandings of political authority that developed in Angola in the months before independence and which persisted throughout the war. What happened in Angola in 1975 may be understood in terms of a crisis of authority that resulted from a reversal during the Portuguese revolution of attitudes towards the imperial project and the contradictions between the old regime's refusal to acknowledge political claims from the African territories and the new regime's refusal to own any responsibility for the actions of its predecessor.

The future of its colonies had been a central political question in Portugal as critics of the dictatorship began, hesitantly, to articulate alternative visions. Although the first stirrings of change in Lisbon came early in 1974 with the proposal by António de Spínola, formerly the vice chief of the Defence Council of the Portuguese Armed Forces, to reconfigure the empire as a global federation, this gradualist approach was soon overtaken by the coup. The officers known as the Armed Forces Movement (MFA) who led the coup knew better than anyone that the colonial wars were unwinnable and favoured full decolonisation.[30] Spínola became head of state simply by virtue of the fact that President Marcelo Caetano agreed to surrender to him during the coup, but ideological differences with the MFA led to his ousting in September 1974. A commitment to decolonisation united the otherwise disparate Portuguese left. Mário Soares, Foreign Minister at the time, made the MFA's priorities clear in an interview in May:

> Q: What do you judge to be the most critical problem that Portugal will
>   have to confront in the coming months?
> A: Freedom for the African colonies. We must start to work immediately for
>   a ceasefire accord with the guerrillas. We cannot wait twelve months for
>   an elected government to deal with this.[31]

In Maxwell's account, tensions between Spínola and the MFA represented 'conflict between revolutionary and evolutionary change in Europe and

---

[30] António Spínola, *Portugal e o futuro* (Lisbon, 1974). Kenneth Maxwell, *The Making of Portuguese Democracy* (Cambridge, 1995) provides a comprehensive account of the coup.

[31] Mário Soares, *Democratização e Descolonização: Dez Meses no Governo Provisório* (Lisbon, 1975), 37.

between immediate decolonization and gradual disengagement in Africa'.[32] The MFA and thinkers associated with it saw decolonisation as an emancipatory moment for Portugal as much as for the colonised, a matter of a new Portugal freeing itself from a past imposed on it by earlier generations. Francisco da Costa Gomes, who succeeded Spínola as president, made Portugal's commitment to decolonisation clear in an address to the United Nations on 17 October 1974 but distanced his regime from responsibility for it, saying, 'We will be as dynamic as is demanded by the impatience of one who takes up a task delayed by many years, and as patient as is necessary to the happiness of people who suffer in their flesh the consequences of the *previous* Portuguese political situation.'[33] Gomes's standpoint won praise as that of 'the president of a poor country that put itself on the side of the countries of the Third World'.[34] Melo Antunes, a leading MFA ideologue, said, 'One of the worst forms of colonialism is paternalism. It will be for Angolans to choose the model they wish to follow.'[35] Macqueen links this to the fact that the Portuguese regime was founded on the same 'revolutionary legiti-macy' that was asserted by the anti-colonial movements.[36] The left's analysis saw colonialism as embedded with capitalism and fascism in the system that had been overthrown on 25 April. By this logic, the new regime was automatically on the side of the colonised, but it also had doubts about its own legitimacy to lead the process of decolonisation. The tension between these two attitudes is evident in the decisions and the actions of Portuguese officials in the months that followed.

White settlers in the Portuguese colonies in Africa typically reacted to the coup with surprise and fear.[37] But in the months after the coup, the new political establishment regarded settlers' claims as an atavistic embarrassment. Soares made this clear in an interview with the Spanish newspaper *Pueblo* in June 1974. When the interviewer mentioned that Soares had been accused of 'dealing with Mozambican matters without having set foot in Mozambique', Soares replied that this accusation had come from a settler 'linked to colonial exploitation and domination'. Soares insisted that he himself was 'consid-ered a friend by [the anti-colonial] movements ... while the person in ques-tion is considered an enemy'.[38] This attitude on the part of Portugal's new

---

[32] Maxwell, *Portuguese Democracy*, 96.

[33] *Diário de Notícias*, Lisbon, 18 October 1974, 1 (my emphasis).

[34] Josê Pires, *Angola! Angola: Testemunho Sobre o Problema Colonial* (Lisbon, 1975), 185.

[35] Macqueen, *Decolonization*, 180.

[36] Macqueen, *Decolonization*, 89; See also Jean-Michel Mabeko-Tali, *Dissidências e Poder do Estado: O MPLA Perante Si Próprio (1962–1977)*, II.°Vol., (Luanda, 2001),39.

[37] Mabeko-Tali, *Dissidências*, II.°Vol., 24.

[38] Soares, *Democratização*, 60–61. Soares's dismissal of all whites in Angola as linked to the old regime contrasts with Francisco Pimenta, 'Angola's Whites: Political Behaviour and National Identity', *Portuguese Journal of Social Science* 4.3 (2005) 169–193, which finds that whites in

rulers served to alienate the settlers further. Fearful whites in Angola turned to violence against black Angolans, and in poor suburbs of Luanda, people responded to the threat by organising themselves into neighbourhood committees.[39] This marked the start of local urban mobilisation that would soon form the basis of conflict between the MPLA and FNLA in Luanda.

ANGOLA AFTER THE COUP

The way in which the liberation movements engaged with Angolan society in the year that followed the coup further contributed to determining the character of later politics in Angola, both in its regional differentiation and in its elite character. At first, political mobilisation was notionally free and competitive, though regional concentrations reflected the origins of the movements' founding elites: the FNLA in the Bakongo north, the MPLA in Luanda and its hinterland and UNITA in the Central Highlands. We have already seen how members of a self-identified intellectual elite believed, with some justification, that they had had access to anti-colonial ideas that were inaccessible to others. Similarly, educated people explained their political adherence after 25 April 1974 as the result of conscious and informed choice while believing that the less educated had no choice but to support whichever movement dominated the area where they lived. Bernardo, a young activist at the time who later made a career in government service, said he had chosen the MPLA because of the socialist platform that it adopted 'to convince the people and the national and international community what the object of its struggle [was]' and to 'put an end to exploitation'. Such choices, he said, were made by 'the more enlightened people', while for 'the less enlightened I think not, because up until then, alternation of power had been unknown in the country … because the country was emerging from colonialism and obscurantism. This made it difficult for the people to know the difference'.[40] Paulina, a former civil servant of the same generation, said she had chosen the MPLA's 'progressive vision' that 'helped me shape my ideas' over the 'emphasis on culture' that dominated UNITA's discourses.[41]

Some rank-and-file UNITA members also suggested there had been an ideological element to UNITA's recruitment. A former lieutenant recalled he had joined UNITA as a student in 1974 because 'it was the movement that

Angola had, to differing degrees, come to identify as African and held political opinions ranging from conservative to radical.

[39] Mabeko-Tali, *Dissidências*, II.°Vol., 32.
[40] Interviewee 31, Huambo, 10 May 2008.
[41] Interviewee 150, Huambo, 3 July 2009.

would free the Angolan people ... from the claws of Portuguese colonialism'.[42]
By contrast, those people who identified less strongly with either party were
more sceptical about the existence of ideological differences between them.
A schoolteacher recalled that 'each party had its way of explaining what its ideology was and each person considered this and according to his understanding, went to whichever was better for him.... Each [party] said that if it were
to govern the country, it would do better for the people'.[43] Abel Chivukuvuku,
who joined UNITA as a young man after the Portuguese coup, explains adherence to the movement in the 1974 to 1975 period principally as the result
of UNITA's local origins, 'UNITA didn't even need to mobilise as such....
I think it happened the same way in Luanda [with the MPLA], or in Uige,
Mbanza Congo [with the FNLA] – people just felt, "this is our organisation".
And for the fact that the elites of the area just joined, everybody joined.'[44]
Although the mission nationalism of the Central Highlands had produced
and inspired Savimbi, he had raised his army in the east, and it was only in
1974 that UNITA acquired a mass support base in the Central Highlands.
In the words of one informant, 'UNITA came out of the bush as a bunch of
rag-tag guerrillas. It was only then that the mission school kids piled in.'

In summary, people who identified with the MPLA during 1974 and 1975 saw
themselves as having a clear ideological commitment to the party – often having been introduced to the MPLA by its radio broadcasts – and this kept them
attached to the MPLA even when UNITA came to be the dominant military
movement. UNITA adherents desired national liberation, but their choice of
UNITA was determined as much by the movement's roots in a certain stratum
of local society as by any ideological agenda. Most of the people quoted so
far had been in towns or at mission schools as independence approached. In
the villages, by contrast, no one spoke of the liberation movements recruiting
people before independence. One village elder, although loyal to UNITA,
echoed the attitude of many villagers when he remarked, 'In 1975 UNITA was
here, but troops only occupied where the whites lived.' He meant that UNITA
was in the region but based in the towns.[45] The determinants of political affiliation were more complex than mere lines on a map: although UNITA was
the creation of Central Highlands elites, it was not guaranteed support among
town dwellers who knew of the longer-established MPLA. Moreover, although
UNITA's leaders would later evoke Maoist strategies of peasant resistance as

[42]   Interviewee 72, Huambo, 3 July 2008.
[43]   Interviewee 26, Huambo, 18 May 2008.
[44]   Interview, Abel Chivukuvuku, Luanda, 14 July 2009. Chivukuvuku was by the 1990s a promin-
       ent figure in UNITA but left in 2012 to found a new political party.
[45]   Interviewee 40, Huambo, 4 June 2008.

they sought to mobilise the rural population, in the Central Highlands in the mid-1970s UNITA's focus was primarily urban. Most accounts of the MPLA similarly concur that it was at heart an urban movement that had had limited success in establishing liberated rural zones during the anti-colonial war. The MPLA quickly lost interest in those areas as soon as the Portuguese coup allowed it to mobilise in the cities.[46]

Although the legal framework for the transition to independence was prescribed in the Alvor Accord, signed by the FNLA, MPLA, UNITA and Portugal on 15 January 1975, the prescriptions of the accord amounted to little alongside the positions of the Portuguese and Angolan elites: from the side of the Portuguese, an unwillingness to exercise authority, and from the side of the Angolan movements, the absence of a common vision of nationhood and a lack of popular accountability stemming from the limited reach of early mobilisation.[47] The Alvor Accord demanded the establishment of a Transitional Government on 31 January with equal representation from the three movements, a Portuguese-appointed High Commissioner to resolve interparty disputes and the formation of a united army alongside the phased withdrawal of Portuguese troops.[48] Accounts of the months after Alvor concur that the transitional executive barely functioned, while Portuguese officials used the executive's de jure existence as a way of distancing themselves from responsibility for events in Angola.[49]

This was to lead to a sequence of events that was not so much a process of decolonisation as the independence movements' assumption of state prerogatives piece by piece, including the deployment of violence in the name of defending communities. It is in this assumption of prerogatives that we can see the origins of the ways in which the liberation movements exercised and sought to justify their control of territory and people over the course of the war that ensued. The MPLA was able to incorporate the self-defence committees that had emerged in response to settler violence, while the FNLA regarded them with suspicion on ideological grounds.[50] The first months of 1975 saw

[46] Mabeko-Tali, *Dissidências*, II.°Vol., 25.

[47] On the mutually exclusive character of the rival Angolan nationalisms, see Mabeko-Tali, *Dissidências*, II.°Vol., 115–116.

[48] Government of Portugal, *Angola – The Independence Agreement* (Lisbon, 1975).

[49] Mabeko-Tali, *Dissidências*, II.°Vol., 102–104. On the Portuguese position, a CIA informant's comment seems pertinent: 'Portuguese forces remain reluctant to act unilaterally to impose order. They prefer to leave that responsibility to the transitional government.' US NARA RG263, CIA, National Intelligence Bulletin, 2 May 1975. Piero Gleijeses, *Conflicting Missions: Havana, Washington and Africa 1959–1976* (Chapel Hill, NC, 2002), 258 also notes Portugal's unwillingness to intervene to stem conflict.

[50] Mabeko-Tali, *Dissidências*, II.°Vol., 56–58.

skirmishes between youths and soldiers aligned with the MPLA and FNLA. Tensions grew to the point where soldiers from the two armies each attacked offices of the other party towards the end of March 1975. Almost immediately, the Portuguese Armed Forces (FAP) faced accusations of failing to intervene, and soldiers from all three liberation movements joined Portuguese troops in trying to restore order.[51] In the following days, the High Commissioner ordered that weapons be surrendered either to Portuguese forces or to UNITA patrols and that only UNITA was to participate in joint patrols with the Portuguese army. The MPLA and FNLA nevertheless continued to operate separate patrols, an indication both of a lack of Portuguese authority and of mutual suspicion that was soon to provoke further violence.[52] The conflict intensified after 8 July, and in the course of the fighting, both MPLA and FNLA supporters attacked the Portuguese High Commission.[53] The right-wing Lisbon newspaper *Tempo* commented sardonically on the Portuguese forces' abandonment of their responsibility to keep order, saying that it was only when FAPLA attacked a FAP vehicle that FAP retaliated 'in a belated act of Portuguese sovereignty and proof of the existence of Portuguese troops in Angola'.[54]

When relative calm returned to Luanda in mid-July, this signalled not a settlement but an effective victory by the MPLA over its rivals – an early instance of a tendency by the nationalist movements to establish outright territorial control by force of arms, a tendency that would determine the character of the conflict over the ensuing months. FAPLA joined the FAP in patrolling to 'prevent acts of banditry', while MPLA militants were rounding up looters and 'protecting houses and goods that had been abandoned'.[55] Whereas a few months earlier, UNITA had been trusted by the Portuguese as a peacekeeper because it had not been involved in the violence in Luanda, the authority that the MPLA had attained by July reflected the fact that it had, with the assent of the Portuguese authorities, established a monopoly of force in Luanda.

UNITA was a marginal player in Luanda, but for UNITA as for the other movements, politicisation happened as part of a process that also involved

---

[51] DN 25 March 1975, 1.
[52] DN 27 March 1975, 10. Marcum, *Angolan Revolution II*, 260 and Mabeko-Tali, *Dissidências*, II.°Vol., 38, both note that UNITA's initial lack of involvement in the conflict in Luanda allowed Savimbi to present himself as above the fray, a position that seems to have succeeded with the Portuguese willingness to incorporate UNITA into peace-keeping operations.
[53] US NARA RG263. CIA, *DCI Briefing for 14 July SRG meeting*. Marcum, *Angolan Revolution II*, 260 notes that 'on July 9, heavy fighting broke out and spread swiftly throughout the country. Within a week, the MPLA had forced the FNLA out of Luanda. The FNLA ... eliminated all remaining MPLA presence in the northern towns of the Uige and Zaire districts'.
[54] *Tempo*, 21 August 1975, 20: a retrospective comment on the previous month's events.
[55] DN 12 July 1975, 1, 14 July 1975, 1, 16 July 1975, 1.

militarisation. This established an association between politics and the military life that persisted until the end of the civil war. The South African Defence Force's (SADF's) authorised account of its intervention in Angola records that Savimbi began receiving weapons from South Africa as early as October 1974, three months before the Alvor Accord. According to this account, the SADF took the initiative in contacting Savimbi in July 1974.[56] UNITA continued expanding its army and its base of cadres, sending trainloads of people from the Central Highlands to its army bases in the east.[57] According to the former UNITA General Geraldo Sachipengo Nunda, the Alvor Accord's requirement that each movement deliver a quota of soldiers to the single army prompted a rush for recruitment, even at a time when there was little ideological animosity among the movements.[58]

Political violence in the Central Highlands became serious only when the conflict in Luanda provoked an exodus of people whose family origins were in the Highlands. People in Huambo spoke of 'massacres' in Luanda that had forced people with roots in the Central Highlands to flee the capital. Press reports tell of 'countless refugees' arriving in Huambo from Kwanza Norte (in the Luanda hinterland), 'some ... with the intention of staying in Huambo only until such time as the confrontations finish.... Others are not thinking of going back to the north'.[59] Thousands more were reported to be heading from Luanda to Lobito and Huambo, the result of 'serious incidents' in Luanda between 8 and 17 August that made people flee 'the shooting, the grenades, the mortars, tribalism, banditry'.[60] Some were attacked by MPLA supporters as they reached the Kwanza River, the notional borderline between northern and southern Angola. Nunda recalls this incident as the time when 'the logic of war emerged. From then on, the lines were divided'. The MPLA at the time emphasised the expulsion of FNLA soldiers as part of the MPLA's exercise of sovereignty in the capital and ignored the fact that civilians, too, had been forced to leave Luanda. On 29 July, an MPLA statement declared that 'the people of Luanda observed the expulsion of ELNA [FNLA army] forces with joy',[61] though a further battle between MPLA and FNLA forces on 8 August 'prompted the Portuguese to accede to MPLA

---

[56] F. J. du T. Spies, *Operasie Savannah: Angola 1975–1976* (Pretoria, 1989), 61.
[57] Interview, Chivukuvuku.
[58] Interview, General Nunda, Luanda, September 2009.
[59] *Província de Angola* 24 July 1975, 1. The period from the coup until July 1975 was the only time in Angolan history when all political parties enjoyed something close to equal access to the media, and this makes newspaper sources particularly interesting. *PA* published the movements' statements verbatim.
[60] *PA* 27 July 1975, 3.
[61] *PA* 29 July 1975, 7.

demands that the FNLA's ministers be evacuated from the capital'.[62] UNITA members of the Transitional Government left Luanda around the same time. Some Portuguese supporters of UNITA warned officials in the movement that they would be in danger were they to remain in Luanda and provided an aircraft to take them to Huambo.[63] Events in August spelled the end of the Transitional Government and of the Alvor Accord.[64]

In the Central Highlands, UNITA responded with violence against MPLA supporters. Moco, at the time a young MPLA militant in the Huambo area, was imprisoned for a while by UNITA, whose 'dominance was ideological, physical, military, everything. MPLA militants were seized, they were killed.... This was practically pay-back for what happened to the UNITA militants who had been in Luanda'.[65] News reports in late June describe Savimbi being greeted in Huambo by 'a throng calculated at many dozens of thousands of people who applauded him deliriously'.[66] UNITA proceeded to consolidate its control of the region by expelling MPLA forces from Kuito early in August.[67] The MPLA, previously concerned only with opposition from the FNLA, began now to speak of UNITA as a rival, accusing UNITA and the FNLA of 'intimidating and terrorising our militants... and stopping the advance of our people in the struggle against imperialism' and accusing UNITA of attacking MPLA activists in the Central Highlands repeatedly during July and August.[68] If UNITA was a latecomer to a conflict that initially involved the MPLA and FNLA, this was the consequence of its weak presence and lack of ambitions in Luanda at a time when the other two movements were investing their efforts in securing a city that they knew was the key to controlling the independent state. Although UNITA elites emphasised their movement's local origins in the Central Highlands, most people in that region remained distant from politics until the conflict reached the interior, and the experience of violence served to politicise people who had previously felt they had no stake in the contest between the rival movements. Interviews with people who remember the period suggest that some remained apathetic until the 'massacres' and population movements of July and August 1975 made it impossible for town dwellers in the Central Highlands to ignore the conflict.

[62] Tony Hodges 'How the MPLA Won in Angola', in Colin Legum and Tony Hodges, *After Angola: The War Over Southern Africa* (London, 1976), 53.

[63] Interview with Jaka Jamba, Luanda, September 2009.

[64] Mabeko-Tali, *Dissidências*, II.ºVol., 110–111.

[65] Interview with Moco.

[66] *PA* 29 June 1975. Huambo is referred to by the colonial name of Nova Lisboa.

[67] Hodges 'How the MPLA Won', 53.

[68] *PA* 9 August 1975, 1.

Accounts of the later years of the Angolan war emphasise the role of foreign intervention in the context of the Cold War in fuelling the conflict. It therefore seems apt to note at this point that the antagonism described so far developed at a time when none of the Angolan movements was heavily armed. UNITA received some arms from South Africa in October 1974, yet when South African instructors arrived a year later, they found UNITA's forces still lacking in materiel and training.[69] The MPLA began to receive support from its principal backer, the Cuban military mission, only in late August 1975.[70] UNITA's dominance of the Central Highlands by August 1975 and the MPLA's taking control of Luanda around the same time were due above all to local mobilisation accompanied by the active or tacit approval of the Portuguese state.

The territorial character of the Angolan conflict had been established by August 1975. The country was becoming divided into what the press and the Portuguese authorities termed 'zones of influence': a euphemism for outright control by one of the nationalist movements.[71] By the end of the month, the MPLA controlled the coast from Luanda southwards and the Luanda hinterland as far east as the border with Zaire at Luau. The FNLA held the northern coastal strip and the adjacent interior, while UNITA occupied the southern interior. From then on, while the FNLA and UNITA maintained a strategic alliance, the relationship between the MPLA and the other movements became wholly antagonistic, and any semblance of the cooperation agreed to at Alvor disappeared. UNITA and the MPLA simultaneously denied the 'balkanisation' of Angola while blaming each other for it.[72] In Luanda, the MPLA began to institutionalise its control of the city. Its behaviour and rhetoric became less that of a liberation movement than that of an authoritarian government, even before it was recognised as such. Lopo de Nascimento, prime minister in the Transitional Government, declared that the elections agreed to at Alvor were now 'out of the question owing to the situation in the country'.[73]

---

[69] Spies, *Operasie Savannah*, 69–70.

[70] Gleijeses, *Conflicting Missions*, 247–349, questions the findings by Hodges and by Marcum that the MPLA was receiving large quantities of Soviet weaponry by April 1975 and suggests that the MPLA's most significant source of arms in early 1975 was either Yugoslavia or Algeria.

[71] For example, in early September, the National Decolonisation Commission noted 'the introduction by the liberation movements of large quantities of armaments since 25 April... a lack of political tolerance that is manifesting itself in violence ... the existence of so-called zones of influence and of supposed military superiority ... [and] the arming of the civilian population (*PA* 5 September 1975, 7). Marcum (*Angolan Revolution II*, 263) notes that the liberation movements were 'dug into their ... bastions' by September, though Hodges ('How the MPLA Won', 52) suggests that this process had begun in early July.

[72] *PA* 14 August 1975, 7–8; 15 August 1975, 9; 21 August 1975, 9.

[73] *DN* 1 August 1975, 7.

A news report suggested that the neighbourhood committees formed earlier in the year had by now become 'People's Defence Committees [CDP] ...: a paramilitary organism made up of workers [that] guarantees the conditions for the existence and defence of the institutions of People's Power.... All armed individuals that do not belong either to the FAPLA or to the CDP are considered illegal armed bandits'.[74] The MPLA had begun explicitly to assume for itself a monopoly on violence in those areas that it controlled, adopting a state-like prerogative while Angola legally remained under Portuguese sovereignty. The movement also called upon the population to 'go back to work' after the disruption caused by the conflict and assumed the task of 'organising the country' through the party's Mass Organisation Committee.[75] The MPLA seized control of Angola's state broadcaster and of the newspaper *Província de Angola* in order 'to serve ... the people, and not to serve reactionary forces'. The newspaper's daily military situation report, which previously had come from the High Commissioner, now began also to include a statement from FAPLA, and the editorial line began to favour the MPLA and promote 'generalised popular resistance'.[76] By 9 September, the MPLA had reconstituted the government, with MPLA incumbents in positions formerly occupied by UNITA and FNLA appointees.[77] A CIA brief noted that MPLA officials had 'worked hard to cultivate the impression that their organization is the only liberation group capable of running an independent Angolan government'.[78]

The personal and ideological links between the Portuguese left and the MPLA may have eased the MPLA's assumption of power in Luanda.[79] Both sides spoke a similar language of class struggle and anti-imperialism. Admiral António Rosa Coutinho, the first new governor to be appointed to Luanda after the coup, was open in his support for the MPLA, a fact that led to his recall after the Alvor Accord.[80] Mabeko-Tali argues that although the MPLA was divided over participation in the Transitional Government, the uncompromising attitude that became predominant was based at least in part on intelligence provided by the MFA regarding the relative weakness of the FNLA.[81] No less important than its ideological affinity with the MFA, however, was the fact that the MPLA's primary support base was in Luanda, that

[74]　*PA* 20 August 1975, 3.
[75]　*DN* 27 August 1975, 10; 16 September 1975, 7.
[76]　*PA* 21 August 1975, 2.
[77]　*PA* 9 September 1975, 1; *DN* 9 September 1975, 7.
[78]　US NARA RG263, CIA National Intelligence Bulletin, 18 October 1975.
[79]　Macqueen, *Decolonization*, 164, 173; Jean-Michel Mabeko-Tali, *Dissidências*, II.°Vol., 34.
[80]　Macqueen, *Decolonization*, 176.
[81]　Mabeko-Tali, *Dissidências*, II.°Vol., 115–118.

it controlled the important ministries of the Interior and Communication in the Transitional Government and that it had the support of those Angolans employed in the colonial civil service who remained in their posts as the Portuguese departed. Its control of security and propaganda allowed it to consolidate its base in Luanda even while FNLA and UNITA members still remained in the Transitional Government. Even some opponents of the MPLA acknowledged that it was better equipped to rule than either the FNLA or UNITA.[82] Macqueen suggests that by July 1975, Portugal was less inclined to side with the MPLA than had been the case a year earlier.[83] Whatever the motivation, it is clear that Portugal did little or nothing to challenge claims of sovereignty by the MPLA in and around Luanda from mid-1975, the heart of the colonial state, where Portuguese authority was at least notionally present until the scheduled date of independence.

As the MPLA assumed control in Luanda, so in Huambo did UNITA begin to assert its authority as the MPLA was chased out of town. It is uncertain how much authority the colonial state wielded at this point. In a single report, we may read that 'the Portuguese army is in control of the situation' but also that 'with the withdrawal of MPLA forces from the capital of Huambo, UNITA and FNLA forces have come to control the two main centres of the Central Highlands, Nova Lisboa [Huambo] and Silva Porto [Kuito]'.[84] Portuguese 'control' here seems to mean simply maintaining a military presence and not interfering as the Angolan movements battled for dominance. Neither the FNLA nor UNITA was as effective as the MPLA in taking over state functions and asserting itself as a government in areas it controlled. Among interviewees who remembered 1975 in Huambo, those who supported UNITA spoke of UNITA-aligned teachers and nurses keeping schools and clinics operating until UNITA was expelled from the towns in February 1976. MPLA supporters, by contrast, insisted that if services functioned at all under UNITA, it was thanks to Angolan employees of the colonial state staying in their posts rather than because of any new initiative by UNITA. Isolation from seaports and the departure of Portuguese businesses devastated the regional economy. *Província de Angola* reported that 'Huambo remains almost isolated from the rest of the world' with telephone and telex lines down and no fuel to generate power for the VHF radio station.[85] The paper quoted people who had come from Huambo as saying, 'there is no longer beer, nor sugar, nor any kind of

---

[82] *Tempo* 21 August 1975, 12.
[83] Macqueen, *Decolonization*, 182.
[84] *DN* 12 August 1975, 2. 'Huambo' in this report refers to the district of which Nova Lisboa was the capital. After independence, the city too became officially known as Huambo.
[85] *PA* 28 August 1975, 8.

the most essential foods', and nor was there petrol. UNITA and the FNLA were nevertheless willing and able to take hold of state resources for their own purposes, and the Portuguese authorities were unwilling or unable to resist. In September, the state airline, TAAG, announced that it would henceforth only operate flights to MPLA zones after the FNLA and UNITA requisitioned TAAG aircraft in Uige and Huambo.[86] This was at a time when there was still a Portuguese military presence in Huambo. UNITA kept part of the Benguela Railway running and pressed it into the service of the movement.[87] In Kuito, UNITA took over the local branch of the state bank, and cash continued to circulate in the town.[88] Whether in Luanda or elsewhere, this assumption of state functions by the liberation movements must be seen in the context of the departure of Portuguese functionaries and the reluctance or inability of the remaining Portuguese security forces to intervene. However great Portugal's rulers' distaste for the past, they could not avoid the legal realities they had inherited. Civil servants in Angola were employees of the Portuguese state, accountable to bosses in Lisbon: hence, relinquishing sovereign powers meant the dismantling of the state in Angola. State employees were assigned priority in the repatriation programme, and if jobs were unavailable in Portugal, they were retained on half pay when they arrived.[89]

The vacuum left by the retreat of the state was even more evident in more peripheral regions of Angola, where security forces were withdrawn and civilian functions shut down as Portuguese staff departed months before Independence Day. The SADF account suggests that Portugal had abandoned Angola's southern frontier as early as August 1975. South Africa and Portugal had previously cooperated to protect the dams that spanned the South West Africa–Angola border on the Cunene River, but 'by August 1975 the steady dismantling of the Portuguese administration was unmistakeable'. As UNITA forces seized two border control points in early August, 'the Portuguese detail at the posts went to seek safety with the South African Police in Ovamboland'.[90] The departure of the Portuguese soldiers opened the way for the SADF to assume military positions in Angola on 12 August. An editorial in *Diário de Notícias* fumed at a violation of Portuguese sovereignty, but Portuguese forces appear not to have resisted.[91] Portuguese troops were simultaneously withdrawing from northern

---

[86] *PA* 5 September 1975, 2.
[87] Bridgland, *Jonas Savimbi*, 164. The Benguela Railway connects the towns of the Central Highlands with the ports of Benguela and Lobito.
[88] Spies, *Operasie Savannah*, 75.
[89] National Security Archive, George Washington University, file Angola 24365. Cable, AmConsul Luanda to SecState, 7 Aug 1975.
[90] Spies, *Operasie Savannah*, 46.
[91] *DN* 12 August 1975, 1.

Angola. A report on 6 August describes the evacuation of Uige and Negage, two strategic towns in the coffee-producing areas where the FNLA was dominant: 'As is usual, a large part of the civilian population accompanied the Portuguese troops [in a] column, comprising hundreds of vehicles.'[92]

One settler who returned to Portugal contrasted the phased withdrawal of troops agreed to at Alvor with the reality, where

> military and logistical support for Portuguese troops in Angola disappeared – they were in danger of becoming isolated.... Whenever the Portuguese troops abandoned a certain city or position, the white population would also leave .... Blacks who were not allied with the movement that controlled that area would also leave.[93]

As we have seen, there were ideological reasons why the revolutionary government in Portugal was hesitant to exercise its powers of sovereignty in Angola. But its apparent lack of interest in events in Africa can also in part be attributed to a political crisis in Portugal itself, fuelled not only by domestic concerns but also by settlers' fears and their anger at what they perceived as abandonment by the government. As its forces relinquished control, Portugal announced plans to airlift 270,000 people from Luanda and Huambo in the three months before independence, twice as many people as had left in the 15 months since the coup.[94] According to General Nunda, UNITA forces assisted the evacuation operations in Huambo; it is entirely plausible that the airlift would have required at least the collaboration if not the active coopera- tion of UNITA. In the months that followed, the airlift came to be the main preoccupation of the colonial government, until in early October the authori- ties declared the evacuation of Huambo to be complete. The concluding of the airlift in the city spelt the end of the Portuguese presence in the southern half of Angola, more than a month before independence.

The account of events presented so far indicates that the delimitation of terri- tory between the MPLA and UNITA that had occurred by the end of August 1975 was the result of local political mobilisation and decisions taken autonomously by the leadership of each movement and was established without organised military confrontations. Instead, the dominant movement in each region gradu- ally assumed control of territory and sometimes took over state functions in the face of an ever-diminishing Portuguese military and administrative presence.

---

92 *DN* 6 August 1975, 7.
93 *Tempo* 21 August 1975. Mabeko-Tali, *Dissidências, II.°Vol.*, 35 also attests to the Portuguese fail- ure to resist the takeover of territory by the FNLA.
94 National Security Archive, file Angola 24365. Cables, AmConsul Luanda to SecState, 7 August 1975 and 30 September 1975.

Violence was in the form of skirmishes between the soldiers of the different movements or attacks on civilians who were assumed to be associated with an opposing movement. As noted, the MPLA and UNITA began receiving help from military instructors, respectively Cubans and South Africans, from August or September 1975, and South Africa unilaterally moved its troops north of the Cunene River. But in August, the Angolan movements still retained the military and political initiative. This was to change over the following two months as foreign involvement came to dominate the political calculus of Angolan actors as both the MPLA and UNITA looked abroad for support. In October, the large-scale South African invasion profoundly changed the character of the conflict. A UNITA unit led by a South African major and supported by South African advisors stopped the MPLA's attempt to advance from Benguela towards Huambo.[95] This was followed by the SADF Taskforce Zulu, which entered Angola on 14 October and expelled the MPLA from the coastal strip as far north as Novo Redondo (Sumbe). Cuba, despite the MPLA's requests for help in the face of the South African invasion, was more hesitant about sending soldiers to sovereign Portuguese territory. The first Cuban fighting force arrived on 9 November and was despatched southwards to halt the South African advance. Two days later, Portugal conceded sovereignty to 'the Angolan people', a deliberately ambiguous formulation that sealed the existing reality of territorial contestation.[96] The MPLA's President Agostinho Neto declared the independence of the People's Republic of Angola in Luanda, while Savimbi declared the Democratic Republic of Angola in Huambo. Cuban Special Forces checked the South African advance by blowing up bridges on the River Queve and later in a decisive battle at Ebo on 23 November.[97] Meanwhile, the FNLA army that was approaching Luanda from the north was routed by Cuban missiles. In this way, the military initiative passed to the MPLA, leading to the SADF's withdrawal from Angola between January and March 1976 and to UNITA's flight from the towns of the interior in early February.

The developments that this chapter has described from the 1960s until early 1976 established the terms on which politics in Angola would be understood in the years of war that followed. A complex of ideas that linked the control of territory and of people, through the notion of statehood, to political legitimacy had been established before either UNITA or the MPLA was receiving any significant foreign assistance; South Africa and Cuba, respectively, sent troops to Angola only in October and November 1975. First, a relatively privileged

---

95 Gleijeses, *Conflicting Missions*, 269; Spies, *Operasie Savannah*, 76–82.
96 Macqueen, *Decolonization*, 196.
97 Gleijeses, *Conflicting Missions*, 298–317.

group of people had access to anti-colonial ideas at least ten years earlier than the majority of the region's population. This came from their links with the church or with people who had travelled to other parts of Angola or through listening to radio broadcasts. People in this category, based in towns or at the missions, believed they possessed a political consciousness that was unavailable to mere peasants. Later chapters will make clear that political officials on both sides treated politics as an urban and elite business, in which farmers were the objects of strategic decisions made by others.

Second, geography determined that there was only minimal direct contact between the nationalist movements and the people of the Central Highlands before 25 April 1974. Popular mobilisation, when it eventually happened, was oriented towards building a following for each party in towns and cities. The rural population of the Central Highlands was marginal to processes of politicisation. UNITA itself emphasised its rural roots, yet it was a rural movement only in the sense that it mobilised among peasants in eastern Angola before independence (as indeed the MPLA did too) and more widely after independence. It did not emerge in response to specifically rural grievances against the Portuguese colonial state. Moreover, while the received accounts of Angolan nationalism associate UNITA with the Central Highlands, the MPLA could claim clandestine followers in the region even before UNITA's foundation in 1966. The political fault lines in the Angola war were not in the first place along lines of region and ethnicity, and nor were they along lines of class or of rural versus urban interests.

Third, even with independence in sight, each party further developed the armed forces that it had established during the anti-colonial struggle. These forces were deployed against supporters or perceived supporters of other parties, including civilians. This served to entrench a pattern of territorial control and to deepen mutual fear and suspicion. Political militants targeted people not on the basis of their political views but on the basis of their origins, yet they sought to justify their violence by imputing political affiliation on the basis of where people came from.

The final point is about the establishment of political exclusivity in various parts of Angola. The MPLA moved to take sole control of the government and other state institutions in Luanda. In the Central Highlands, UNITA's adoption of the formal instruments of power was less consistent, but it remained the dominant military force in the region. On the eve of independence, the MPLA, UNITA and the FNLA each enjoyed exclusive control in a particular region of Angola. This control was secured through a monopoly of violence, but each side asserted its legitimacy by acting to a greater or lesser degree in a state-like manner. Each movement claimed legitimacy throughout Angolan territory and spoke of its rivals as illegitimate and alien to Angola.

These developments during 1974 and 1975 served to establish two important themes in the discourses that surrounded the Angolan civil conflict: first, an association between political movements and territory and second, the assignation of identity to people on the basis of the movement that controlled the territory where they lived. The following chapters will demonstrate how these themes evolved in the years after independence and continued to define how politics was understood on both sides of the conflict in the Central Highlands.

2

UNITA 1975–1976: From the Cities to the 'Long March'

The hasty departure of the Portuguese administration and security forces from Huambo in October 1975, alongside the violent struggle between the liberation movements to take control, ensured that Independence Day made little difference to people's everyday lives in the Central Highlands. By 11 November, UNITA had effectively been in control of Huambo for at least a month. Less than three months later, UNITA's leaders, soldiers and part of the civilian population fled from the cities of the Central Highlands as the FAPLA and their Cuban allies advanced from the coast. This chapter is concerned with the few months during which UNITA controlled the cities of the Central Highlands, with its subsequent retreat and with how this period was remembered in the years that followed. UNITA supporters would recall the final months of 1975 as evidence that UNITA was able to take responsibility for the running of the institutions left behind by the colonial state, while others remember the period simply as an interregnum between the departure of the Portuguese and the arrival of the MPLA.

Yet even if for practical purposes, 11 November was just another day of de facto UNITA rule and of little certainty about the future, in legal terms it remained the date on which Portugal formally surrendered sovereignty over Angola. UNITA marked the occasion with independence celebrations in Huambo that asserted UNITA's position at the centre of an independent Angolan nation. Fred Bridgland, who was covering events as a journalist, describes a 'desultory' ceremony at midnight on 10/11 November at Huambo's football stadium, during which the Portuguese flag was lowered without a single Portuguese person present, and a UNITA military police officer took the salute as the UNITA flag was raised. Gunfire had broken out several hours earlier as UNITA soldiers celebrated and continued throughout the night.[1] Savimbi had been busy with another engagement on 10 November

---

[1] Fred Bridgland, *Jonas Savimbi: A Key to Africa* (Edinburgh, 1986), 132–133.

1975. A South African Defence Force account relates that the UNITA leader, having requested a meeting with South African Prime Minister J. B. Vorster, was flown that morning to Pretoria via the Caprivi Strip in northern Namibia. After meeting Vorster and other senior government officials, he returned to Angola the same day, having secured Vorster's commitment 'not to withdraw the South Africans from Angola immediately provided that Russia and Cuba's help to the MPLA did not grow to the point that South Africa could not deal with the onslaught without the help of a foreign power'.[2] It was only the next day that Savimbi declared the independence of the Democratic People's Republic of Angola at the same stadium. Savimbi began by chiding the soldiers for their unruly behaviour. 'If tonight, or at any other time from now onwards any UNITA soldier fires a shot without an order, it will be his last shot [...] If we catch you firing your gun, you will not move again from that very spot.'[3] The remainder of Savimbi's speech included attacks both on the former Portuguese colonists and the MPLA. He sought to cast doubt on the MPLA's authenticity as Angolan by stating that 'Portugal wished to decolonise by leaving us here with its godchild named Antonio Agostinho Neto.'[4] He nevertheless expressed willingness to contest elections with the MPLA as soon as it 'decides to consider other liberation movements as patriots'. He also emphasised the MPLA's Soviet links as evidence of the movement's non-Angolan nature. 'While the MPLA goes on thinking that only through Russian arms can they offer an ideology, we will say "no" and we will continue to fight.' The speech also set out a vision of the role of the state in relation to the people, declaring a 'people-oriented socialism' in which political leaders would take their cue from people's demands. 'They want jobs, schools, sanitation. We depend on the people. From the institutions here they deserve respect, kindness and consideration. The people must be cherished.'[5] Public celebrations began the same day. General Peregrino Isidro Wambu Chindondo, who was 15 years old at the time and whose older brothers were already in UNITA's army, remembers 'a big rally on the eleventh, well organised. UNITA was a great political force at that time. There were difficulties but the message that UNITA transmitted was that there would

---

[2]   FJ du T Spies, *Operasie Savannah: Angola 1975–1976* (S. A. Weermag, Direktoraat Openbare Betrekkinge, 1989), 149; John Marcum, *The Angolan Revolution, Volume II (Exile Politics and Guerrilla Warfare, 1962–1976)* (Cambridge, MA, 1978), quotes a newspaper source also mentioning the 10 November visit.

[3]   Bridgland, *Jonas Savimbi*, 134 – ellipsis in original.

[4]   Bridgland, *Jonas Savimbi*, 134–135.

[5]   Bridgland, *Jonas Savimbi*, 135.

soon be an agreement between the estranged brothers [i.e. the rival parties]. But this was only reached years later'.[6]

The symbolism of the independence ceremony, echoing similar ceremonies that had marked the end of colonial rule across Africa throughout the 1960s, was itself a declaration of how UNITA saw its own status. From Savimbi's speech, several themes emerge that form the basis of how UNITA asserted its own legitimacy and defined its role in relation to the Angolan nation. The first is the stating of UNITA's anti-colonial credentials (even if, in reality, UNITA had done little to hasten the departure of the Portuguese) and the painting of the MPLA as colonial stooges. Second is Savimbi's preoccupation with maintaining order, which is linked to his assertion of the legitimacy of violence carried out in the name of the political movement (hence his threat of capital punishment), as opposed to the illegitimate violence perpetrated by soldiers without orders. The third theme is Savimbi's ambitious conception of the duties of the dominant political movement with respect to its people. These characterisations of UNITA's role as set out by Savimbi call on three distinct but interrelated norms of statehood: the idea common to post-colonial Africa of the state as the token of the aspirations of a nation whose identity was formed in a process of anti-colonial struggle; the Weberian idea of the state as the entity that defines which violence is legitimate and which is not; and an idea derived from the developmental ideologies of late colonialism and the first decade of African independence of the state as an entity with a duty of care and responsibility for the betterment of the people. These norms were not adopted only by UNITA. Interviews quoted throughout this book will show how political leaders and ordinary people regardless of their political affiliation evoked the same norms as measures of a political movement's legitimacy and its prerogatives in relation to the people under its control.

Savimbi's claims to statehood bore no relation to the reality in which UNITA found itself. With the departure of public-service personnel from the cities of the interior, UNITA inherited physical infrastructure but hardly a functioning state. Moreover, its claims of national inclusivity were hollow considering that it continued to be at war with the MPLA. UNITA's alliance with the FNLA counted for little after the forces commanded by the FNLA's leader, Holden Roberto, were put to flight north of Luanda in the days after independence. Savimbi's entente with Daniel Chipenda, the former MPLA faction leader who led what remained of the FNLA forces in the south of Angola, lasted barely two months after independence.[7]

---

6 Interview with Wambu, Luanda, September 2009.
7 Marcum, *Angolan Revolution II*, 276.

What, then, did UNITA achieve, and is it in any way accurate to talk about government in the Central Highlands during that period between the departure of the Portuguese and the arrival of the MPLA? Separating fact from prejudice is never simple when interpreting interviews, and more than thirty years after the events, people's memories of UNITA's brief time in the cities of the Central Highlands were especially clouded by political preference and by the experience of subsequent events. Their recollections of the period are useful as repositories of the preferred discourse of one or other party more than as accurate records of events. For those who supported UNITA, its legitimacy as a government resided as much in what it aspired to do as in what it actually did. The accounts of UNITA supporters tell us much about the interlinked ideas concerning Angolan history and UNITA's place within it that were fundamental to their acceptance of and support for UNITA. A *soba* who had been loyal to UNITA since before independence recalled UNITA's efforts in terms of the principles that the movement espoused rather than in terms of concrete progress: 'Savimbi fought for Angolans to have no limits on their education … Savimbi wanted everyone to study to whatever level, without paying money. In the days of Savimbi we understood for the first time that one could get medical treatment without paying.'[8] Other party members of the same generation recalled that 'nothing changed with independence – the Portuguese left then the war began' – but that 'UNITA defended the people's goods' and 'the administration functioned – in 1975 we had functionaries in all the areas'. The shops continued to function, 'everything in the service of the party'.[9] General Wambu recalls that schooling continued during the period of UNITA control 'with some difficulties, because we had lost some teachers who had gone to Portugal. But new teachers came. […] There were many shortages – books, notebooks – because at that time the academic year began in October, so we were in the first term'.[10] As long as it had a presence in the cities, UNITA's first task was to assert its control over the relics of the colonial state and to maintain minimal levels of services. As noted in the previous chapter, it kept the Benguela Railway operating, albeit in the service of the party rather than as a public transport amenity.[11] In Kuito, UNITA took control of the local branch of Banco de Angola, and people continued to use cash.[12] Estêvão, a long-time UNITA loyalist, pointed to the significance of the cities within UNITA's political logic: 'The MPLA called in the Cubans

---

[8]   Interviewee 86, Huambo, July 2008.
[9]   Interviewees 82 and 83, Huambo, June 2008.
[10] Interview with Wambu, Luanda, September 2009.
[11] Bridgland, *Jonas Savimbi*, 164.
[12] Spies, *Operasie Savannah*, 75.

[to take Huambo from UNITA in 1976] because it knew that who controls Huambo, controls the south of Angola.'[13]

If the accounts of UNITA supporters provide an idea of how UNITA presented its role, we need to listen to those with a more sceptical attitude to obtain a more tempered view of whether it succeeded. Bernardo, the former civil servant quoted in the previous chapter, suggested that Savimbi's declaration of statehood was nothing more than empty rhetoric:

> Even if it's known that Savimbi proclaimed the Democratic Republic of Angola, I know nothing of this because UNITA governed in a climate of war. UNITA didn't have a flag of the republic, only the movement's flag. If UNITA installed the Democratic Republic of the South I didn't know of this, because having a republic means having a flag, constitution, government recognised not only at the local level but also internationally. This didn't happen. I think we're dealing with a kind of speculation here.

Bernardo sets out the criteria whereby a movement may become a state: these include the visible symbols of statehood but also international recognition. Even though these were lacking, Bernardo nevertheless acknowledges that UNITA made 'efforts' and performed 'certain tasks … in the midst of the conditions of war … safeguarding certain health services, certain education services. These functioned, but not to the extent that people would have wished them to be in peacetime – they were services in a climate of war'.[14] But if UNITA's failure as a provider was at least in part due to the context of war in which it operated, this fact alone does not make him any more sympathetic to UNITA. His assessment of the UNITA occupation between 1975 and 1976 seems to have been coloured by his own long association with the MPLA state, and as the next chapter will make clear, his assessment of the MPLA's subsequent efforts at state building were more positive.

Others who did not share Bernardo's ideological antipathy to UNITA also recalled that UNITA made an inadequate government during those months in the cities but suggested this was simply because it lacked the necessary skills and outside support. The recollections of Ricardo, a schoolteacher from Huambo who had been 30 years old at the time of independence, were typical. His attitude to party politics was ambivalent: he regarded UNITA's identity claims among southern Angolans as valid but also felt an affinity with the MPLA since he and his wife had spent their careers in government service since 1976. Life under UNITA, Ricardo recalled, 'was difficult … we didn't have petrol, nor salt nor soap'. Although UNITA had tried to establish a

[13] Interviewee 60, Caála, June 2008.
[14] Interviewee 31, Huambo, May 2008.

government, 'it was a government that didn't work properly for people to live well'. Hospitals stayed open, 'but there were few medicines in the hospital and few doctors, only nurses'. The schools operated, but without proper wages for the teachers.[15] The description by a Protestant preacher from Huambo, Pastor David, gives a further indication of how people who were not strongly politically committed spoke of UNITA's time in the cities in 1975:

> [UNITA] had their government, they had their administrators around the country. The question of electricity – except that later they cut it off. The question of water – then they cut it off. But in principle they tried to organise, to put in order everything that the Portuguese government left. But they didn't have the technicians to maintain it.[16]

Pastor David suggests that maintaining the legacy of the colonial state is the minimum criterion for evaluating a political movement in power: he explicitly judges UNITA's success as a state against the colonial state and finds it wanting. As we shall see later, UNITA adherents also evoked memories of colonialism as a yardstick for judging the MPLA's effectiveness. The fact that the UNITA officials and some of the FNLA officials in the Transitional Government had settled in Huambo after leaving Luanda provided for a certain degree of continuity, at least as far as incumbency in office was concerned. Paulina, who already had strong pro-MPLA views at the time of independence, also suggested that whatever government structures might have existed under UNITA were simply the remnants of what had existed before.

> There was a government with two parties, with portfolios divided between UNITA and the FNLA. I worked with the Agriculture Ministry, which went to the FNLA. I felt the minister didn't feel good [about working with UNITA], but being from the FNLA he had more trust in me. [In terms of governance] UNITA did nothing. I preferred to stay at home.[17]

People's views about UNITA's attempts at governance have been coloured by their present-day political affiliations, yet beneath the differences of interpretation, there is a consensus on certain facts: UNITA (and initially FNLA) officials took seats in government offices, but the administration had neither the human nor the material resources to function effectively.[18] The best that the

---

[15] Interviewee 48, near Huambo, June 2008. The lack of basic manufactured commodities such as salt was a recurrent theme in recollections of life in UNITA areas throughout the war.

[16] Interviewee 19, Huambo, May 2008.

[17] Interviewee 150, Caála, August 2008.

[18] A visiting journalist described Huambo in January 1976 as a town where economic activity and public services had all but ceased. 'The War in Angola: View From 2 Sides', *New York Times*, 23 January 1976.

administration could hope for would be to keep the functions inherited from the colonial government operating at a minimal level. Where this happened, it appears to be thanks to public servants who remained in their posts rather than to any original initiative by UNITA. Dedicated UNITA sympathisers saw an inherent value in the movement's occupation of government structures and its maintenance of at least the rituals of governance: structures and rituals that reflect colonial-era norms. Those less devoted to UNITA also invoked these norms to demonstrate UNITA's lack of success. As Chapter 5 will make clear, Savimbi later sought to present UNITA as a rural guerrilla movement whose aims were at one with those of the peasantry. Yet during these months after independence, UNITA's norms and priorities echoed those of urban colonial statehood. Sceptics, as well as dedicated MPLA supporters, expressed their reservations about UNITA not in terms of any lack of inherent worth but rather in terms of UNITA's lack of capacity – or lack of ability – to be an effective government. The minimum norms by which people made this judgement had to do with the maintenance of institutions put in place under colonial rule.

DEPARTURE FROM HUAMBO AND THE 'LONG MARCH'

By January 1976, Savimbi had already decided that retreat from the towns that UNITA had occupied was inevitable, as South Africa withdrew direct military support for UNITA while Cuba continued to provide military backing and developmental assistance to the MPLA state. Savimbi informed UNITA officials that they were 'rowing against the tide' in trying to resist the MPLA. UNITA was aware of the proposed Clark Amendment to the United States International Security and Assistance and Arms Control Act, which became law later that year and which banned US assistance to non-state armed groups operating in other countries.[19] South Africa had ordered the withdrawal of

---

[19] Samuel Chiwale, *Cruzei-me com a História* (Lisbon, 2008), 215–216. The amendment successfully sponsored by Democrat Senator Dick Clark against the wishes of the Ford administration had started life as the amendment proposed by Senator John Tunney to the Defense Appropriation Bill: George Wright, *The Destruction of a Nation: United States' Policy Toward Angola since 1945* (London, 1997), 68–77. B. J. Vorster's conditional promise made to Savimbi on 10 November 1975 (Spies, *Operasie Savannah*, 149), that South African forces would remain in Angola as long as it was equal to the task of keeping the Cuban forces at bay, had apparently been eclipsed by the military progress made by the MPLA and its Cuban allies. The strength of UNITA's own forces at this point is indicated by Spies's account of the UNITA troops trained by South African instructors at Capolo, near Kuito, between September and November. 'By the time the South Africans evacuated the base on 8 November 1975, the following UNITA force had been trained: three infantry battalions each comprising three companies, three 81mm mortar platoons, three 60mm mortar platoons, three 4.5 inch mortar

its troops on 14 January, and they retreated to within fifty miles of the border
with Namibia. The last South African soldiers would later leave Angola on
27 March.[20] A man who had been part of Savimbi's proto-government in
Huambo recalled Savimbi admitting that UNITA had lost the conventional
war because 'We don't know how to choose our friends. The United States is
not our friend. If we'd chosen the Russians we'd be in Luanda by now.'[21]

According to Samuel Chiwale, who was later to become UNITA's military
commander in chief, UNITA began withdrawing from the towns in January
1976, ahead of the advance by the MPLA and the Cubans. Once the MPLA
had entered Huambo and Kuito in February, Chiwale writes, 'the abandonment was total: we had lost "our" capital'.[22] Some 5,000 UNITA troops left
Huambo as the MPLA and Cuban forces approached early on 9 February
1976 and retreated east to Vila Nova.[23] Unrecorded numbers of civilians went
with them. UNITA did not maintain a clear categorical distinction between
people serving in civilian and military roles, but interviews make clear that the
majority of those who withdrew from the cities with UNITA were not armed.
This exodus was confirmed by interviewees who stayed behind in Huambo, as
well as those who left with UNITA. According to an interviewee whose political sympathies were pro-MPLA:

> This is normally the strategy when troops leave: they have to take the public
> with them for defence. We saw when the government was coming, UNITA
> said 'come with us because they are from the other side, they are the enemy' –
> this is always a strategy.

Despite his own opposition to UNITA, this man admitted that some civilians
went voluntarily with UNITA, while others were taken by force.

> Some could leave more easily than others – it depended where they were in
> relation to the advancing army. It can be overwhelming, a military clash – so

platoons, three 50 inch Browning machine gun platoons and crew for eleven 106mm canons.
Also, 60 UNITA solders had been trained as a leading group and another 60 as instructors. [...]
They took over training after 8 November 1975'.

[20] Piero Gleijeses, *Conflicting Missions: Havana, Washington and Africa 1959–1976* (Chapel
Hill, NC, 2002), 341–343.

[21] Interviewee 149, Lisbon, May 2009.

[22] Chiwale *Cruzei-me*, 217. I quote extensively from Chiwale's book in this chapter, while
acknowledging the need to read his account sceptically. I accept his accounts of dates, the
movement of people and the logic of UNITA strategy as generally reliable. On matters such as
the principles that UNITA supposedly upheld or the details of its interaction with the farming
population, I regard Chiwale's account, just as I regard interviews with UNITA officials on
such matters, as an indication of how UNITA liked to see itself rather than a record of how it
was. The same applies to my citations from Muekalia and from Bridgland, whose account of
this period is attributed to interviews that he conducted with Savimbi and with Nzau Puna.

[23] See also Bridgland, *Jonas Savimbi*, 174.

without knowing UNITA's programme, one might find oneself on one side or the other.[24]

This recollection of a 'clash', however, is inconsistent with most accounts, which indicate that UNITA's forces had left the city before the Cubans and the MPLA arrived. Pastor David, when asked whether the Cubans' entry into Huambo had been accompanied by much violence, replied:

> In the city, no, because they didn't find many people. The large majority fled. But those whom they [the MPLA and the Cubans] found on the road died, those who were trying to flee died. But here in the city, no. Only a few people stayed behind – including myself.

The pastor said that he was at liberty to stay in Huambo because 'I wasn't involved in any movement – I had no reason to leave'. He added that while UNITA forced its own members to leave, many others who had no formal link with the movement 'went voluntarily, because they were very frightened – they always fled because of fear'.[25] The message spread by UNITA, that the people of the Central Highlands had reason to fear the MPLA and the Cubans, had provoked anxiety beyond UNITA's immediate circle.

Simão, a former UNITA lieutenant, presented the version of events that was current within UNITA in the years that followed. This version emphasises the Cuban role in such a way as to construe UNITA's adversary as foreign, but it does not speak of UNITA being expelled from Huambo violently.

> There were no confrontations but there was a lack of understanding between presidents [Neto and Savimbi]. Agostinho Neto fetched the Cubans – the Alvor Accord never happened. In 1976 the Cubans were the greater force and we had to leave for the bush.[26]

An MPLA sympathiser interviewed in Huambo emphasised how UNITA used coercion in keeping people under its control but also acknowledged that UNITA had some support and emphasised the dilemma of people who might not have had strong political sympathies with either party, caught between the armed forces of the two sides.

> When the MPLA caught UNITA here, UNITA withdrew, and many intellectuals went with UNITA. Those who stayed were those like me who were in the seminary.... And then the war started, because [...] UNITA took,

---

[24] Interviewee 22, Huambo, May 2008.
[25] Interviewee 19, Huambo, May 2008.
[26] Interviewee 72, Caála, July 2008. The reference to the Alvor Accord refers to the failure of the agreement for the liberation movements to share power in the transition to independence.

invited everyone to leave the cities and go to the bush, to the villages. [...]
They said there would be a fierce war here in the city. So these people went
to the villages and UNITA stayed between the villages and the city, so the
people couldn't go back to the city – so they started to withdraw [further into
the countryside]. [To go back] would be difficult because it was as though the
city was sealed. The [UNITA] security forces got to work – everyone they
took, they considered a soldier as they couldn't go back. If they went back
they would be considered UNITA [by the MPLA] and could be killed.[27]

While civilians' decisions were determined by fear and by the immediate need
to avoid being caught between the two military forces, UNITA's leadership was
faced with a strategic decision about where to head to, a question that had to
be considered in terms both of the military situation and of the organisation's
vision of its future. With the MPLA and the Cubans advancing from the west
and north-west, the options seemed to be the east (Moxico province) and the
south-east (Cuando Cubango). Savimbi and Miguel Nzau Puna, respectively,
took charge of these two regions.[28] Savimbi, still in Bié following his departure
from Huambo, 'ordered his soldiers to disperse to their old forest bases and
advised UNITA's civilian followers to return to their relations in villages. As far
as possible, the enemy must be left with empty towns to conquer'.[29]

Savimbi and a group of officers travelled east, flying first to Luena, the
major town of eastern Angola. However, they had barely arrived before
the town came under attack by the MPLA and Cuban forces, and the group
made for Lumbala Nguimbo. They remained there for one month, during
which time the UNITA officers rallied soldiers in the area who had joined
UNITA during the anti-colonial war. A Cuban air attack on Lumbala Nguimbo
on 13 March prompted a rapid evacuation of 4,000 soldiers, and civilians left at
dawn the following day to Sessa, a former colonial forestry settlement.[30] From
here, Savimbi despatched troops to establish bases in locations farther west
and ordered them to carry out guerrilla attacks.[31]

By 24 March, Savimbi was ready to move on, having assembled a column
of about 1,000 to accompany him, of which 'some 600 were guerrillas and the
rest civilians, including women, children, several African Protestant pastors

---

[27] Interviewee 3, Huambo, May 2008. The tendency of the MPLA authorities to identify anyone
   outside the city limits as being attached to UNITA will be discussed in the next chapter.
[28] Chiwale *Cruzei-me*, 217. Marcum, *Angolan Revolution II*, 195–196 suggests that UNITA had by
   1970 already had some success at building political structures among peasant communities in
   the east, though only in the relatively small areas that it had secured.
[29] Bridgland, *Jonas Savimbi*, 195.
[30] Bridgland, *Jonas Savimbi*, 196–198; Chiwale, *Cruzei-me*, 217–219. Bridgland refers to Luena
   and Lumbala Nguimbo by their colonial names, respectively Luso and Gago Coutinho.
[31] Bridgland, *Jonas Savimbi*, 200.

and three black Catholic priests'.[32] The journey that followed was to become mythologised in UNITA's accounts of its own history. In Chiwale's words, 'The tough journey to flee from the tentacles of our executioners came to be known in the history of our party as the Long March, because of the similarity to that of Mao Tse Tung and his companions.'[33] A former member of the Transitional Government took a more cynical view of this label: 'UNITA called it "the great march", but that was more a question of marketing. Savimbi had no need to do that. He could have gone to Namibia. But then he wouldn't have been able to go back to the guerrilla war.'[34]

Many of those who accompanied UNITA as it withdrew from the cities in 1976 were urban people with urban expectations and priorities who had no idea that aligning themselves with UNITA would involve taking on the life of an itinerant guerrilla army. Jardo Muekalia recalls being one of a group of mission-educated teenagers who set off to join UNITA motivated by a desire for adventure 'like the characters in the cowboy books that we were reading at the time'.[35] Bridgland writes that people carried with them 'their best town clothes' and 'platform-heeled shoes', and that after a day's marching, Savimbi had to lecture them on the need to travel with only the essentials.[36]

Chiwale recounts the shock of those UNITA urbanites who had left town in their cars, only to be told by Savimbi one morning that all vehicles were to be burnt:

> [T]he order dropped on us like a bomb: those present looked at one another, incredulous; someone might have thought we were not in command of our mental faculties. Honestly, it cost me immensely to throw my BMW and a Citroen, both almost new, onto the fire. The people, still perplexed, commented on what happened, which led Dr Savimbi to say: 'As from now we are going to exchange conventional war for guerrilla war, otherwise we will be wiped out by the machine of those who are pursuing us. If anyone thinks we are going to need these cars, this is completely mistaken; a guerrilla's car is his feet.'[37]

Chiwale also reports the conversations of young people and students who had never expected to find themselves in the midst of a war. 'This is what happens when you follow these old men! Now what will become of our lives?

---

[32] Bridgland, *Jonas Savimbi*, 201.
[33] Chiwale, *Cruzei-me*, 221.
[34] Interviewee 149, Lisbon, May 2009. Other interviewees and printed sources spoke of the 'Long March'.
[35] Jardo Muekalia, *Angola: A Segunda Revolução* (Lisbon, 2010), 49.
[36] Bridgland, *Jonas Savimbi*, 201.
[37] Chiwale, *Cruzei-me*, 221.

How are we going to do this by going on foot, then without planes to bring us food and things for first aid and personal hygiene, how will we survive?'[38] These observations speak not only of the unfitness of the urban recruits for guerrilla war but also of a profound difference in class background and outlook between the peasants who were necessary to Savimbi's vision of struggle and the urban people who were recruited to wage that struggle. The presence of mission-educated professionals was as much a part of the practicalities of Savimbi's plan as the presence of peasant farmers. Later chapters will demonstrate how UNITA's politics during the civil war need to be understood in terms of UNITA's efforts to forge a perception of common interest between these two groups.

UNITA's strategies for setting up new political structures that defined its relationship with rural communities will be discussed in Chapter 5. During those first few months of the 'Long March', however, UNITA benefited from the structures that had been set up during the war against the Portuguese.[39] Another former UNITA official recalled life at the bases:

> It wasn't difficult to survive. We had a line of 'zero bases' which had been set up during the armed struggle against the Portuguese army. Every day, each person worked three hours in agriculture, including the officials like me. [...] Another source was the Cuban columns – we ambushed them for food. But still, it was tough. When I went to the guerrilla war I weighed 80 kilograms – when I left, I weighed 50 kilos.[40]

This man added that the bases remained in place while Savimbi was being pursued and were sufficiently well concealed to avoid attack until 1979, when South West Africa People's Organisation (SWAPO) guerrillas revealed the location of the bases to the Cuban forces.[41] However, the meandering route taken by Savimbi's column during the five months of the march meant that weeks could go by without the marching party having contact with a base. Chiwale and Bridgland both write of the group surviving by hunting and gathering and occasionally benefiting from the hospitality of villagers.

> [The chief] was one of our allies, living almost in the beard of the enemy: a few metres from the chief's seat there was an encampment of Cubans and FAPLA, which was protecting the road. [...] 'I cannot convey my happiness and satisfaction to have you here', he said, smiling. 'So I invite you to spend

---

[38] Chiwale, *Cruzei-me*, 222.

[39] Chiwale, *Cruzei-me*, 218.

[40] Interviewee 149, Lisbon, May 2009.

[41] This detail reflects SWAPO's decision to turn away from UNITA and to ally itself with the MPLA. See Gleijeses, *Conflicting Missions*, 275–276.

the night with us; have no fear, for these people are trustworthy. No one will go and report you'. […] They served us plates of cassava porridge and sweet potato with goat and pork. […] What at first appeared to be simply an opportunity to satisfy our hunger turned into a feast.[42]

Chiwale never speaks of having to use threats or coercion to obtain food, and Bridgland's informants seem to have been similarly silent on this matter. These accounts must be read sceptically as a record of events but are important as an indication of UNITA officials' convictions about the nature of their movement: central to their belief in their movement's legitimacy was the idea that it could survive on the voluntary support of villagers. Remarks made by the UNITA official Tito Chingungi in his interviews with Bridgland give an indication of how UNITA perceived its relationship with the peasants at the time.

The President [Savimbi] lectured that UNITA had no prospect of success unless the people were with the movement. They [the villagers] would ask awkward questions and there was no way those questions could be avoided. They would ask, for example, whether the war would finish soon or whether it would be long.

The President said it would be long. There would be no quick victory. He told the chief that one day the enemy would discover that his village was helping UNITA and it would be attacked. The village should start building up food stocks in the bush for when the day came that they needed to flee.[43]

As Chapter 5 will show, UNITA's encouragement of war preparedness and its efforts to present itself as a defender against an external threat remained an important element in its interaction with the rural population throughout the war.

Some six months after retreating from the towns of the Central Highlands, Savimbi and the last remnants of the group that had accompanied him were once again in Huambo province after a circuitous journey from Luena, during which enemy attacks and fear of discovery had necessitated repeated changes of plan. Savimbi decided to head for Cuelei, a UNITA base that had been established during the anti-colonial war and which was still under the command of UNITA officers. They arrived there in August.[44] Despite the panic that had accompanied the exodus from the towns, UNITA's officers found that they were able to move and to mobilise people freely in the rural areas of the Central Highlands, even while the MPLA was in control of the towns. This was to last at least until the following year.

---

[42] Chiwale, *Cruzei-me*, 232.
[43] Bridgland, *Jonas Savimbi*, 216.
[44] Bridgland, *Jonas Savimbi*, 218; Muekalia, *Segunda Revolução*, 55.

In March 1977, UNITA held its Fourth Congress in the Benda district of
Huambo province. On the ideological level, the congress affirmed UNITA's
commitment to opposing 'Soviet penetration' in Angola and in southern Africa
more widely.[45] This resolution was strategic in terms of soliciting support from
South Africa and the United States but was consistent with the nationalist
character that UNITA strove to present inside Angola. The account by Jardo
Muekalia seeks to justify opposition to the MPLA in terms of longer historical
narratives. The MPLA's soliciting of Soviet and Cuban support, in Muekalia's
logic, was symptomatic of its lack of deep historical roots in Angolan society.
For Muekalia, the uneven penetration of colonial rule over Angola led to the
creation of a class of 'acculturated' blacks distinct from the 'indigenous' majority who were seen by the Portuguese simply as a labour force. This distinction,
he argues, was perpetuated by an MPLA that stemmed from the assimilated
class. 'For reasons of mentality, those who held power were incapable of seeing the others as fellow citizens.'[46]

More significantly, the congress endorsed a strategy for UNITA's survival.
In Chiwale's recollection, 'given that the war would be long, organisational
structures were conceived that would be able to sustain it through an efficient
system of health, so that children, and not only children, would have access
to basic literacy and to health'. UNITA's leaders were aware of the need for
a cadre of educated people to maintain the schools and health posts that the
organisation saw as the basis of its legitimacy. Chiwale writes that Savimbi
told him:

> 'We must have here the best teachers from [the missions], as well as the
> priests and pastors of those missions, otherwise we're not going to go any-
> where. Only they will manage to transmit, with wisdom, the knowledge that
> the youth need for their intellectual, cultural and military training.'
>
> 'I agree completely with you, sir', I replied, 'but we don't have these
> people here.'
>
> 'If we don't have them, then we must go to fetch them wherever they may
> be and place them in the bush to work for our revolution.'
>
> It was not difficult to put this plan into practice. It was ordered that Captain
> Geraldo Sachipengo Nunda would go to these locations to make aware the
> elites linked to education, to health and to the church, and convince them
> to join us.
>
> The plan produced results: a while later we received, with open arms, the
> most noted pastors from Central Angola with their families [...] and some

---

[45] Chiwale, *Cruzei-me*, 246. See also Muekalia, *Segunda Revolução*, 78–84.
[46] Muekalia, *Segunda Revolução*, 91–92.

[Catholic] priests. There was the same success with teachers [...] and in the area of health we had the same good fortune.[47]

If Chiwale describes this process as voluntary, Nunda himself – speaking in 2009, two decades after he broke from Savimbi – makes clear that the teachers were tricked.

> We knew that Agostinho Neto had invited the religious leaders who were at Dôndi – the leaders of the Evangelical Church ... The director of schools was there too. The Dôndi hospital continued to function, and the seminary and the church structures. Dr Savimbi knew that this posed a danger because, through these religious leaders, the MPLA would manage to mobilise the church elites at Dôndi, and also the political elite of that area. The party-political positions [between UNITA and MPLA] were still not very far apart. People who were mobilised by UNITA would be UNITA, those mobilised by the MPLA would be MPLA. [Savimbi] sent me to Dôndi to find a way of fetching the leaders. He didn't say to me 'you will fetch the leaders for them never to return'. I went to tell the leaders that Dr Savimbi was in an area not far away, just so you can go and meet him, three days away on foot. But go and talk to him, and afterwards I will bring you back. When we arrived there [where Savimbi was] he told me, 'go and fetch their wives – you will find a way of bringing their families here'. Eventually I understood that I hadn't fetched the pastors for them to return afterwards. They stayed there, and I went to the mission to fetch the families and bring them to the position where the UNITA leadership was. [...] [Savimbi] told the old men to write letters to the families. We took the letters and delivered them to the mamas.[48]

People who were familiar with Savimbi's thinking in the years after independence suggest that the UNITA leadership required a strategy that would accommodate both the need to operate in an environment where the population was large enough to allow UNITA to recruit people to its cause – what Savimbi called 'the theory of big numbers' – and the need for a central political base that was safe from attack by the MPLA government.[49] Jaka Jamba attributes this analysis to conversations that Savimbi had with Mao Tse Tung during a visit to China in 1967.

> Savimbi said that when he had met Mao he had become an admirer – he said that Mao had asked 'do you have mountains?' and he [Savimbi] had

---

[47] Chiwale, *Cruzei-me*, 244. 'Make aware' translates *sensibilizar*.

[48] Interview with Nunda, Luanda, September 2009. Dôndi, near Katchiungo in Huambo province, is the best known of the Protestant missions in the Central Highlands and was where Savimbi was educated.

[49] Chiwale, *Cruzei-me*, 243–244, 253.

replied, 'no, the mountains are more towards the coast'. [Mao] said 'to do this
task, you need a zone that is not very accessible'. Savimbi said, 'there's a part
in the east with woodland', and Mao said 'that is where you must have your
base'. On the other hand, there was the question of the relationship between
the guerrillas and the people – like a fish in water, one has to have a good
relationship with the people.[50]

Maoist ideas, including that of self-reliance, informed Savimbi's strategy of
mobilising rural communities during the anti-colonial war.[51] After independence, according to General Nunda, the movement's leaders initially believed
it would be possible to maintain a secure base in the Central Highlands,
founded on a consensual relationship with the local population in the rural
areas even while the towns of the region were in MPLA hands.

> As the Central Highlands were the most populated part of the country, and
> almost self-sufficient in food, until 1977 life was almost normal in the parts
> of the Central Highlands controlled by UNITA. Schools continued func-
> tioning, health posts continued functioning, with the secret system to buy
> medicines in the towns.[52]

During 1977, when Savimbi and other officials could move freely in the
Central Highlands, they travelled around the region and held rallies that
served, in Chiwale's words, 'to mobilise the masses and their elites,[53] a phras-
ing which, again, encapsulates UNITA's dual strategy of popular and elite
mobilisation.

Nunda explained the need for professionals in UNITA's ranks in terms of
his own understanding of Mao and the need to provide services as a way of
cementing support. 'The Chinese revolution taught that a guerrilla movement that wants to take power has to create support bases.' This required the
service of skilled individuals whose role contrasted with that of the peasantry,
which 'was more the population where soldiers were recruited, the population
that organised food for the troops, and also carried weapons for the troops'. In
later years, UNITA officials would employ the same logic in trying to justify
the capture and abduction of professional people to Jamba.

Savimbi's interest in Mao persisted at least until the late 1970s. Chiwale
recalls Savimbi saying in 1977,

---

[50] Interview with Jaka Jamba, Luanda, September 2009.

[51] Marcum, *Angolan Revolution II*, 195.

[52] Interview with Nunda, Luanda, September 2009. Nunda later became a senior UNITA gen-
      eral before joining the government forces after the Bicesse accord and eventually becoming
      commander-in-chief of the Angolan Armed Forces (FAA).

[53] Chiwale, *Cruzei-me*, 246.

We are not going to reject certain theses of Marxism completely, particularly
that which says power must be seized from the bourgeois class and handed
over to the worker and peasant class. [...] Marxism gives us a base, it's a good
principle, but to apply it mechanically [...] in a socio-economic and cultural
context like ours would be a mistake. [...] If [for the MPLA] the revolution
moves from urban centres to the periphery, our perspective is the opposite,
that is, one has to move from the countryside to the city, since in Angola [...]
we don't have a working class in the real sense of the word.[54]

The last visit to China by a senior UNITA delegation was in 1978. It included
the general chief of staff, Valdimar Chindondo, secretary for foreign relations
Ornelas Sangumba, Tito Chingunji and Samuel Chiwale.[55] This delegation
returned to Angola with promises of weapons, but Savimbi turned his back on
China in the years that followed as he consolidated his links with the South
African military.[56] Savimbi's pragmatic, even cynical, attitude towards questions of global ideology is nowhere better illustrated than in Chiwale's recollection of Savimbi mourning the death of Mao in 1976 even as he enjoyed
the hospitality of the South African Defence Force in Namibia and discussed
'the strategy to adopt to put down the red invasion' with the then-Defence
Minister P. W. Botha and his most senior generals.[57] Where Maoist thought
had an influence on UNITA, it was in the practicalities of waging a guerrilla
war rather than in a vision for a future Angola. According to Jaka Jamba:

> As we were establishing the guerrilla struggle, theories that influenced us the
> most were those that came from the people who had been best at making
> this kind of war. Hence the passion for China: theirs was the kind of rebel-
> lion that ended with them taking power. It wasn't about big doctrines, like
> Stalinism – more just the theory of guerrilla warfare.[58]

However, even as UNITA was turning away from China and towards the West
in the late 1970s, circumstances made it all the more urgent that Savimbi make
a reality of the dual strategy that he had discussed with Mao ten years earlier. As

---

[54]   Chiwale, *Cruzei-me*, 250. See also Muekalia, *Segunda Revolução*, 94.
[55]   Interviews with Abel Chivukuvuku and General Nunda, Luanda, 2009. Nunda suggests that
       after this visit to China, Savimbi became increasingly mistrustful of his previous confidantes,
       including those who had gone to China. He sees the trip as having led to the estrangement
       between Savimbi and Chiwale that resulted ultimately in Chiwale's detention, described earl-
       ier in this chapter.
[56]   According to Chivukuvuku, the UNITA leadership came under attack at a place where they
       had assembled in October 1978. The group scattered, and Savimbi was evacuated by a South
       African helicopter.
[57]   Chiwale, *Cruzei-me*, 239. Chiwale names Botha as prime minister, though in fact he took up
       this office only in 1978, two years after the meeting that Chiwale recalls.
[58]   Interview with Jaka Jamba, Luanda, September 2009.

the MPLA state increased its efforts to extend its influence over the rural parts of the Central Highlands, the need for a secure rear base became more apparent to UNITA, even if for strategic reasons this had to be many hundreds of kilometres from the well-populated Central Highlands, where UNITA would continue to recruit and to launch attacks on the government-held towns. The bases that UNITA established in the bush in the Central Highlands will be discussed in Chapter 5, while Chapter 6 will examine the significance of the headquarters that it established at Jamba.

This chapter has examined the character and identity of UNITA and the nature of its relationship with the people who were attached to it and how these were shaped by the control of territory in the months before, during and after Angolan independence. Prior to April 1974, Savimbi had led a guerrilla movement in the east of Angola. As soon as UNITA was able to operate openly and legally, it rapidly gathered a following from among the educated people of the towns and missions whose political socialisation had taken place outside of UNITA but who saw UNITA as a political realisation of a nationalism rooted in the Central Highlands. Although UNITA officials would later make much of the movement's relationship with rural communities, UNITA's first priority was to take control of the functions abandoned by the colonial state, and this meant concentrating its efforts in the cities. The self-styled Long March was a backup plan adopted after it became clear that the balance of military force did not allow UNITA to pursue its preferred vision of urban-based state building. Some peasant communities offered support to UNITA, but this was the result of UNITA's success in convincing them that it was their best defender against a largely absent and unknown MPLA. If the allusions to Mao suggested a political imaginary of rural class struggle, this had little to do with reality. Savimbi would speak of a strategy that included both a class of skilled professionals who would contribute to UNITA's project of building legitimacy through service provision and a class of farmers whose acceptance of UNITA would allow the movement to maintain a presence over much of rural Angola. Yet UNITA remained the offspring of the professional class, and that class would maintain a privileged position in terms of UNITA's identity and priorities. These tensions in the character of UNITA would persist throughout the conflict.

3

The MPLA and Urban State Making

The entry of a column of Cuban and FAPLA soldiers into Huambo in February 1976 marked the arrival of the legally recognised Angolan state in the Central Highlands. As the previous chapter noted, it was only after 1977 that the FAPLA and Cuban soldiers made any attempt to attack UNITA positions outside the cities. However, even after it began to take military action against UNITA, the MPLA never consolidated its control over the countryside, and its dominance was challenged by UNITA's return to war in 1981. The MPLA leadership had ideologically driven ideas about the role of the political party and the state, ideas that defined the prerogatives and responsibilities of the party or state towards the people and the rights and duties of the people with respect to the state. At the same time, the realities of war had an impact on the kind of state building that the MPLA was able to engage in and how this was received and perceived. This chapter examines the ways in which the MPLA went about constructing a state and asserting its legitimacy. I consider state-building not only in the sense of the creation of physical infrastructure and a coercive apparatus but also in the sense of how these activities were accompanied by the construction of a set of meanings that were consistent with broader narratives about the MPLA's historic and current role. This discourse defined a particular kind of relationship among the state, its citizens, the MPLA, and the Angolan nation. This chapter contrasts the ways in which different interviewees spoke about the work done by the party-state so as to present both the discourse of MPLA officials and devotees and that of people who lived in the city but had a less close relationship with the party. In this way it offers an indication of how far the official discourse shaped people's understanding of their own rights and responsibilities as citizens and of the position of the MPLA in relation to the Angolan nation.

Between August 1975 and February 1976, the MPLA had had no visible presence in the towns of the Central Highlands. From the point of view of those residents who had not been active supporters of the MPLA, the MPLA entered as a military movement that only later acquired a political character. Pastor David remembered that the MPLA 'came with tanks, with the Cubans, so UNITA didn't resist, it left. The MPLA came, and started looking around to see if there were still any UNITA people there, and established, more than anything else, its military bases: it occupied strategic areas of the city, and later civilian structures started to appear, but first the military structures'. Later, with Cuban support, the MPLA 'established all the structures for the functioning of governance [...] the water started to function, the electricity started to function, the shops started opening – then the communications, the postal service began to work and then they put buses on those roads they had managed to open – they went to other cities like Benguela, Lobito and Bié. Life started functioning normally'.[1]

There were also a substantial number of MPLA supporters who had remained in Huambo during the period of UNITA control, people who had embraced the MPLA after listening to its radio broadcasts or hearing its message during the period of mobilisation that followed April 1974. They had no choice but to keep their opinions to themselves during the months of UNITA's exclusive occupation from mid-1975 but welcomed the arrival of the FAPLA with gratitude and a sense of justice being done. Being sympathetic to the MPLA's aims, these people put a stronger emphasis on its civilian developmental role rather than on its military character. According to Bernardo,

> The MPLA had barely arrived before it started concerning itself with taking over the state administration. [...] Schools, hospitals began to work and the whole administration started to gain its previous force. They paid civil servants' salaries and tuition became free: everybody studying, everybody working and everyone on the move. [...] Children went to school and received books for free. There were the Pioneers [MPLA children's brigade] who received clothes for free. Everything free. This was always the philosophy of the MPLA: keep struggling for the people to have a better life.[2]

The availability of foreign exchange from oil revenue allowed the state to take responsibility for social services and for the provision of basic foodstuffs, as well as funding the military and the privileges of the MPLA elite.[3] The

---

[1]   Interviewee 19, Huambo, May 2008.
[2]   Interviewee 31, Huambo, May 2008.
[3]   Christine Messiant, 'Deconstructing a Nation' in Christine Messiant, *L'Angola Postcolonial: 2. Sociologie Politique d'une Oléocratie* (Paris, 2008), 232.

departure of Portuguese business people, as well as bureaucrats, meant that the new MPLA state had little choice but to 'establish state control over an increasing number of abandoned enterprises in order to maintain vital economic activities'.[4] Marcolino Moco, who was a provincial official in the years following independence, viewed the state's involvement in the economy as the consequence both of ideology and of necessity.

> On the one hand, the war itself: with the departure of the Portuguese who were the shop owners, the factory owners – everything collapsed. There was a period of nationalisation. But afterwards, this persisted, and broadened.[5]

At the same time, the need for army escorts for transport between the coast and the interior towns implicated the state in the delivery of goods from one region to the other. The party implemented a system of state shops that sold basic foodstuffs at a low price, which were accessible only to people who held ration cards. Those who had cards were state employees. Certain goods, such as soap, toothpaste and soft drinks, were delivered to public functionaries when available, in quantities commensurate with the recipient's professional rank. During the 1980s, special shops were established where higher-ranking civilian and military officials could obtain a wider variety of goods. The fertility of the land and climate in much of the Central Highlands and the presence of agricultural plots within city limits ensured that vegetables and grain were produced inside the cities and bartered on the informal market: this was technically illegal, since all goods were supposed to be sold to the state, but there was little that farmers could buy with the cash paid by the state buyers. In Messiant's analysis, the use of oil revenues to import food from abroad allowed the state to abandon the farming population. Inefficiency in the administration and a declining oil price saw a deterioration in the quality of state services over the 1980s and a concentration of wealth in the hands of the party and government elites. Most city dwellers obtained everyday goods through informal trade, and those who through state or party connections had privileged access to these goods were the main beneficiaries of the black market.[6]

The bureaucratised system of food production implemented by the MPLA is remembered both as an example of the party's efficacy in creating structures that served the public interest and as an example of inefficiency and

---

[4] Franz-Wilhelm Heimer, *The Decolonization Conflict in Angola 1974–76: An Essay in Political Sociology* (Geneva, 1979), 83.

[5] Interview with Moco, Huambo, August 2009. See also Jean-Michel Mabeko-Tali, *Dissidências e poder do estado: O MPLA perante si próprio (1962–1977), II.º Vol. 1974–1977* (Luanda, 2001), 174.

[6] Messiant, 'Deconstructing a nation', 232.

discrimination in the interests of a privileged stratum. Paulina, who was deeply loyal to the MPLA's principles, expressed misgivings about its practices:

> For basic, necessary goods you needed a card. [...] Later the special shops started, for skilled and mid-level workers, and the bosses. It was terrible discrimination. Everything was cheap because it was subsidised. Things like sugar or rice you could get in the people's shops. The special shops had butter, milk, imported beer.[7]

Paulina explained the philosophy behind the MPLA's food-provision strategies as follows: 'Whoever had a job was ours, and had the right to goods.'[8] She contrasted the availability of foodstuffs in government shops with the situation in UNITA-held areas: 'In a UNITA area you'd be in trouble if you were caught with salt or cooking oil.' The shortage of basic manufactured goods in many of the areas controlled by UNITA was a recurring theme in the comparisons that people drew between the effectiveness of the two rival movements. A UNITA officer interviewed by Leon Dash in 1977 complained that peasants who went to live in government-controlled areas had been 'bought by the government with blankets and salt ... or forced into the army'.[9]

Chapter 2 showed how UNITA's first brief attempts at asserting itself as a state were defined by its presence in the cities. The MPLA state in the Central Highlands took on an even more strongly urban character, which persisted throughout the war. A number of factors combined to determine the urban nature of the state-building project. The fact that the MPLA's anti-colonial guerrilla struggle had not extended to the Central Highlands ensured that the MPLA in the region was entirely an urban movement. Moreover, Mabeko-Tali suggests that even in the border regions where the MPLA had established liberated zones, the party was not inclined to consolidate its support and instead chose to invest its efforts in building urban support.[10] Messiant suggests that the presence of MPLA cadres in the colonial administration meant that MPLA was better placed than UNITA or the FNLA to take over the functioning of a largely urban colonial state once the Portuguese departed.[11] Most importantly,

---

7   Interviewee 150, Caála, July 2009. The appearance of the special shops may be seen in the context of the increasingly elitist nature of MPLA politics through the 1980s, as noted by Nuno Vidal, 'The Angolan regime and the move to multiparty politics', in Patrick Chabal and Nuno Vidal (eds.), *Angola: The Weight of History* (London, 2008), 128–130.

8   'Ours' here means 'of the MPLA'. This idea of political belonging will be explored more fully in the following chapter.

9   Leon Dash, 'A prisoner's hard road to reeducation or death', *The Washington Post*, 10 August 1977, A18.

10   Mabeko-Tali, *Dissidências, II.ºVol.*, 25.

11   Christine Messiant, 'Angola, les voies de l'ethnisation et de la décomposition', in Christine Messiant, *L'Angola Postcolonial: 1. Guerre et Paix Sans Démocratisation* (Paris, 2008), 33–130. Originally published in *Lusotopie* I 1–2, (1994), 155–212.

it was the war itself that set the geographical limits on the MPLA's ability to construct the apparatus of statehood, as well as determining the character of the institutions that it created and nurtured. Towns were defensible, while any state presence outside the city limits was liable to attack after UNITA resumed its offensives in 1981. Although the war provided an incentive for state intervention in the economy, it also imposed limits on the intervention: 'As the war closed in more and more, it made it difficult for the state to broaden its role as a distributor. The factors worked against each other.'[12] Roberto, a lawyer who had been a young man in Huambo in the early years of independence, suggested that state building in the Central Highlands was unable to progress beyond 'maintaining what had existed in colonial times, because the action of the guerrilla war didn't permit more than that. It required a great effort to maintain Bailundo and Mungo [administrative centres in Huambo province] because they were completely surrounded by UNITA's forces'. In these areas at the edge of the state's reach, its functions amounted to little more than 'maintaining an administrative presence, the schools, the hospital, the infrastructure that the colonist had left'.[13]

Pastor David recalled the MPLA state as being 'an island', with state functionaries unable to travel more than 20 kilometres from an administrative centre.[14] Travel between the 'islands' was possible only as part of a military convoy. Even in those rural areas that were close enough to the towns to fall under the MPLA's military control, the efforts of state building through service provision that were noted by urban dwellers were barely present. Maria da Conceição Neto notes that even before UNITA went on the offensive in the early 1980s, the MPLA's rural development efforts were inadequate.

> UNITA had little military power during the first years of the war. However, the MPLA lacked the capacity to provide a development project that was sufficiently attractive to the rural population [...] It also did not understand the cultural, social and political reality of Huambo [province], and so failed to see that economic and social advancement was much more enticing for that population than the uncertainty of war.[15]

Farming communities, even those on the outskirts of the Central Highlands towns, had had no contact with political movements during the anti-colonial

---

[12] Interview with Moco, Huambo, August 2009.

[13] Interviewee 3, Huambo, May 2008.

[14] Interviewee 19, Huambo, May 2008. This characterisation of the independent state in wartime echoes the description by René Pélissier, 'Part two', in Douglas Wheeler and René Pélissier, *Angola* (London, 1971), 232 of a colonial state in which 'each white settlement was an island in an African sea', linked only by air until the roads were built.

[15] Maria da Conceição Neto, 'Angola: The historical context for reconstruction' in Paul Robson (ed.), *Communities and Reconstruction in Angola* (Luanda, 2001), 65–66.

struggle, and they remained marginal to processes of state building that followed independence. A farmer who had spent her whole life on the periphery of Huambo, in an area that had been under MPLA control since February 1976, recalled that after independence, 'each depended on his or her own efforts'.

> Peasants had to cultivate land to get something to eat. Many who had children … didn't have the possibility for their children to study – the facilities didn't exist because of the war. As time went by, the non-governmental organisations brought materials for schools and hospitals and the government managed to do more for the schools. With time the country managed to send children to schools.[16]

Since those people whose livelihood depended on agriculture saw little positive benefit from the presence of the MPLA, it made little difference which party was in power as long as they were not being preyed upon by soldiers. A man who in 1975 had been a teenager at a mission school spoke of UNITA 'governing at the provincial level', but by this he meant no more than that UNITA was occupying the provincial capital rather than fulfilling any kind of function in his home area. Asked if the arrival of the MPLA government in February 1976 had brought about any changes where he lived, he replied that 'the village was outside the city – we stayed in the village'. It is true that the majority of the rural population was beyond the reach of the Angolan state for much of the war. However, even in the limited rural zones that were under the safe military control of the MPLA, the state was barely present. Rural people perceived state building to be something that happened elsewhere and happened to other people.

MASS ORGANISATIONS AND POLITICAL EDUCATION

Within the 'islands' of MPLA control, the creation of functioning schools, hospitals and shops was accompanied by a programme of political education aimed at promoting the single party as the unique and legitimate representative of the Angolan nation. Marcum argues that during 1976, while UNITA fell apart politically as a result of being on the defensive militarily, the MPLA 'drew strength from its longstanding commitment to ideologically grounded political education and mobilization', something made possible by the MPLA's control of the towns.[17] Civic structures linked to the party such as

---

[16]   Interviewee 30, Huambo, May 2008. This woman lived in a village where an NGO had conducted adult education programmes for more than a decade.

[17]   John Marcum, *The Angolan Revolution, Volume II (Exile Politics and Guerrilla Warfare, 1962–1976)* (Cambridge, MA, 1978), 278.

OMA (*Organização da Mulher Angolana* – Angolan Women's Organisation), OPA (*Organização dos Pioneiros Angolanos* – Angolan Pioneers' Organisation, for children) and JMPLA (*Juventude do MPLA* – MPLA Youth) sought to create opportunities for participation in party activities. The following account by Maria da Conceição Neto, who was living in Huambo in the mid-1970s, illustrates how these organisations brought activities identified with the party into civic and social life and into state functions such as the provision of education and health care.

> 'Mass organisations' had the role of 'conveyor belts' for directives from the top of the party. [...] The youth organisation (JMPLA) changed from a 'mass organisation' to a 'nursery for cadres', a kind of antechamber leading into the party; in the process any less orthodox or controlled initiative for youth was stifled or marginalised. In spite of everything, the activities of the mass organisations were for many people important experiences of community action. Through them were carried out campaigns of literacy, sanitation and vaccination. They involved all sections of the population in socially useful activities, and through them were awakened ideas of citizenship.[18]

Moco described the role of the mass organisations as 'fundamental'. 'A child who went to school was automatically with OPA. It was a system of total integration.'[19] Interviews with people who were teenagers or students in the late 1970s illustrate how the close identification between party and state and the state's control of employment opportunities were a strong incentive for people to embrace the party. Verónica, a teenager in the 1970s who had no strong partisan views but whose family included both UNITA and MPLA sympathisers, recalled:

> After UNITA left it was all MPLA propaganda. People were persuaded to participate in government organisations, though not obliged to. There were privileges attached to participating, like uniforms or activities. There were OMA meetings in the schools that were sometimes obligatory. If you didn't go, it counted against you. At rallies (*comícios*) each school and each business kept a note of who was there – teachers, pupils, workers. If you didn't go you would lose a day's salary. But some went voluntarily if they were party members.[20]

Rui, a teenager in the 1980s, described recruitment to the MPLA as 'obligatory' on the grounds that the party's structures were so pervasive in the schools.

[18] Neto, 'Angola', 45.
[19] Interview with Moco.
[20] Interviewee 108, Luanda, October 2008.

There was a social structure linked to the JMPLA – it was called the AEEM (Association of High School Students / *Associação de Estudantes de Ensino Médio*) and this association was an appendage of the JMPLA. Even if you weren't incorporated as an activist you still would be involved in activities that were those of the JMPLA. In such a way that all of us [young people] were part of the JMPLA, whether directly or indirectly.[21]

A Catholic priest from Bié drew comparisons between the systems of politicisation under the MPLA from 1976 onwards and under UNITA when it returned to the cities in 1993.

People couldn't choose. The movement that was there controlled everything. It was the same when UNITA came: everyone joined the UNITA structures. [...] OPA promoted patriotic education. People couldn't go to church, because they planned events on a Sunday. Going to church was not prohibited, but party activities took place at the same time. They gave us [in OPA] uniforms. Those who excelled were sent to Cuba to study. This was organised by party activists. [At school] history changed. They even changed the exercise books, taking away the multiplication tables [formerly printed inside the cover] and replacing them with the national anthem. In the workplace, if you didn't belong to the party you couldn't be promoted. If you criticised the system openly you were seen as being UNITA.[22]

Participation in party activities should not be confused with party membership. Accounts of the MPLA in the early years of independence reveal tensions between the desire for ideological coherence and for cross-class inclusiveness, the latter being the legacy of 'People's Power' urban mobilisation in 1975.[23] MPLA membership dropped dramatically after the leadership purged dissidents and tightened membership criteria in response to the challenge to Neto's leadership led by former government minister Nito Alves in 1977. By the early 1980s, grassroots party adherents enjoyed no special privileges.[24] The mass organisations and the blurring of party, state and people that they embodied nevertheless continued into the era when formal party membership became more exclusive.

The existence of the mass organisations and the inseparability of the party from the civic sphere permitted the dominance of the ideologies that defined the roles of state and party and their position in relation to the Angolan nation. Most evident both in the party's own writings and in the recollections of people

---

[21]   Interviewee 9, Huambo, May 2008.
[22]   Interviewee 105, Huambo, September 2008.
[23]   Keith Somerville, *Angola: Politics, Economics and Society* (London, 1986), 78–99.
[24]   Vidal, 'The Angolan regime', 129–132.

who remember that period were the ways in which these ideologies were articulated in accounts of the historical role of the MPLA and the reasons for the war. Bernardo, as a long-time party loyalist, gave an idea of the MPLA's own preferred version of its function in society: 'to mobilise people for work'.

> It was known that without work the party would not go forward. Mobilise the country for work and to study, because studying was a revolutionary duty, and mobilising the people for the defence of the country because at that time we didn't only have the problem of UNITA, but also the problem of external enemies. You know we had the problems with South Africa, with Zaire, which attacked us. It was necessary to mobilise the people in such a way that they would be aware of the political-military situation that the country was experiencing. Aside from education, work, health, it was necessary to mobilise the people to guarantee the security of our territorial integrity. Mobilise the youth to join the armed forces to guarantee territorial integrity. That was the great role of the party.[25]

Anselmo, a younger man, had spent the first years of his life in an area that was contested between UNITA and the government before moving to the city with his parents in order for him to go to school and for his parents to resume the teaching careers that they had begun in colonial times. He recalled the late 1970s as follows:

> It was a time of great investment in ideology, particularly in education. I was a member of the Pioneers, then the students' association, and then the JMPLA. I helped organise rallies. The education system functioned, but in terms of transmitting the ideas of the dominant power. We were most affected by the war after 1983, when there were attacks [by UNITA] on Huambo city. [...] There was an internal reaction against counter-revolutionaries, people suspected of working for UNITA. There was a lot of talk of South Africa, of Ronald Reagan and the Clark Amendment.[26]

In the youth organisations, a figure called Ngangula featured in political education. He was a young boy who had supposedly been captured by the Portuguese and been killed when he refused to reveal where guerrillas were hiding. According to a priest who had been a child in the 1980s:

> Now that I know, I'd say he was a fictional character, just so that children would have a model, a fictional character, so that we couldn't do anything

---

[25] Interviewee 31, Huambo, May 2008.

[26] Interviewee 104, Huambo, September 2008. The 1976 Clark Amendment, which prohibited US assistance to armed groups abroad, was repealed under the Reagan administration in 1985: George Wright, *The Destruction of a Nation: United States' Policy Toward Angola since 1945* (London, 1997), 118.

without reference to him. They had to create this image – this reference for childhood patriotism.[27]

MPLA propaganda after independence recalled the party's role in the anti-colonial struggle and emphasised the external nature of the enemy that the MPLA was confronting. MPLA versions of history made much of Savimbi's pact with the Portuguese army during the war of independence.[28] The fact that UNITA enjoyed the support of apartheid South Africa and the United States was fundamental to the MPLA's analysis of world events. In Moco's words:

> When UNITA allied itself with South Africa, which at that time was hated for its policy of apartheid, it was a mobilising factor to say that UNITA was not worthy of being a liberation movement, but was a movement that, first, helped to prolong colonialism, and second, tried to help apartheid, racism, and tried to destroy Angola to help foreign interests.[29]

The party's alignment with the left in international politics originated in its opposition to the Salazar regime and was reinforced by its acceptance of Cuban assistance in the late 1960s and again at the time of independence. Yet, as Mabeko-Tali has noted, the MPLA's assertion of 'revolutionary legitimacy' came in the absence of a clear ideologically driven programme.[30] The nationalisation of business led to the growth of an 'administrative bourgeoisie' which came to dominate the party and became increasingly corrupt. A 'pragmatist' tendency in the MPLA, represented by Agostinho Neto, acknowledged the cross-class nature of the party but did not assuage rank-and-file militants' resentment of the privileges enjoyed by the emerging party elite, grievances that fuelled the uprising on 27 May 1977 led by Nito Alves, the former MPLA guerrilla commander who briefly served as interior minister after independence.[31] The repression of the uprising was consolidated with the adoption of Marxism-Leninism at the MPLA's First Congress in 1977, a move that was

[27] Interviewee 193, Kuito, August 2009.
[28] On the MPLA's use of history, see Christine Messiant, 'Chez nous, même le passé est imprévisible', in Christine Messiant, *L'Angola Postcolonial: 2. Sociologie Politique d'une Oléocratie* (Paris, 2008), 153–202. On Savimbi's cooperation with Portugal see William Minter, *Operation Timber: Pages from the Savimbi Dossier* (Trenton NJ, 1988).
[29] Interview with Moco.
[30] Mabeko-Tali, *Dissidências, II.ºVol.*, 153. Mabeko-Tali provides the most thoroughgoing account of the internal divisions that afflicted the MPLA throughout its history and which are beyond the scope of this book, though they continue to be a matter for debate. See also Somerville, *Angola*.
[31] Paul Fauvet, 'Angola: The rise and fall of Nito Alves', *Review of African Political Economy* 4.9 (1977), 88–104; Dalina Cabrita Mateus and Álvaro Mateus, *Purga em Angola: Nito Alves, Sita*

driven not by a logic of class struggle but by a concern to tighten central control following the challenge posed by Alves and his followers.[32]

Those interviewees who were both educated and committed to the MPLA on ideological grounds would articulate the connection among party, state and military explicitly in terms that were influenced by Marxist thinking. But where socialist ideas were most clearly invoked was not in ideas about class struggle, but rather in a discourse of socialist internationalism that served to position the party and the Angolan nation in relation to global politics. The importance both of Cuban technical expertise in the MPLA's state-building project and of Cuban soldiers and military advisers in the defence of the state made visible the international dimension in the ideologies that surrounded the party's functions, even if, in most interviewees' accounts, socialist ideology was a secondary strand alongside ideas about the party-state's developmental and defensive role.

The fact of being at war was itself an essential element in the MPLA's strategies of legitimation. Supporters of the MPLA spoke of the party as the defender of the nation in a way that conflated the functions of party and military: 'In 1980, when UNITA intensified the guerrilla war, it was the task of the party to defend the city: to create a system to protect its leaders.'[33] Supporters of the MPLA would consistently say that the party's role during the war was 'to defend the people'. The narratives that the MPLA propagated about its role as the defender of Angola from alien enemies served to construct the MPLA's deployment of violence as defensive and legitimate and UNITA's violence as aggressive and illegitimate. In Maria de Conceição Neto's account,

> 'Reactionary violence' was met with 'revolutionary violence'. The various participants saw violence to be not just necessary but legitimate; they claimed that it served 'the interests of the Angolan people', whom everybody claimed to represent.[34]

A schoolteacher from Huambo spoke of the expulsion of UNITA from the city and the subsequent clashes between the rival armies as follows:

> Of course, this [violence] happens. At that time, UNITA considered this [territory] its own property that it wanted to defend. But in order to defend territorial integrity, the government had to come and conquer all the spaces

---

Valles, *Zé Van Dunem, o 27 de Maio de 1977* (Lisbon, 2007); Lara Pawson, *In the Name of the People: Angola's Forgotten Massacre* (London, 2014).

[32] Mabeko-Tali, *Dissidências*, II.°Vol., 229–239.

[33] Interviewee 150, Caála, August 2009.

[34] Neto, 'Angola' 43.

that UNITA had occupied, and this had to be done in battle. Each one defends, and withdraws when it sees the other side is advancing.[35]

If establishing a state is the establishment of a monopoly of legitimate violence, such accounts remind us that this task is an ideological one as much as a military one, a task of defining which violence is defensive and therefore legitimate.

MILITARY CONSCRIPTION

Military conscription, for which every Angolan male was liable from the age of 18, helped to blur the distinction between the military and the civilian domains by ensuring that every man spent time as a soldier. For those who were drafted into the army, the experience helped to determine how they perceived the authority and the legitimacy of the state. Rui recalled that 'at 18 years old I was already a soldier in FAPLA, which was the army of the single party. [...] At 19 I was already an officer. And no officer was outside of the party structure. That could not be imagined. If one happened to be at the battlefront, as a matter of principle one had to be a member of the party. I went to a military unit whose commando was more inside the city because it was part of the justice system: the military court. I was part of the MPLA youth and part of the party itself'.

Most former soldiers spoke of having received political education while in the army. Some of them still understood their military service in terms of the perspectives that this political education provided. Albano, a farmer from the outskirts of Huambo, insisted that 'I joined the army so that we could remain independent', an interpretation that was linked to his belief that 'if it wasn't for the MPLA we wouldn't have become independent. The MPLA has brought us to this time of peace'. He recalled that 'we learnt to work together with others, live well with others, remain respectful towards others, and work so that our country could remain free and just'.[36] Lucas, who had served in the FAPLA in the mid-1980s, recalled that 'there were political chiefs in each battalion so as to have good political and military education. We were taught to live among the people. We were taught: "we are soldiers, we are FAPLA, our mission is to defend our population, to respect the elderly – we are friends. The soldier is the defender of his people"'.[37]

---

[35] Interviewee 22, Huambo, May 2008.
[36] Interviewee 29, Huambo, May 2008.
[37] Interviewee 121, Chicomba, November 2008.

Men who had professional skills could sometimes avoid conscription. Mário, a former schoolteacher, said that when he finished his education in 1978, aged 20, 'if you were a teacher you were considered a frontline combatant, and benefited from postponement'. Mário was eventually summoned for military service in 1983, when the intensification of the conflict prompted the armed forces to recruit men regardless of whether they were working in favoured professions such as education.[38] His account illustrates the privileged position of the military in state discourse and practice. The importance of teaching is justified through the military metaphor of a 'frontline' activity, but teachers lost their exemption as soon as there was a shortage of men for the real business of war. Yet many men, particularly those without the skills that could win them exemption or a place in the officers' ranks, experienced conscription as an arbitrary and often violent process. They would frequently use verbs like '*raptar*' (seize) or '*apanhar*' (catch) when they spoke of being drafted, exactly the same words that people would use to talk about abduction by UNITA. Although men officially became eligible for military service at age 18, there are frequent accounts of boys being conscripted from age 15, usually because they were physically large for their age. Once in the army, men might be posted to a remote garrison where they might stay for an indefinite period. According to a rifleman who had served fourteen years in the FAPLA: 'The law didn't mean very much. If you knew someone who could arrange something you might get out.' A captain who had served eleven years in the military added: 'Service ended when you were killed or lost an arm or a leg.'[39]

Conscription, by incorporating the majority of Angolan men into the armed forces at some point in their lives, created a further opportunity for political education in a society where the penetration of the party into civilian life meant that such opportunities were already plentiful. Yet men's experience of conscription illustrates the disjuncture between state propaganda and their experience. Most men had little choice but to resign themselves to the fact of spending years in the ranks of the military. Political education could not stop them from recognising the arbitrariness and injustice of the way in which conscription operated. Yet the political legitimacy of the MPLA was, as we have seen, closely bound to its identity as the defender of a nation against an external threat, since the narratives that the FAPLA used to bolster soldiers' morale were identical to the narratives that the MPLA called on to sustain its legitimacy in government.

---

[38] Interviewee 22, Huambo, May 2008.
[39] Group discussion 125, Chicomba, November 2008.

This chapter has shown how in the civilian sphere and the military sphere alike, the MPLA consolidated its power over the parts of Angola that it controlled throughout the civil war by implementing a state-led vision of development and shaping public discourse concerning the role of the state and the party in the realisation of such a vision. It did this through political education in the ranks of the military or through party-linked civic structures in wider society, in which civilians had little choice but to participate. The MPLA presented itself as a provider of public goods and as a force that both elicited international solidarity and mobilised Angolan citizens in pursuit of a project of modernisation to the benefit of the nation. The party presented itself as Angola's sole liberator from colonialism, which granted the MPLA a special relationship with the Angolan nation. At least in these two aspects, the discourse associated with the MPLA's state-building endeavours had much in common with that of other African liberation movements that had assumed power from the late 1950s onwards. What distinguished the MPLA from most independence movements, however, was the fact that it remained at war after independence. By emphasising the continuity between the MPLA's role in the anti-colonial struggle and in the war against UNITA and the fact that UNITA had the support of a racist regime in Pretoria and an imperialist regime in Washington, the MPLA presented its own interests as the interests of the Angolan nation. More than that, it constructed an Angolan nation in its own image by portraying any support for its opponents as an act of treason rather than as an act of political opposition.

This discourse achieved a degree of hegemony in that it came to shape a perception of common interest among those who were in the city, beyond those who were actively involved in the work of the party. Beyond the inner core of party functionaries, there were people who accepted the MPLA's account of its role and its legitimacy without actively endorsing it. Among soldiers, the systematic political education that they received in the army could not stop them from recognising the arbitrariness and injustice of the way they were treated as conscripts, but it could nevertheless convince them that the cause they were fighting for was a just one. Those who rejected outright the MPLA's account of itself were those who had a prior and active commitment to UNITA, though they had to keep their views to themselves.

The discourse on the Angolan nation that the MPLA presented was an all-encompassing one. It made no reference to questions of ethnicity or race, defining instead a citizenship linked to the MPLA's defence of an embattled nation and to participation in an MPLA-led state-building project. Yet these aspirations to articulating an inclusive nationhood were constrained by the fact that the MPLA's politicisation efforts took place within the confines of the towns. Acceptance of the MPLA account of nationhood was contingent on people having a similar experience of a process of urban state building and on people being contained in a secure zone that allowed the state to define its own use of violence as defensive. This contradiction between inclusivity and exclusivity shaped the attitude of state officials towards people who lived in areas beyond the perimeter of the towns. The following chapter explores the complex processes through which political identities were constituted and assigned at the margins of the state's control.

4

Migration, Relocation and Identity

The area within the Central Highlands that was controlled by the MPLA state in the late 1970s and 1980s was confined to pockets of territory centred on towns. The boundaries were never strictly delineated: there were some areas that were notionally under government control but where UNITA soldiers could pass at night. In the early 1980s, the South African Defence Force returned to Angola and took control of the extreme south of the country. This renewed South African support enabled UNITA to reorganise its forces, and it began more systematically to attack government-held towns and installations.[1] During this time, large numbers of people arrived in government-held centres: Angolan government records for the period are not available, but data assembled by the United Nations suggest that 500,000 people had been displaced by the war by 1985.[2] Some of this movement was voluntary, but the government also employed a strategy of evacuating people from villages that fell on the margins of government influence and leaving them in locations that were more securely under its control.[3] Interviewees recalled some efforts to move people into government-held territory in the late 1970s, although these efforts appear to have become more systematic after 1980, in response to UNITA's increasing military strength at the time. Similarly, part of UNITA's strategy was 'to move peasant villagers away from areas where they [could] be easily approached by government forces'.[4] In this

[1] Victoria Brittain, *Death of Dignity: Angola's Civil War* (London, 1998), 10–19; Assis Malaquias, *Rebels and Robbers: Violence in Post-colonial Angola* (Uppsala, 2007), 40–41; Jardo Muekalia, *Angola: A Segunda Revolução: Memórias da Luta pela Democracia*, (Porto, 2010), 165; Piero Gleijeses, *Visions of Freedom: Havana, Washington, Pretoria, and the Struggle for Southern Africa 1976–1991* (Chapel Hill, NC, 2013), 118.
[2] United Nations Economic and Social Council 1987, *United Nations Children's Fund Programme Committee 1987 Session: Country Programme Recommendation: Angola*. E/ICEF/1987/P/L.7
[3] Maria da Conceição Neto, 'Angola: The historical context for reconstruction' in Paul Robson (ed.), *Communities and Reconstruction in Angola* (Luanda, 2001), 68.
[4] Leon Dash, 'A Warrior Sits in Judgment on Women Held for Witchcraft', *The Washington Post* 11 August 1977, A24.

chapter, I examine the experience both of forced relocation as a war strategy and of voluntary migration in response to the threat of war. I also analyse the political meanings that officials of the MPLA government attached to geographical space and the identities that were imposed upon people on the basis of where they were located.

Of the people who arrived in the towns in the late 1970s or early 1980s, some came from areas that had never been controlled by any movement other than UNITA since 1975, while others had spent the previous few years in areas that were contested between the two sides.[5] Some of them described being rounded up by soldiers in the countryside and brought into the towns. Others, particularly those who had been in contested areas, said they had gone to the towns voluntarily, not necessarily because they had any prior preference for the MPLA but simply because going to the town offered a respite from the violence of the contested zone. Anselmo's family, schoolteachers and part of 'the rural elite from colonial times' in his words, was among those who had moved in order to get away from the constant threat posed by living in a conflict area. Anselmo's childhood had included periods in UNITA- and in MPLA-controlled areas, and although his education in had been entirely in the state schooling system, he maintained a neutral view of the two rival movements.

> At the time of independence my family left the village and we lived in the *mata* under the control of the guerrilla movement, until we left the guerrilla movement in 1979.[6] It was a rural economy, so at that time there was not much difficulty in feeding ourselves – not like later. But UNITA didn't have much capacity to control the population. The government troops put a lot of pressure on us. The result was the destruction of the rural zone, and the population became divided: some went to Jamba and others to the cities. [Where one went to] was the result of circumstances – through being closer to one side or the other.
> [...]
> The zone that was under the influence of the city was the zone of instability. We had to leave secretly, so as not to be intercepted. In 1979, we came to Vila Nova.[7] My parents were teachers. They presented themselves to the authorities, said they had abandoned the guerrilla movement, and were integrated into the civil service.[8]

---

[5] At this stage of the war, people would distinguish between the conflict zone and UNITA-held areas in their accounts of the conflict; this changed after 1990, and the UNITA zone became synonymous with the conflict zone, as later chapters will make clear.

[6] I use 'guerrilla movement' to translate '*guerrilha*' in Portuguese, which refers to a campaign or a movement, in contrast to the English meaning of 'guerrilla' as an individual combatant.

[7] Present-day Katchiungo in Huambo province.

[8] Interviewee 104, Huambo, September 2008.

As Vila Nova came under military pressure, the family moved to Boas Águas, closer to Huambo, and as the war intensified further, they moved to Huambo in 1984.

João, a schoolteacher in Kuito, told a similar story, although he suggested that his status as a state employee made him more vulnerable to capture by UNITA, while the *povo* (people, meaning peasants) were left alone. João had been posted after independence to a school in a *comuna* – that is, to a centre that was lowest in rank in the administrative hierarchy and which typically would have provided state services in the form of a primary school and a basic health post.

> In 1985, we functionaries had to abandon the area and go to where there was protection. But the *povo* stayed there. You know, the people weren't controlled. It didn't matter whether UNITA appeared or the government. But functionaries, if you stayed you were captured.[9]

As state employees became concentrated in the provincial capitals, there was no difficulty in finding employment. 'Teachers from *comunas* could be absorbed into the city because teachers were in short supply,' João said. State resources were scarce, and one effect of the war was further to concentrate the presence of the state in urban areas.

João's claim that the '*povo*' were left alone by the warring parties is contradicted by numerous accounts from farmers who were instructed to move by the government: this will be explored further in the following chapters. What is more certain is that while teachers and other professionals found themselves welcomed and incorporated into state structures, the same was not true for farmers, who in most cases were resettled either on the outskirts of towns, sometimes within established *bairros*, or next to main roads. One area where people had found themselves vulnerable to both rival armies was a valley some 20 kilometres from the city of Huambo. On the far side of this valley were mountains where UNITA established bases. In the years immediately following independence, this area was under the firm control of neither the MPLA nor UNITA. A chief from the area, who had been a child in the mid-1970s, described the experience of living between two armed forces before the MPLA state obliged the people from his village to move to a roadside location:

> Often when I was a child FAPLA would come to attack, then UNITA would come to attack, killing people, taking away crops, chickens, cattle. FAPLA said 'if you stay here there will be contact with UNITA'. FAPLA would say 'you are UNITA' and UNITA would say 'you are FAPLA'.[10]

9 Interviewee 191, Kuito, August 2009.
10 Interviewee 39, near Huambo, June 2008.

Another man from a nearby village added:

> All [the soldiers] robbed, raped, killed – they're soldiers. In 1977 the govern-
> ment withdrew the people to the road so as to guard the people. [The gov-
> ernment] asked for help from the Red Cross: schooling, soap, clothes. The
> Red Cross was invited by the MPLA. [After the evacuation] the war was out
> there, not in the village. The MPLA was in the city, UNITA was in the bush.[11]

Several significant points emerge from these accounts. First, the government
presented humanitarian aid in such a way that it was associated with the
MPLA. In this way, people who previously were unconnected to either side
were drawn into a political relationship with the government/MPLA, even
if they remained marginal to a state-building process that was concentrated
in cities. This use of humanitarian assistance for political purposes would
remain part of the MPLA's strategy until after the end of the war. Second,
the interviewee accepted the fact that the government moved the people to
'guard' them, a justification that can be understood only within a wider set of
narratives about the government's use of force being protective and defensive
against the aggressive and destructive force that was deployed by UNITA.

A third point concerns the way in which government and popular discourse
attributed political meanings to town and countryside. This theme occurs
repeatedly in interviews with people from all levels of society and from urban
and rural areas.[12] In the interview with the villager quoted earlier, the MPLA
is associated with cities and UNITA with the bush. The original location of
the village, before the removal to the city, was conceived of as an intermedi-
ate position between city and bush. These meanings were fluid and relative,
depending on the point of view of the speaker. A man who had spent most of
his life in a village outside Huambo city recalled that after 1976, his village
had suffered raids by UNITA but never occupation. 'UNITA never entered
the village because we weren't very far from the city.'[13] In other words, he perceived his village as being safely under government control on the basis that it
was close to the city. This contrasts with the account of Anselmo quoted earlier. Having spent part of his childhood in a UNITA-controlled area, Anselmo

---

[11] Interviewee 38, near Huambo, June 2008.
[12] This is strikingly similar to Brinkman's observations about the anti-colonial war in south-eastern
Angola, in which '[w]ithin the context of Angola as a whole, the entire South-East was classified as "bush", while officials in the region's towns would use the word "bush" for everything
outside the urban sphere. Seen from the village, every place connected with the colonial system was called "town"'. After independence, the MPLA state came to be associated with the
towns, and UNITA with the bush. Inge Brinkman, *A War for People: Civilians, Mobility, and
Legitimacy in South-East Angola during MPLA's War for Independence* (Cologne, 2005), 97.
[13] Interviewee 44, near Huambo, June 2008.

believed that the instability he had experienced was the result of being close to the city. 'The zone influenced by the city was the zone of instability.'[14] To both men, the dangerous places were those on the margins of the zones of military control.

The political meanings attached to space also became, in the minds of the military, attached to the people living in a particular area. Soldiers in FAPLA had orders to bring to the cities anyone who was found in the bush in the course of their operations. A former FAPLA soldier recalled the procedure as follows:

> We'd collect them – it wasn't their fault they had been captured [by UNITA]. We'd take them to the base and inform the authorities. Then a vehicle would come to take them to the *município* [the district administrative centre] where the government would give them food and other assistance.[15]

Another former soldier, asked how soldiers were supposed to identify the enemy in the bush, replied:

> Those who are with the MPLA are in the environs of the city – beyond that is the bush, thirty kilometres away – anyone there is the enemy. Even if he doesn't have a gun, he's one of the enemy people. The commander would send these people to the *município*. But if he had a gun he couldn't stay with the people [in the *município*], he might run away. So he would be sent to the province [i.e. the provincial capital].

Yet efforts to keep the peasants away from their farms were not always effective: 'some of them stayed thirty or only twenty days and then they went back to the bush'.[16]

Armed or unarmed, any person who did not go along with the FAPLA soldiers would be suspected of active collaboration with UNITA. Another former conscript into FAPLA recalled:

> We knew that there were [UNITA] troops among the people. People paid dearly for this. In confrontations no distinction was made. Both UNITA and MPLA troops killed many people. UNITA had bases, but there were moments when it hid itself among the people. [When FAPLA came to remove people,] whoever stayed behind, wasn't people any more.[17] This policy continued until 2002 in the east. If you hid and didn't go, you weren't people any more, you were *tropa* [one of the troops].[18]

[14] Interviewee 104, Huambo, September 2008.
[15] Group discussion 125, Chicomba, November 2008.
[16] Interviewee 126, Chicomba, November 2008.
[17] 'Quem ficou, já não era povo.'
[18] Interviewee 142, Luanda, July 2009.

Someone who was '*povo*' was liable to capture by either side: war booty rather than a belligerent. Someone who was '*tropa*' was perceived as being more closely integrated into UNITA, even if, as will be discussed in the next chapter, participation in UNITA's army was never voluntary. This categorical distinction made by the FAPLA soldiers echoes a distinction that was made within UNITA itself and which will be discussed in the next chapter, the distinction between those individuals who had defined military or civilian roles within UNITA and the '*povo da UNITA*' who tilled fields in areas under UNITA control and who supplied food to the military bases.

Although the task of bringing people into government-controlled areas was usually the duty of soldiers, it was not always a violent business. This is seen in the recollections of Adriana, who, aged 12, had left Kuito with her family when UNITA fled the city ahead of the advancing MPLA and Cuban forces in 1976. Her story concerns events in 1979, when she was taken by the FAPLA to a government-controlled *comuna*, or local administrative post. In contrast to the stories quoted so far in this chapter, told by farmers who were caught between the two armies, Adriana's family was part of a community that had never known any Angolan movement other than UNITA. They accepted UNITA's narratives to the point of fearing the MPLA. Adriana recalled:

> One night, while we were in the *matas*, the elders found out that in that area there were FAPLA troops, MPLA troops. The men said: 'generally when the troops find people, the men are killed – so you women stay here'. [...] Our fathers and brothers went to another area while we remained. In the morning there was an attack on the base, and the people went fleeing. [...]I grabbed my things and went to look for my mother. [...] I met troops – the FAPLA. They caught me and took me along. On the way from the village where they caught me to the *comuna* that they had come from, we suffered many attacks. The UNITA troops chased us – all along the way we were attacked. I was well treated [by FAPLA] – they did nothing to me, I did very well. [...] In the *comuna*, I didn't know anyone there, so I stayed with a family I didn't know for about six months, until [...] my mother came looking for me and found me.[19]

Adriana, who later became a government official and a loyal MPLA supporter, was nevertheless conscious of the situational nature of political identity during the war. Asked whether her parents had been followers of either party, she replied:

> In the conditions in which we were taken, of necessity one had to identify oneself as an adherent of UNITA. If you identified yourself the other way

[19] Interviewee 180, Kuito, August 2009.

you would be dead. As long as we stayed with UNITA, we were UNITA. But when we came back here with the MPLA, we became MPLA.

This apparent contradiction between viewing one's political identity as the outcome of deep-seated belief in a political cause and being aware that one's political identity could change according to circumstances is at the heart of how Angolans understood political affiliation during the civil war and is also central to understanding how political identity became a tool of political strategy. The remarks by former soldiers earlier in this chapter indicate how, in the terms of government discourse, anyone living outside of a government-controlled area became an 'enemy person' or a 'UNITA person'. Adriana's remarks suggest that people had to express identification with the political movement in whose territory they were living. Examining how people recollect the years of war in Angola, we may discern a number of different discourses on the relationship between territorial control and political identity. The government, particularly the military, labelled people on the basis of their location in a way that silenced the possibility of political choice by the person in question. According to Moco:

> During that period of almost thirty years, people lost the notion of being independent persons. They would say, 'I'm UNITA' or 'I'm MPLA'. This has been disappearing since 2002, but there was a time when it was like that. I, Marcolino Moco, was either MPLA or UNITA – there was no middle way. People became possessions. During the time of the single party, people were all with the government.[20]

When asked what it meant to be 'with the government', Moco explained,

> To obey all the government's instructions, collaborate with the government – though it wasn't really the government, it was the MPLA. The MPLA was the government, it was the same thing, a fusion.

Moco's definition captures one of the contradictions in how political identity was constituted. In one sense it was assigned on the basis of where one was; in another sense, it had to be demonstrated by obeying and 'collaborating'. Space became associated with political identity, since within any one political space there was no possibility of expressing any political choice. According to a farmer on the outskirts of Huambo, who had been a teenage girl at the time of independence:

---

[20] Interview with Moco. 'With the government' translates *'do governo'*, literally 'of the government'.

> In those areas [away from the city] UNITA controlled its people. Here in the government area, the government also controlled its people. Each party in the area where it was, controlled its people.[21]

Yet people also spoke of having chosen to identify with one or the other party, even if they acknowledged their lack of genuine choice, and recognised that political identity could change. A man who had been a student near Huambo during the independence years, when asked about which party he supported at that time, replied,

> If I had been more mature, I would have depended on ideology. [...] But from 1976 we identified ourselves with the MPLA, because in the city there was only the MPLA. I was of the age for military service but I only went to the army in 1984 because I had been at the seminary. I spent eleven years in the army and all this time I identified with the MPLA party.[22]

People who passed from one zone of control to the other, like Adriana, had a keener sense of how political control required that they assume one or another political identity. This appears in Rui's recollection of travelling by train from Luena in eastern Angola to Huambo as a child with his mother and siblings, soon after the MPLA took control of Huambo:

> We lived constantly in a situation of war that is very hard to understand. For instance, when we left Luena for Huambo my mother had to identify with two movements – because from Luena to Katchiungo the train came under the control of UNITA, and from Katchiungo to here [Huambo] the train came under the control of the MPLA. [...] People were obliged to say they were with one or the other to preserve their lives. [...] We were three children and [my mother] had to protect us. Honestly, in those days it was very complicated to say 'I'm from one side or the other'.[23]

Another man, who was working as a driver in Kuito at the time of independence, said he had no particular political affiliation but emphasised how one's affiliation was assumed on the basis of having or not having a UNITA membership card:

> Whichever [party] was here you needed to have their card to save your life. When the MPLA came in, whoever was caught with a UNITA card was in

[21] Interviewee 30, Huambo, May 2008. I have translated '*controlar*' in Portuguese as 'control', but the two words do not have identical meanings. Portuguese '*controlar*' often has to do with watching over someone or something, as opposed to the English sense of managing or commanding.

[22] Interviewee 21, Huambo, May 2008.

[23] Interviewee 9, Huambo, May 2008.

trouble – they would be considered a sympathiser. Like trees bending in the wind – the people had to lean whichever way.[24]

In a situation of close political control, how one presented oneself was not a matter of choice. Small groups of people nevertheless continued to work secretly for UNITA within communities that were under the control of the government, including the city of Huambo. In August 1980, the Huambo provincial court sentenced nine people to death and a further seven to prison terms ranging from two to twenty years for having belonged to 'clandestine networks of bombers linked to UNITA puppet groups' who attempted to plant bombs on at least three occasions during 1979.[25] According to the state newspaper, *Jornal de Angola*, most of them had first joined UNITA in Huambo in 1974; some had left with Savimbi in 1976 and later returned to the city. Colino Ricardo began in 1978 'to make trips to the city of Huambo where he managed to contact former UNITA sympathisers and people with families or friends in the bush, to recruit them to the bombers' network'. Francisco Chitombi had also left Huambo with UNITA in 1976 but later returned and joined an urban guerrilla cell. Francisco Chiungo had been in UNITA from 1974 but remained in Huambo in 1976 and even joined the Civil Defence, which organised civilians to be vigilant against UNITA. After being 'captured' by UNITA in 1978, he returned to the city to recruit secretly for the underground movement. Chitombi and Chiungo were caught when a detonator that they were carrying exploded as they made their way to plant a bomb at the railway station in Huambo.[26] Others used their own or their employers' vehicles to take essential goods to the guerrillas. One man was said to have used the petrol station where he worked 'as a transit centre for goods sent to the *matas*'. UNITA's delegation in Lisbon issued a statement in which it accepted responsibility for the bombings.[27]

People who were active in the UNITA underground justify their activities in the same terms in which UNITA sought to mobilise people throughout the Central Highlands, which were raised in Chapter 2 and will be discussed further in later chapters. According to a chief in an urban *bairro* of Huambo, aged over 70 at the time of the interview:

> As a *soba*, despite being a UNITA adherent, I decided to stay here [in the city] with UNITA in my heart to encourage the people. I worked secretly, enlightening the people that they must wait for UNITA. We took pencils,

[24] Interviewee 193, Kuito, August 2009.
[25] *Jornal de Angola*, 17 August 1980, 1.
[26] *Jornal de Angola*, 23 August 1980, 4.
[27] *The Times* (London), 30 July 1980. Excerpted in *Facts and Reports* 10 (O-P), 8 August 1980. Holland Committee on Southern Africa.

educational material and books [to people in the bush] – a long way, sometimes as far as Bailundo [100 kilometres away].[28]

A woman in her sixties, who had been active in UNITA's structure for women,
Liga da Mulher Angolana (LIMA) said she had joined UNITA in Huambo in
1975 but had been visiting Benguela when Savimbi retreated from Huambo.
She went home to a city now under government control but remained loyal
to UNITA.

> UNITA leaders would appear secretly and give us courage. We sent flour,
> cooking oil, salt, schoolbooks to the bush. This was prohibited, and [the gov-
> ernment] security caught a lot of people. In 1978 we saw people being shot
> for this, at the *palácio* [the government building in Huambo]. Pamphlets
> used to come from Jamba. When Savimbi had a rally in the bush people
> went, recorded it and brought the cassettes home. Everything that he did in
> the bush, we knew about.[29]

Verónica, a schoolteacher, recalled that her own brother had worked secretly
for UNITA throughout the 1980s without her knowledge and that when
UNITA 'came out of the bush' in preparation for the 1992 elections, her
mother had donned her old UNITA t-shirt and wrap from LIMA, insignia that
she had kept hidden for years.[30]

What these accounts illustrate is that political identity was not entirely a
function of political control. Some people could make choices about the party
they supported, even if they could not show their support publicly.[31] During
interviews, I routinely asked what it meant to be 'a government person' or
'a UNITA person'.[32] The responses broke down into two main groups, with
people either saying that this depended on the party that one supported or on
the party under whose control one lived. But some interviewees were aware
of the contradictions that could arise from the different ways in which party
identity was determined. Bento, a catechist who had grown up during the war,
acknowledged that there were two bases on which the authorities would judge
an individual's political affiliation:

> One would have to speak well of the party and receive them. But some
> people don't change, for many motives. Also, because of [professional]

---

[28] Interviewee 86, Huambo, July 2008.

[29] Interviewee 82, Huambo, July 2008.

[30] Interviewee 108, Luanda, October 2008.

[31] All of the accounts that I heard of such dissidence were from the towns. It is possible that the
social environment of the village ruled out the possibility of working for the party that was not
in control: see the comments in the methodology section of the introductory chapter about the
restrictions on public discourse in rural Angola.

[32] '*Pessoa do governo*' / '*pessoa da UNITA*'.

function – not being MPLA could be very difficult. [But] in the war, on the basis of where one lived, one was considered to be MPLA or UNITA.[33]

Bento's own life was an illustration of the disjuncture between political identity as assigned and political identity as lived. He had some sympathy for UNITA, linked to the importance that he attached to his southern Angolan identity and his Christian faith. However, he had lived exclusively in government-controlled areas during the war and had served in the FAPLA. In his description of processes of political identification, 'speaking well' and 'receiving' suggest the necessity of demonstrating, like Rui's mother on her train journey in 1975, that one was associated with the party that happened to be in power.

CONCLUSION

This chapter has considered the complexities of political identity and its relationship to political control in the context of a government strategy to relocate people in order to cut off material support for UNITA. To understand the nature of the association between person and party and how those in power required it to be demonstrated requires us at the very least to disaggregate the ideas of political membership and political support and to understand them in the context of wartime Angola. 'Support' in a non-democratic situation does not have its liberal connotations of free choice and moral identification: it becomes as much a matter of performance as of belief.[34] As will be discussed in the next chapter, loyalty to UNITA in the rural areas that it controlled was judged in terms of how people delivered the food and labour that UNITA needed, yet to deliver these goods was obligatory: 'support' was understood to be not a sentiment but a behaviour that did not necessarily coincide with subjective belief. In government-controlled areas, similarly, people's political identity was judged on behaviours such as working for the civil service or attending MPLA events that were all but obligatory: 'obeying' and 'collaborating', as Moco expressed it. When interviewees were asked specifically about their 'support' for one or other movement, it was in these terms that they understood the question and offered answers.

---

[33] Interviewee 141, Luanda, July 2009.

[34] Stathis Kalyvas, *The Logic of Violence in Civil War* (Cambridge, 2006), 92–94 warns against '[c]onceptualizing support in attitudinal terms', a practice that ignores the fact that the preferences expressed by people may be conditioned by the need to survive under threat from a dominant political-military movement and wrongly implies 'that people actually "choose" what faction to support based on its political and social profile or ideology – as if they were voting in elections'.

However, 'support' referred only to one kind of political relationship. When interviewees spoke generally about their and others' relationships with political movements, without being prompted by a question about 'support', the words they usually chose were *aderir* ('adhere', or more colloquially, 'join') and *aderência* ('adherence'). These suggest a relationship with a movement not necessarily defined either by agreement with its aims or by active participation and a relationship that was not necessarily voluntary. In its broadest definition, 'adherence' meant nothing more than accepting the authority of the movement that was in charge. Bento's assertion that 'some people don't change' speaks of the possibility of retaining political beliefs contrary to the party that was dominant in an area. Government discourse nevertheless categorised people primarily on the basis of where they were: 'government people' or 'UNITA people'. People's actual beliefs, if they were not pro-MPLA, could not be expressed and therefore could not be quantified, although people could fall under suspicion of belonging to UNITA if they did not take part in MPLA activities. At the same time, the government discourse allowed for the possibility of bringing people who had formerly been with UNITA into government-controlled areas on the assumption that they had been with UNITA involuntarily and that simply the change of location could transform them into *'povo do governo'* (government people). Ambivalence towards these people remained, however: anyone who chose to remain in a rural area that was notionally under UNITA control was suspected of being actively part of UNITA.

This is not to say that everyone was motivated only by the need for survival or that political choice was never a factor. Indeed, the interviews quoted throughout this book demonstrate that some people in UNITA and in the MPLA were motivated by deeply held convictions that persisted through changes of political control. MPLA supporters quietly retained their beliefs through the months of UNITA occupation in Huambo, and UNITA supporters who lived in the towns continued to risk their lives working underground for their organisation. What is more, when people spoke of their beliefs having changed, this did not always have an opportunistic motivation. People who had spent long periods with UNITA and had been exposed only to UNITA's narratives genuinely feared the MPLA and believed that UNITA was the better defender of their interests. These beliefs were liable to change once people encountered the MPLA state and became familiar with the MPLA's narratives, provided that their experience of the MPLA state was a positive one. People with skills and education that could be used by the state had reason to identify positively with the MPLA, particularly since its state-building efforts in the towns were something that remained only a distant aspiration for UNITA at the bush bases. Farmers, who had a more marginal relationship with both of the political movements, generally had little to gain from moving to a government-controlled area: at best, for farmers who had previously been caught between the two movements, the move to a government zone represented an improvement in security but little more than that, and it was in these minimal terms that farmers in the peri-urban zones expressed their approval of the MPLA.

Concerning the strategy of moving people into government-controlled areas, several possible motives suggest themselves. Some writers have suggested that the possession of people has an intrinsic symbolic worth that in itself makes the power of the political movement legitimate.[35] The testimony presented in this chapter suggests that in the situation of war in which the Angolan state found itself, its primary reason for moving people was first of all instrumental: to cut off support for the guerrillas by emptying the countryside. Beyond this, however, the movement of people was also the first condition for efforts to forge a political relationship between the MPLA party-state and people who previously had been beyond the reach of the state. The first part of this relationship consisted in the provision of humanitarian assistance to people who arrived in the towns, even if much of the aid in fact came from foreign donors working under the auspices of the MPLA state. Later chapters will show how parties invoked the provision of food as a basis of political legitimacy throughout the war and after. The second part of this political relationship was defined in terms of security, in the capacity of a political movement to protect the people of a particular area against an enemy. This, however, needed more than guns: it also required the creation of a perception of fear, which in turn required the construction of an enemy in the eyes of people who, left alone, would have maintained an equal and sceptical distance from both movements. This chapter and the previous one have shown how the nationalist ideology with which the MPLA sought legitimacy required the presence of UNITA as an enemy whose foreign and colonial links the MPLA took pains to emphasise. The following chapters, in which UNITA's wartime ideologies and practices are discussed further, will show how UNITA's quest for legitimacy similarly required it to present the MPLA as an alien enemy.

---

[35] Brinkman, *A War for People*; Thomas Blom Hansen and Finn Stepputat (eds.), *Sovereign Bodies: Citizens, Migrants, and States in the Postcolonial World* (Princeton, NJ, 2005).

5

UNITA in the Central Highlands, 1976–1991

UNITA's turn to guerrilla war in 1976 was a reaction to unexpected events. Most of the people who had allied themselves with UNITA in the towns and missions of the Central Highlands in 1974 and 1975 had done so in the expectation that UNITA was about to take command of an independent Angolan state. As Chapter 2 demonstrated, the calculations of the UNITA leadership were founded on an understanding of the need to maintain a presence among the rural population of the Central Highlands as well as to establish a rear base in the remote south-east of Angola. This chapter will consider the ways in which UNITA sought to build a political relationship with the people of the Central Highlands between 1976 and the peace process of the early 1990s. It draws on interviews with people who occupied different places in the UNITA hierarchy, from the leadership to peasant farmers who lived under UNITA control. The purpose of examining accounts by people from across the hierarchy is to illustrate both the ideological and the strategic approach adopted by the UNITA leadership and how the ideas and practices associated with UNITA were accepted and understood by the population at large. Some communities experienced UNITA only as a violent and predatory force, and the purpose of this chapter is not to cast doubt upon these accounts. The processes of political engagement that are outlined in this chapter are those that UNITA adopted in those areas where the military situation was sufficiently stable to allow it to engage in a peaceful manner with the local population.

The previous chapter showed how MPLA government discourse created a dichotomy of 'government people' versus 'UNITA people'. This chapter will disaggregate the idea of 'UNITA people', showing how UNITA discourses created different categories of identity within the areas it controlled, as people were classified in terms of their relationship to the movement, a distinction that has its origins in the dual strategy of elite and peasant mobilisation discussed in Chapter 2. The focus will be on the relationship among three broad categories of people: the UNITA leadership, the people who had accompanied UNITA's columns that left the towns and the peasant farmers who lived in the zones over which UNITA established or attempted to establish its control. I will relate interviewees' accounts of UNITA's practices and political discourses to the formation of identities based around the movement. All of the accounts indicate that the core element of UNITA's presence in a rural district comprised bases that had a military character but which also were central to UNITA's attempts to provide services, particularly health and education, to villages within the area of influence of the base. The interviews sometimes pointed to contradictory interpretations of the role of military and civilian members of UNITA and of the villagers who lived in areas controlled by UNITA. These apparent contradictions, as I will discuss later, demonstrate how the categories of 'military' and 'civilian' were less clearly differentiated in UNITA areas than was the case in the part of Angolan society controlled by the government. They also offer insight into the ways in which UNITA viewed its relationship with the people it controlled and how those people came to see themselves in relation to UNITA.

Estêvão, a farmer, declared himself to have been 'captured' by UNITA from a government-held area but soon became integrated into UNITA's political and economic structures and was appointed as a 'director' of a village, continuing to live in the village but serving as the point of contact between his fellow villagers and the UNITA officials from the nearby base. When interviewed in 2008, he continued privately to express strong loyalty to UNITA, although he believed that it would not be safe to make his continued support for UNITA publicly known.

> From 1975 to 1979 I was with the government. From 1979 to 1991 I was placed in a village after they [UNITA] captured me and made me go to the bush. I was director of a village. UNITA chose men who had vision. There were between one and three directors controlling each village. The leaders lived in bases and the population lived in the villages. When they [the leadership] came from the bases to the villages, they would contact the director [of the village]. They would ask, for example, 'were there MPLA troops here?' And they would make a report. Only soldiers lived at the base – but that included the wives of soldiers. It was rare for a soldier to have a wife in the village. If a woman stayed outside the base, she could talk [to the enemy].[1]

---

[1] Interviewee 60, Huambo, June 2008. In this extract I have translated '*mulher*' variously as 'wife' and as 'woman' as seemed appropriate in English, though the same word was used in Portuguese.

As a 'director', Estêvão's role was to liaise with the traditional authorities, but 'the orders came from the party'. The essential point here is that villagers were militarily useful, in this instance as sources of information, but that people who were part of UNITA's political or military structures saw the villagers as people who had a relationship with UNITA rather than as being an integral part of UNITA.

Costa, a former soldier, had joined UNITA's army 'from my own convictions' in 1975, aged 20. He remained with UNITA until the end of the war in 2002, when he went to one of the quartering areas established in the terms of the Luena peace accord.[2] When interviewed in 2008, he was spending much of his time at the local UNITA office in a town in the Central Highlands and considered himself a party activist. Costa explained that the bases housed 'no civilians', but they were home to the 'party secretariat,' whose members were considered soldiers although their function was political. This merging of political and military functions was characteristic of UNITA's organisation. The purpose of the secretariat was 'to organise the masses, to explain the cause, why we were here to defend Angolans' while the task of UNITA's 'military protection' was 'to allow the people to be able to work in peace'. Military patrols would go out from the base to cover the 'consolidated' area surrounding it – that is, that area deemed to be beyond the reach of government troops – with details of five to ten soldiers stationed at outlying bases on the edge of the 'consolidated' area. According to Costa and other interviewees, some bases had to relocate every few months when the government became aware of their location, but the farmers in the surrounding villages 'didn't move much: there were attempts to capture people but our troops defended them'.[3] The mobility of the bases was in contrast to the more permanent settlements at Jamba that will be discussed in the following chapter.

Because Costa was still an active UNITA party member at the time of the interview, it is likely that his account contains elements of UNITA's preferred view of itself. Two elements are most apparent. First, as had been the case during its brief period in the cities, UNITA portrayed its role as defending the people and defending the peace. Second, the interview suggests that UNITA knew that political education was necessary if people were to be convinced of the justice of UNITA's cause. The content of this education will be discussed later in this chapter.

---

[2]   This agreement is discussed in Chapter 9.
[3]   Interviewee 63, Caála, June 2008. As discussed, 'consolidated' is relative. In this case it refers not to the Jamba area but to a part of the Central Highlands that was relatively safe for UNITA.

Chapter 2 made clear how Savimbi and other UNITA leaders believed that providing services was essential in establishing a political relationship with people. Interviewees who had lived under UNITA control before 1990 mostly recalled that UNITA either provided or attempted to provide basic social services, principally health and education, to people in villages as a central element of its vision of the political relationship that it sought with the people. Estêvão, the former village 'director', described the relationship between a base and the surrounding villages as one of benevolent service provision: 'Teachers and nurses [...] lived at the bases and left the bases to help the people in the villages. Medicine was free and pupils didn't have to pay for classes.' He said UNITA would allocate between one and four teachers to a village, depending on the size of the settlement.

The superior training and expertise of the teachers employed by UNITA was a claim frequently made by the movement's followers. UNITA set a high value on the fact that some of its teachers had been trained in the colonial education system. 'This is why teaching in the bush was different from in the city,' according to Costa. 'UNITA had more teachers from colonial times. When the Portuguese left UNITA already had teachers, who were obliged to go to the bush.' A report by *Washington Post* journalist Leon Dash describes how even before independence, UNITA teachers were teaching from the Portuguese government school textbooks but pointing out and correcting those parts that they believed to be colonial and racist propaganda.[4] Even in the bush, appeals to legitimacy could be made in terms of UNITA's ability to mimic the colonial state. Yet this superior expertise was set alongside the teachers' self-sacrifice in forgoing the comforts of city life. In Costa's words, 'There were no salaries, just barter – there was no money. They would receive food or salt.'[5]

While little distinction in status was made between the people who performed military and social service roles within UNITA, the more important distinction was between the people who lived at the base and had arrived there from the towns along with UNITA's columns, and the villagers who were originally from the area. The base was dominated by people who had left Huambo or other towns of the Central Highlands in 1976. They referred to the villagers as 'the found people' [*povo encontrado*], that is, the people living in the area before the arrival of UNITA, or more commonly and simply, 'UNITA people' [*povo da UNITA*].[6] This second category became 'UNITA people'

---

4   Leon Dash, 'Angolan Guerrillas Run Schools and Clinics in Forest', *The Washington Post*, 24 December 1973, A9.
5   Interviewee 60, Huambo, June 2008.
6   Interviewee 69, Caála, July 2008.

simply through being in an area controlled by UNITA, the same basis of categorisation that appeared in government discourses, as noted in the previous chapter. People from the villages would go to live at the base only if they had been recruited into the army or, more unusually, if they had acquired the skills necessary to join the ranks of UNITA professionals.

In addition to the fields worked by peasant farmers who lived near the base, some bases also had collective fields, which were cultivated by people who lived at the base. Amélia, who spent three weeks as a captive at a UNITA base near Bailundo in 1984, remembered an orderly system for the distribution of food from the collective fields.

> Everyone received the same quantity. A commander or official from UNITA would call the people to receive. A pregnant woman would get an extra ration. What interrupted the system of food supply was the war. If you were concerned with having breakfast, lunch and dinner sometimes that wasn't possible.[7]

But even if the people of the base produced some of their own food, the organisation of food for the base was nevertheless the main material basis of the distinction between the two categories of people: the people outside the base produced and donated food, while the people inside the base produced some food but also consumed food produced by others. Extracting food from the farmers was both a practical task and a political one for UNITA, since UNITA officials had to convince people that it was in their own interests to give up part of their harvest.

Former UNITA central committee member Horácio Junjuvili, when asked how UNITA persuaded people to give produce to the soldiers, spoke of a system that linked security, administration and politics, underpinned by the possibility of violence.

> In the *mata* UNITA had a tripartite structure: Army, administration, and party. The army made war, protected the population. The administration dealt with agriculture, stock-rearing, health and education. Other professionals were in the party to mobilise, encourage, recruit personnel. [...] Survival would be easier with a better relationship with the people. If you mistreat the people, the people go away. And also, UNITA's discipline was very strict. One had to respect the people and their goods. [...] A village might have a field of cassava or whatever – if you destroy this field and the people flee, you eat cassava one day and then the animals destroy the rest. Better that you maintain relations with the people because they will look after what they have. When

---

[7] Interviewee 88, Luanda, July 2008.

you arrive, ask, and they give. It's true that when UNITA began to grow it no longer had enough professionals to be allocated everywhere. And in this case there was violence.[8]

The logistics of extracting food was one of the tasks of people at the base, in cooperation with designated individuals in the village. A woman who had lived at UNITA bases throughout the civil war recalled having been 'responsible for organising food, in the fields, with people who cultivated. I arranged food for the troops. The responsibility of each farmer was to deliver x kilograms.'[9] A former UNITA soldier, who had been in the army from the late 1970s, spoke of the relationship between UNITA officials at the base and nearby farmers ('*povo*') in a way that conflates the farmers' interests with those of UNITA and plays down the role of the farmers' labour.

> Food appeared in abundance. People cultivated – other goods came for free, in the name of UNITA. UNITA always depended on its own efforts. The peasants lived in peace through their own efforts. The peasants lived in good legality. The troops ate well through the efforts of the party. In the villages there were *sobas*, and the peasants were organised. The relationships [between UNITA and the *sobas*] were all-embracing, revolutionary, tangible. There were never any problems between UNITA and the *sobas* because UNITA defended what belonged to Angola. There was never any ill-feeling.[10]

The farmers' contribution is subsumed under the 'own efforts' of UNITA, and food simply 'appeared', abundantly. This account also suggests a seamless relationship between a moral order that existed before the arrival of UNITA, under the authority of the *sobas*, and a moral order that incorporated UNITA. The choice of the word 'legality' to denote this order is clearly an idiosyncratic usage, but it echoes a comment by another former UNITA soldier: 'The order of the bush was better than the order of the city – people had order because people ate well.'[11] Both these remarks link the availability of food to the maintenance of social order.

UNITA officials also claimed an active role for the movement in agricultural production by teaching agriculture. Junjuvili described the system as follows:

> The so-called branches or UNITA committees were organised. All the villages had committees, and one of the tasks of the committees was to collect

[8] Interview, Horácio Junjuvili, Luanda, July 2009.
[9] Interviewee 73, Caála, July 2008. The value of 'x kilograms' varied from time to time and place to place.
[10] Interviewee 67, Caála, July 2008.
[11] Interviewee 61, Caála, July 2008.

food that would be kept there to give to whoever passed by. Whoever passed by would go to the committee and would eat – committees produced, they created production centres where there were ploughs and animals to pull them. In 1982 I was appointed commander of Region 63, north of Menongue, and we turned that area into the biggest maize producer in all of Huambo, Cuando Cubango and Bié: no one produced more than we did. [...] UNITA introduced hybrid seeds from South Africa. Good seeds.[12]

Those who fought in UNITA's army echoed the idea that UNITA needed to intervene technically rather than just take an existing surplus. According to Costa,

[UNITA] had an economic base to sustain the troops, to feed them. UNITA organised the peasants to cultivate. This helped UNITA in its great battles. All the population wanted to join us, to be part of us. There was education so that the people wouldn't be hungry. It was necessary to explain how to cultivate – that was the policy.[13]

This creation or imagining of a role for UNITA in agricultural production hides the fact that the peasant farmers had been self-sufficient for food before UNITA arrived and that they gave UNITA more than they ever received. The 'organisation' of agriculture described by the UNITA loyalists was above all a matter of extracting. There was little that a movement like UNITA could do in terms of providing basic foodstuffs. In favourable circumstances it could (and, as we shall see, sometimes did) supply manufactured items such as clothing, soap and salt, which had to come from the cities or from the coast, but this was not always possible.

Similarly, the political and service structures of which UNITA officials spoke so proudly were not consistently present in the areas where UNITA operated. This is evident in the account of a woman whose home area in Bailundo district fell under UNITA control soon after independence when she was 18 years old. She speaks of UNITA above all as a military organisation that offered nothing to the civilian peasant population:

The government hadn't yet arrived there. There was only one party, UNITA. We worked in the fields. We had lots of food but we lacked soap and salt. And clothes. There was no school, nor a hospital. When people were sick, they would be cured with herbal remedies.[14]

---

[12] Interview, Junjuvili.
[13] Interviewee 63, Caála, June 2008.
[14] Interviewee 17, Huambo, May 2008.

Another farmer, Ana, had previously lived in a village some thirty kilometres from Huambo from which the government tried to evacuate people to the city as part of its counter-insurgency measures of the early 1980s. She and her husband, however, resisted the government's evacuation attempts and moved further away from the city, to a part of the countryside where the FAPLA never gained control. Her account illustrates that in an area that was contested by the two sides, the farmers had little to gain materially from UNITA's presence.

> People didn't like being with UNITA because they had neither salt nor cloth-ing. But they gave food [to UNITA], voluntarily. During the time we were with UNITA, we were always on the move. When the government caught us, we would burn our houses. When the government attacked, we would hold on to part of our food. Then we would come back if the government had gone away. The government took food, cattle, clothes, chickens, whatever they could find. We could spend two years in a place, and we would grow crops. Then, when [FAPLA] came, we would burn the houses.[15]

Pedro, a catechist, was captured by UNITA in 1978. After some months as a prisoner, he spent the years from 1979 to 1990 working for the Catholic Church in UNITA-controlled territory. In contrast with the accounts of UNITA loyal-ists, Pedro's description is more ambivalent, emphasising coercion as well as consensus:

> No one was allowed to leave. [...] There was food, but almost nothing for the prisoners. Those people who had fields would sometimes give us something. The soldiers would ask for food from the natives.[16] They didn't threaten them. The population gave it. When the soldiers captured cattle on this side[17] they would take them back and sell them to the people. They would sell cattle and buy honey and rice, if the people were growing rice. There was no money – just barter.[18] They would also sell soap, if they cap-tured soap. Later I had a field, a small one because I was a prisoner, and I didn't have to give food to UNITA.
>
> When UNITA entered an area it mobilised the population: 'We have come not to retreat, but to save you from the hands of the Cubans and the MPLA. You can't go away. We have a lot of troops to confront the Cubans.' The people were frightened. Some went to the government. Others stayed in the bush. The population was divided.

---

[15] Interviewee 54, near Huambo, June 2008. Compare also the remarks in the previous chapter by interviewees 38 and 39, which suggest that villagers in the contested areas experienced both armies as violent and predatory and experienced no attempts at political incorporation by either side.

[16] *Nativos* – in other words, the local indigenous population.

[17] Meaning 'the government-controlled area'.

[18] He is using 'buy' and 'sell' loosely here to mean barter.

In the beginning UNITA already had teachers and nurses but when there were no medicines they would arrange traditional medicine. As for schools, it was difficult, but there were schools, but not all the time. Later there were schools, only for the soldiers' children, and the teachers were soldiers. A teacher would go to a village and say 'study, study', then at age 15 or 16 they would be captured to the bases to become soldiers […]. UNITA's policy was to mobilise people by saying: 'If I come to power it will be better than with the MPLA. I will take you away from the slavery of the Cubans.' The people accepted this because they were not very wise. Now we are seeing that that was not the case. If the people had known this, they would not have accepted UNITA. No one could have known anything. The three movements said different things and no one knew which was better. We just accepted. If [in a UNITA area] one said 'I'm going to the MPLA' you'd be in prison. You had to keep your mouth shut. If you said you were going to the MPLA you could be killed.

Asked if UNITA had dispensed justice in any systematic way, Pedro replied:

There was a system but it was complicated. Sometimes someone would say 'this man wanted to go to the MPLA' or accuse someone of having salt.[19] You would be put in prison where you would die.[20]

Pedro portrays the system of food provision as still consensual, but as a system of barter rather than the kind of social contract between UNITA and the peasants that was described by many other interviewees. With regard to the people in and around the base, the category distinction that he makes is between 'soldiers' at the base and 'the population' in the villages. This suggests that in his experience, UNITA's teachers and medical personnel served a primarily military function. His account of UNITA's version of history, which cast its role as defending Angolans against the foreign threat of the Cubans, is consistent with the account given by the other interviewees. He is nevertheless sceptical about UNITA's powers of persuasion, noting that some people from the villages chose to leave the UNITA areas and go to the government-held towns and that UNITA relied on force and threat to prevent them from leaving.

The question of regulation and punishment is one that UNITA loyalists were hesitant to talk about, and the accounts by more sceptical observers

---

[19] Possession of salt in a UNITA area led to the suspicion that the person had been in contact with the MPLA, since salt had to come from the coast, which was government controlled. There were also accounts from government-controlled areas that anyone caught carrying large quantities of salt would be suspected of planning to deliver this salt to UNITA in the bush.

[20] Interviewee 128, Chicomba, November 2008. Leon Dash witnessed prisoners being brought out of the subterranean pits that were used as cells: 'A Chameleon of Civil War Is Captive of Ex-Comrades', *The Washington Post* 10 August 1977, A18. This description matches the testimony of other interviewees; see Chapter 5.

are not comprehensive. The journalist Leon Dash, sympathetic in certain respects to UNITA's aims, witnessed some of the ways in which UNITA dealt with people who were captured by UNITA troops during incursions into government-held areas. He describes captives, including soldiers and a civilian woman, showing signs of being beaten. Captives were kept tied with ropes, while longer-term prisoners were held in underground pits. UNITA officials quoted in Dash's report say that civilians and government soldiers would be spared and 're-educated', while commanders and their Cuban allies would be executed. The captives interviewed by Dash apparently knew what to say to increase their chances of survival: they denied any political links with the government and claimed to have been captured from their villages by government or Cuban troops and taken against their will to government-held centres.[21]

UNITA, then, possessed both persuasive and repressive capabilities. Accordingly, the interviews with farming communities that had lived alongside UNITA suggest attitudes that ranged from active identification to simple compliance with instructions in order to avoid punishment. Jaka Jamba, a founding member of UNITA who later became one of the party's most prominent parliamentarians, acknowledged that many peasants for reasons of self-preservation accepted the authority of whichever movement was in command at the time, though he believes some had more lasting convictions:

> When [UNITA] arrived in Bailundo [before the 1992 elections] there were already ladies who had UNITA wraps that they had kept hidden away. When the MPLA came, they had MPLA uniforms. There is a proverb in Umbundu: '*Omunu iyo tu tula. Omunu enda tu tuika.*' Whoever arrives, we help them to put down their basket. Whoever goes away, we help them to put their basket on their head. This means: we stay where we are, and whoever is in power is the one we listen to. But even so, there is still a base, a firmer core, which normally identifies either with the one who is coming, or the one who is going away.[22]

Yet if we are to understand better the distinction between the two ways of being connected to UNITA that Jaka Jamba describes, this characterisation needs further qualification in two important ways. The first concerns the questions of which people were the active UNITA supporters and which people merely accepted UNITA's presence. Among those I interviewed, those who spoke of always having supported UNITA's ideas and practices had, without exception,

---

21   Leon Dash, 'A Prisoner's Hard Road To Reeducation or Death', *The Washington Post*, 10 August 1977, A18.
22   Interview with Jaka Jamba, Luanda, September 2009.

fulfilled some kind of institutional function within UNITA, whether as soldiers, village political officials or traditional leaders. The former soldiers and officials were among those who had remained with UNITA until the last days of the war and continued to be members of the political communities attached to UNITA party branch offices after the end of the war. The *sobas* were living in villages and had been cut off from government patronage as a result of their continuing UNITA affiliation. In contrast to these more active participants in UNITA's work, peasant farmers who had no special status would sometimes speak of having accepted UNITA's authority but seldom acknowledged UNITA to be inherently more worthy of their support than the MPLA or any other political movement.

The second point is that a simple dichotomy of active support versus passive acceptance does not take account of UNITA's efforts to shape the perceptions of the people under its control. If people were reluctant to leave UNITA-controlled areas, this was not because they had any particular preference for UNITA's policies but rather because they were fearful of what they might encounter were they to fall under the control of the government.[23] Their fears were the direct result of having accepted a version of events that UNITA actively propagated in the areas that it controlled. In comparing the accounts of different interviewees who gave more or less positive accounts of UNITA's presence, it becomes apparent how UNITA's preferred discourse served to conceal the fact that as far as food supply was concerned, the relationship between UNITA and farmers was to the benefit of the UNITA professionals and soldiers at the base and offered nothing to the farmers in the villages. UNITA therefore needed to convince peasants that they had something to gain by remaining in the areas controlled by UNITA: UNITA would provide security in exchange for food. The next section of this chapter discusses the content and character of these processes of politicisation.

POLITICAL EDUCATION AT THE BASES

Political education was a part of life at the UNITA bases and in the villages that fell under the bases' influence and was mentioned in the recollections of most interviewees who had spent any time with UNITA. Simão, the former lieutenant, spoke of 'political experts tasked with organising the people to understand the guerrilla war'.[24] An important part of this meant promoting a perception of fear and threat so as to convince people that they needed UNITA as a defender.

[23] See, for example, the account of interviewee 180, quoted in the previous chapter.
[24] Interviewee 72, Caála, July 2008.

> When we were in the bush, the villages were dispersed. If FAPLA was
> coming from one side, the people could leave on the other side. The people
> had places to which they could flee. FAPLA would try to infiltrate and
> capture people. The (UNITA) troops came from the base to instruct the
> people: 'FAPLA's coming, you must leave.' When the enemy was coming,
> they always said we must go, to escape the bullets.[25]

Apart from the cultivation of fear, there was also an ideological element to this
education. Savimbi, in an interview with the journalist Leon Dash, described
UNITA's political task as one of 'nationalization,' by which he appeared
to mean something more like nation building, the creation of a national
consciousness.

> You are trying to get a man to switch from thinking of himself as a Cuanhama
> to thinking of himself first as an Angolan. It's very complicated.[26]

According to Dash, Savimbi personally taught a course for political commissars who were sent from military camps to peasant villages. The claims that
Savimbi had made to national leadership during his proclamation of statehood in Huambo on Independence Day were also implicit in the ways in
which UNITA commissars sought to convince people in rural Angola of the
rightness of UNITA's cause. These included a reading of history that emphasised UNITA's anti-colonial role and its claims to represent the interests of the
majority of Angolans against an MPLA leadership that UNITA spoke of as
alien to Angola. Dash cites a speech by a UNITA commissar who mentioned
Neto's white Portuguese wife as evidence that Neto was a relic of colonialism
who did not have the interests of poor Angolans at heart.[27]

Two key themes in UNITA's political narratives were, first, that Angola's
natural resources were a national patrimony that UNITA sought to distribute
fairly, and, second, that UNITA stood for a participatory democracy. Estêvão,
the former village organiser, said UNITA officials 'explained in such a way that
the people would accept to stay in the bush – it was necessary to nourish the
word of the party'.[28] The message was that 'they were fighting to liberate
the black people of Angola with a different politics'[29] and that 'Angola has
resources that need to be shared, the money that belongs to the majority can't

---

[25] Interviewee 61, Caála, June 2008.

[26] Leon Dash, 'Commissars Heap Scorn on Role of Portuguese and Cubans', *The Washington Post*, 11 August 1977, A24.

[27] Leon Dash, 'Commissars Heap Scorn on Role of Portuguese and Cubans', *The Washington Post*, 11 August 1977, A24.

[28] '*Alimentar a palavra do partido*'.

[29] *Política* can mean 'politics' but also 'policy'.

be kept by the minority'. According to Estêvão, 'people accepted this, and this is why they agreed to stay in the bush, because they believed that one day UNITA would be in power'.[30]

Felipe, a former soldier, recalled that in the process of civic education, 'we learnt about the history of Angola: the arrival of the Portuguese, the enslavement of the people. In 1975 the MPLA refused elections because UNITA had the advantage over the MPLA. Agostinho Neto wasn't confident that he would win, and because UNITA always wanted democracy, Neto went to get the Cubans to chase the people out of the city and into the bush. UNITA went to the bush so as to have another strategy to struggle for democracy.'[31]

The secretaries and organisers – the villagers who served as the contact between UNITA and the villages – were the point at which the welfare and political functions of UNITA merged.

> The secretaries organised food and civic and political education. The message [of this education] was to defend the national cause against our enemy, the Cubans. The intention was not to fight black against black, but to drive out the Cubans so that the indigenous Angolans could retake power.[32]

At the same time, as we have seen, UNITA's cadres were indistinct from the military, and political education included narratives of fear of an outside enemy. The women's structure within UNITA, *Liga da Mulher Angolana* (LIMA), similarly assumed political, humanitarian and military functions. A LIMA member recalled that 'from the age of 18 I worked for LIMA – our tasks were looking after children, instructing activists, arranging food and clothes'.[33] Even if women were not deployed in military combat, military

---

[30] Interviewee 60, Caála, June 2008. The unequal distribution of the benefits from Angola's natural resources is a theme upon which UNITA officials have become particularly vocal since the end of the war. This has coincided with increased foreign investment in the Angolan oil industry and soaring global oil prices between 2003 and 2007. Scepticism is therefore necessary towards interviews conducted in 2008 with UNITA activists who suggest that resource distribution was always part of UNITA's programme; we may see some attempts here to claim a retrospective legitimacy for UNITA's activity over the decades by asserting a continuity in the movement's doctrine from the 1970s until the present. On the other hand, Bridgland (*Jonas Savimbi*, 313) witnessed an example of UNITA propaganda that suggests that as early as 1981, UNITA claimed to be fighting against the looting of Angola's natural resources by foreigners in collaboration with the MPLA.

[31] Interviewee 64, Caála, June 2008. This and similar recollections erase the fact of UNITA's cooperation with Portugal in Operation Timber and that its actions against the colonial state amounted to little more than the sabotage of the Benguela Railway while most of its military efforts before independence were directed against the MPLA. See John Marcum, *The Angolan Revolution, Volume II (Exile Politics and Guerrilla Warfare, 1962–1976)*, 191–197, 211 and William Minter, *Operation Timber: Pages from the Savimbi Dossier* (Trenton, NJ, 1988).

[32] Interviewee 63, Caála, June 2008.

[33] Interviewee 74, Caála, July 2008.

logistics depended on women's labour. A former UNITA military officer described how 'when the troops went to the fronts, the mamas carried flour, carried [military] materiel to them'.[34] The leadership regarded the bases in the Central Highlands as a way of building links with a civilian population that could be relied on to support UNITA by providing food and used as a pool for military recruitment. By maintaining these political links while also maintaining a distinction between the core UNITA population of the base and the peasants who farmed within the base's zone of influence, it was possible for UNITA to keep mobile military units that could move relatively quickly when under threat by FAPLA and still be sure of finding people who would provide them with food, whether the soldiers returned to the base they had vacated or moved to a safer location.

CONCLUSION

The relationships with rural people that UNITA established in the late 1970s and 1980s were underwritten by UNITA's monopoly of force in much of the countryside of the Central Highlands. From the early 1980s, UNITA's military capability owed much to the rear base at Jamba and to South African and US support, but UNITA's military bases in the countryside were set up before this. With or without external support, in order to function effectively and sustainably, UNITA needed to construct a relationship with farming communities that rested on consent as well as on force. UNITA sought to define the relationship by presenting itself as an entity that acted in the best interests of rural people by defending them against a perceived external threat. These discourses were complemented, to varying degrees at different times and in different places, by the provision of basic health and education services.

Nevertheless, this practice rested upon and reproduced the categorisation of people that had begun as UNITA's urban cadres left the cities in early 1976, as outlined in Chapter 2: on the one hand, the political leadership and the cadres who saw themselves as having an institutional relationship with UNITA and on the other, the population of rural areas under UNITA control. UNITA's mode of operating required the creation of a political space that would allow its officials and cadres to intervene within communities that had existed and been self-sustaining before UNITA arrived. In Jamba, by contrast, the creation of a society more or less from scratch was determined as part of a political project. The implications of this will be examined in the next chapter.

[34]   Interviewee 72, Caála, July 2008.

6

UNITA at Jamba

The idea of a rear base in south-eastern Angola began as a strategic military consideration for UNITA, but its implementation became central to the political imaginary that underpinned the movement's legitimacy in the eyes of its followers for years afterwards. After the government began to attack UNITA bases in Huambo province from 1977 onwards, Jonas Savimbi's central base was moved every few months to avoid detection, until UNITA established a base at Jamba in December 1979.[1] The east of Cuando Cubango had been identified as the most suitable region for the headquarters because of its remoteness from the MPLA's centres of power and its proximity to Namibia, then under South African occupation. Scouts went to look for a suitable location with all-round water in 1978, and UNITA first used Jamba as 'a centre for the re-education of convicts',[2] a repressive purpose far removed from the idealised memories of Jamba presented by those who lived there in the 1980s.

The focus of this chapter, however, is less on military calculations than on Jamba's political importance to UNITA. People who remained loyal to UNITA after the war spoke of the significance of a permanent 'capital' as evidence of UNITA's aspirations to statehood. As General Chiwale described it, 'We were sowing the seeds for the creation of a state within a state. Angola was inexorably on the way to becoming a country with two capitals.'[3] For the UNITA official Jardo Muekalia, 'as the capital of resistance, [Jamba] represented the symbol of our force and the expression of our organisational capacity' through the provision of 'electricity, running water ... schools for primary and secondary education, a secretarial school, a Protestant and a Catholic church'.[4] This

---

[1] Fred Bridgland, *Jonas Savimbi: A Key to Africa* (Edinburgh, 1986), 284.
[2] Samuel Chiwale, *Cruzei-me com a História* (Lisbon, 2008), 254.
[3] Chiwale, *Cruzei-me*, 253. Compare Chiwale's remark, quoted in Chapter 2, to the effect that losing a capital in Huambo signified that 'the abandonment was total'.
[4] Jardo Muekalia, *Angola: A Segunda Revolução* (Lisbon, 2010), 129.

chapter examines how Jamba became an embodiment of UNITA's ideas about its role not only as a state but as a particular kind of state, one that assumed responsibility for the welfare of its citizens but also demanded a high degree of obedience to the authority of the leadership. I examine critically how people who lived at Jamba remember and speak about it so as to illustrate the importance of Jamba within the narratives that framed people's understandings of UNITA's political legitimacy.

Understanding the significance of Jamba in relation to the other parts of Angola where UNITA had a presence requires paying critical attention to some of the terminology that was applied to UNITA and to the spaces it occupied, by UNITA's opponents as well as by its followers. This terminology is often layered with overlapping and sometimes contradictory meanings, and the slippages between these meanings are themselves revealing. Jamba's main concentration of population, estimated between 10,000 and 15,000, was within an area that UNITA officers sometimes referred to as the 'consolidated lands' (*terras consolidadas*), the part of Angola where UNITA's military presence was unchallenged.[5] The term 'Jamba' was also sometimes used more broadly to refer to the consolidated lands. 'Consolidated' was, however, a relative term, and people would sometimes talk of pockets of land in the Central Highlands as being 'consolidated', meaning that they were reasonably safe from FAPLA incursions. The word '*mata*' (bush) also takes on layers of political meaning in connection with UNITA and Jamba. Chapter 4 showed how government discourse associated UNITA with the bush in a way that presented UNITA and the people connected with it as a threat to the urban-based state established and defended by the MPLA. But people loyal to UNITA also commonly used '*mata*', without the negative connotation that this term had in MPLA discourse, to indicate the area in which UNITA operated more or less freely, including Jamba. A person who emphasised Jamba's sophistication and urbanness could nevertheless say, 'I was born in the *mata* – at Jamba.'[6] At the same time, UNITA loyalists would talk about 'the interior' when referring to those parts of the country such as the Central Highlands where UNITA's control was not consolidated but where it had bases.[7] This opposition between Jamba and 'interior', as well as the extension of the term '*mata*' to include Jamba, served to construct the idea of Jamba as a provisional capital and a peripheral location in a country where UNITA could not gain a hold of the heartland. The ways in which people speak about Jamba reflect the tensions between its status as a capital and as an outpost in a region that remained foreign to

---

[5] Statistics from Thomas Collelo (ed.), *Angola: A Country Study* (Washington, 1989), 103.

[6] Interviewee 65, Caála, July 2008.

[7] Interviewees 62, 74 and 75, Caála, June and July 2008.

the great majority of people who inhabited it. A man who had migrated to UNITA-controlled territory with his family as a young child and who had grown up in Jamba nevertheless expressed the feeling that he would one day return to his birthplace. 'Jamba was seen as a temporary land. We kept the dream that the enemy that had occupied our lands would withdraw.'[8]

The theme that dominated people's recollections was that Jamba was a place where a benevolent authority provided all the essentials of life in a just and equitable manner. People who lived in Jamba emphasised that food was plentiful there and was available at no cost. Social services such as health and education, according to interviewees, were also available free of charge, more widely and on a more sophisticated level than was the case at UNITA's rural bases. These often idealised recollections, though quite possibly flawed as a record of events, are useful as an indication of the power of the idea of Jamba and all that it represented. I quote here from an interview with Tiago, which typified the flavour and the content of former residents' accounts. Tiago had grown up in Jamba after moving there from Huambo with his parents as a young child. At the time of the interview, Tiago was living in poverty in a provincial town, part of a group of former UNITA soldiers and supporters who spent most of their days at the local branch office and who formed a distinct community defined by their UNITA past and their continued identification with UNITA in the present.

> The way of living was as though it were a city. Health matters were looked after for free, not like it is with the [current MPLA] government. Education too. The first time I ever saw money was in 1995. If an individual were sick, they would go to hospital without paying. We were self-sufficient for food from agriculture, but there was also help from the party. Here [under the control of the MPLA in 2008] a six-year-old who goes to school has to pay fees and pay something [a bribe] to the teacher. The school lunches that the donors provided are being sold on the market. No educational material arrives. The government is saying these things exist, but they don't.
>
> In the area where my father was stationed [Mexico, hundreds of kilometres from Jamba] there was no education. So I lived with my aunt so as to benefit from the education at Jamba. There were films, from which we learnt what a city was like. There were satellite dishes – after 1990 we could see international football.
>
> I studied from first to seventh grade in Jamba. Then I reached military age – service in the military was the duty of every citizen. We received education in the army too. Civic education like in other countries – qualities of behaviour in relation to society. And political education, about our party.

---

[8]   Interviewee 166, Chicomba, August 2009.

We learnt that a misunderstanding between brothers had led to the war. And some lessons about the origins of our kingdoms and the life in colonial times.[9]

Tiago talks of the provision of services, the presence of which supports his characterisation of Jamba as a city. He contrasts life in Jamba both with life under the MPLA and with life in the more peripheral areas of UNITA control. Crucially, Tiago points to the role of UNITA in ensuring the supply of food and other goods. People who lived at Jamba saw themselves as having a relationship with UNITA that involved the obligation to work and the right to receive benefits such as health, education and food, with the party itself at the centre of the relationship.

> Everyone worked for the party. The party supplied all needs – right down to pregnant women, the children in their bellies already had rights. I never saw money there. The party brought things from outside. The people there ate and worked.[10]

Given that Tiago had grown up with UNITA parents, had been educated at UNITA schools and had continued to live alongside other UNITA loyalists, his positive portrayal of Jamba is not surprising. Yet some of the details are confirmed by people who had no particular reason to endorse UNITA's preferred version of life in Jamba. Pedro, the catechist whose account of life at UNITA's rural bases, as we saw in the previous chapter, was ambivalent, presented entirely positive recollections of Jamba.

> Life was good in Jamba. It had all the conditions.[11] Nobody told lies. They had means – vehicles came from South Africa with enough food. [...] It looked like a *bairro* but it was organised like a city. There were roads of beaten earth. The hospitals were well organised. The houses and government departments were built of wood. The hospitals were built underground out of mud bricks, and the operating theatre was made of wood. There was a parish church, St Mary the Mother of God, with houses for the missionaries, and Protestant churches too. I never had any problems with UNITA, but I didn't work for UNITA. I worked with the people, for the church.[12]

Amélia, who had been kidnapped in Huambo province and made to work as a schoolteacher in Jamba, had every reason to feel resentment towards UNITA. Instead, although her experiences ultimately left her cynical towards politicians and politics of any kind, the way in which she speaks of life at Jamba

---

9   Interviewee 66, Caála, June 2008.
10 Interviewee 66, Caála, June 2008.
11 'Condições', particularly in Angola, is often used to denote necessities or amenities.
12 Interviewee 128, Chicomba, November 2008.

draws a connection between her appreciation of UNITA's powers of social organisation and her recognition of the movement's political legitimacy.

> I admired the way they knew how to look after amputees. I admired the way everything was distributed for free. UNITA people embraced a different way of studying. Young people from UNITA studied better than the ones on our side [the government side]. Jonas Savimbi, the president, said 'your weapon is your pencil, and your trench the school'. Savimbi determined the destiny of the party. For this reason people called him a dictator. If he said 'today we're all going to work at cleaning up', then everyone would work. He was an admirable man.[13]

The previous chapter described how at the rural bases, UNITA tried to claim a role for itself in 'organising' agriculture. At Jamba, its claims to intervene in agriculture went further than this: UNITA created posts for experts who were part of the administrative structure that UNITA established. A man who had studied agronomy at Jamba and been appointed a 'director of agriculture' said that his work 'made the peasants produce better harvests'. His work involved travelling over a wide area of south-eastern Angola. 'As part of free Angola, the administration could travel to give instructions, so that the area would become richer, and so that there would be no more problems with food.'[14] Journalists' descriptions of Jamba emphasise the visible efforts that UNITA made to create the appearance of a modern, bureaucratic and service-oriented state in Jamba. Bridgland's account of a 1981 visit includes immigration checks beneath a sign proclaiming 'Entering Free Angola', a secretarial college where a woman in a 'smart Parisian suit and high heels' taught girls to touch-type and a hospital where surgeons performed an appendectomy.[15] Shaun Johnson, an anti-apartheid South African journalist who reported sceptically on an organised media event in 1988, described the immigration forms, a uniformed traffic officer stationed at a traffic roundabout where vehicles rarely passed, a clinic, a uniform factory and a weapon repair workshop.[16] Even if what was reported in foreign newspapers may have less to do with everyday life in Jamba and more to do with a show put on for journalists, it remains significant as an indication of the UNITA leadership's thinking: of how UNITA's leaders chose to demonstrate the movement's legitimacy in terms of its potential as a state and, moreover, as a particular kind of state.[17] Medical facilities and agricultural

[13] Interviewee 88, Luanda, July 2008.
[14] Interviewee 166, Chicomba, August 2009.
[15] Bridgland, *Jonas Savimbi*, 321.
[16] *The Guardian* (London), 27 June 1988. Excerpted in *Facts and Reports* 18 (N), 1 July 1988. Holland Committee on Southern Africa.
[17] When I visited the UNITA quartering area at Calala near Cazombo in Moxico province in June 2002, I saw a traffic-free roundabout like the one Johnson describes, and I was given a

improvement plans can be explained in terms of efforts to create a relationship with the population on the basis of service provision, even if the efforts were possible only thanks to South African supply lines and seemed incongruous in a settlement that was built of mud bricks and thatch. Well-dressed secretaries, traffic officers and immigration controls have no such obvious practical justification but mimic an urban and modern model of statehood, which competed in UNITA's political imagination with ideas of peasant revolution. Similarly, Savimbi's warning to his troops 'that when they did reach Luanda they would be judged by the appearance they presented to the outside world'[18] suggests an appeal to norms that were foreign to the bush environment in which UNITA operated during the war.

POLITICAL EDUCATION AT JAMBA

As was the case in the villages near UNITA bases, schooling in Jamba promoted narratives that posited UNITA as the representative of Angolan national aspirations. These emphasised UNITA's role in liberating Angola from colonialism and sought to legitimise UNITA's continuing war against the MPLA by presenting the MPLA as the agent of foreign interests. Jorge, a former soldier who had spent his childhood in Jamba, said he had 'learnt about what was needed for the well-being of the country – about international history and the history of my country. That our country has wealth but the wealth is not helping everyone, only a minority'.[19]

The political content of schooling promoted the idea of statehood and the idea that UNITA was a democracy and a better alternative to the MPLA government. Filomeno, another former soldier who had grown up in Jamba, said that as a child, 'we had a basic idea that there was a government, but that UNITA was a state within a state. We had political education, which was part of the school programme. We learnt about economics, about rights, equality and citizenship'. By contrast, according to Filomeno, 'the MPLA had the wrong priorities – it was a machine, a prepared structure. They chased UNITA people away and said that UNITA killed – but we wanted democracy'.[20]

tour of the 'hospital' that had been constructed even although the quartering areas were never intended to last more than a year. By this time, UNITA had been cut off from foreign support for years, and the resources available to it were limited to what had survived during the years when the leadership was on the run. Nevertheless, when I arrived for the tour, the hosts made sure I was greeted by a surgeon in gown and mask and a man using a microscope in the grass-hut laboratory.

[18] Bridgland, *Jonas Savimbi*, 328.
[19] Interviewee 75, Caála, June 2008.
[20] Interviewee 65, Caála, July 2008.

Public events in the *terra consolidada* provided further opportunities for political education. Bridgland describes a play performed at a parade at Mavinga in 1981, which presented UNITA as a nationalist movement defending Angolan peasants against an MPLA whose leaders had sold the country to hostile Cuban and Soviet interests.[21] Churches, too, were another vehicle for UNITA politicisation. At UNITA's Fourth Congress, Catholic and Protestant priests led prayers that 'sanctioned the war against the MPLA "in the name of God"'.[22] Bridgland writes of a Protestant minister preaching on peace, saying that despite UNITA's attempts at national reconciliation, 'the power of the devil entered' and people had to 'go into the forests to learn the work of shooting because peace comes with those who are able to fight'. A Catholic priest who had been in Jamba in the 1980s acknowledged the repressive political climate that had existed there but sought to justify it on the basis that 'freedom of opinion in a war regime is a utopia'. Asked about the forced marriages that took place in Jamba, the priest explained them in the following terms: 'There were forced marriages in Jamba just as the rape of women, particularly minors, happens in Luanda, in France, in the United States. The situation of war is what gives rise to the idea of forced marriage.'[23] This echoed UNITA officials' explanations of violence: if UNITA's actions differed from the Christian norms that the movement's leadership professed, this was justifiable as the result of war.

SOCIAL ORGANISATION AND RULE BY FEAR

At Jamba, nobody was local. Its residents were there because they had left their home regions, either voluntarily because of their opposition to the MPLA or because they had been abducted by UNITA. Family and other social structures were shattered in this process, a state of affairs that allowed the authorities to intervene in finding accommodation for children or arranging marriages. Bridgland writes that during a parade at Jamba in 1981, Savimbi presented a teenage recruit who was 'away from his mother and his father for the first time in his life'. He ordered that his officers 'must therefore not neglect his needs. You are now his mother and his father'.[24]

UNITA dealt with unaccompanied children by placing them in institutions or with foster families. The way that Jorge told his story makes it clear that

---

[21] Bridgland, *Jonas Savimbi*, 313.

[22] Leon Dash, 'Commissars Heap Scorn on Role of Portuguese and Cubans', *The Washington Post*, 11 August 1977, A24.

[23] Interviewee 150, written correspondence, October 2009.

[24] Bridgland, *Jonas Savimbi*, 327.

he was kidnapped as a child and abducted to Jamba, although he does not describe his experience as one of abduction:

> I grew up in Jamba. My parents had stayed here in the interior.[25] I went to Jamba as a result of military confrontations. I chose to go to Jamba when I was ten years old. We walked on foot, accompanied by soldiers and other officials – about fifty people together. When we arrived at Jamba we were selected for school. I stayed there for six years and was then nominated for battle.[26]

He lived in an *internato* (school boarding house), although some children who had been separated from their parents were placed in the homes of unrelated adults in Jamba. Amélia, who had been captured and taken to Jamba with one of her own children, spoke of having fostered children in this way: some who had been kidnapped without their parents and one child whose mother had been imprisoned under accusation of witchcraft.[27]

Even if the kind of social organisation that existed at Jamba was remembered positively by people who remained loyal to UNITA after the war, it was underpinned by fear and the daily possibility of violence. Amélia, though she admired certain aspects of life under UNITA, spoke frankly about the atmosphere of terror at Jamba:

> When we arrived at Jamba we were put into a pilot unit where we received political education, from soldiers and cadres. After politicisation, every one became the security of everyone else. Everyone knew that someone else was watching you – each one knew that if you did this or that you'd die. If someone transgressed the limits, they would be brought into a public space and killed. This is how they educated people. Or if someone was caught trying to flee. But we lived normally – adapted, just so as to avoid situations. Crimes included running away. They [UNITA] didn't like violence. For sexual abuse there were isolation camps, for re-education [of the accused]. I also heard of them killing witches but I never saw this. I know the field where they used to burn people but they stopped doing this before I arrived.[28]

If UNITA 'didn't like violence', this obviously refers to violence perpetrated without its authority. An aspect of the state-like functions that UNITA took upon itself was to define and arbitrate when and in what circumstances violence was permissible.

---

[25] As noted earlier, 'interior' (the word is identical in English and Portuguese) was often used to indicate central Angola, seen from the perspective of Jamba.
[26] Interviewee 75, Caála, July 2008.
[27] Interviewee 88, Luanda, August 2008.
[28] Interviewee 88, Luanda, August 2008.

A more personal account of violent political repression at Jamba appears in Chiwale's memoir, published six years after Savimbi died. Chiwale writes of an atmosphere of paranoia and mutual suspicion and of the brutality with which suspected dissenters were treated, including Chiwale himself when he was accused of plotting against Savimbi. 'I noticed that some long-standing companions were avoiding me, as though I had a contagious disease. Then, as if this were not enough, my wife continued to insist on the subject [of rumours of a plot against Savimbi].' Chiwale writes that he was awakened at three o'clock one morning and brought before Savimbi. The UNITA leader accused Chiwale of plotting against him before turning Chiwale over to his security men, who beat him and tried to extract a confession, and then 'released me at five in the morning covered in blood and with my left arm broken'.[29]

The burning of witches at Jamba has been reported in the accounts of UNITA sympathisers as well as its detractors, mostly referring to the period between 1981 and 1985.[30] Chiwale's memoir includes a description of his own aunt being burnt alive, an act that UNITA apparently tried to justify as an aspect of traditional practice. 'A judgement was organised with the participation of elders, officials and cadres from the highest echelons of the party: the innocent were set free and the guilty condemned to capital punishment, that is, death by fire as African customs demand.' Chiwale blames 'people of bad faith who take advantage of the circumstances in order to settle scores' but also rejects the suggestion 'that the witches were thrown into the fire through the unilateral decision of Dr Savimbi' and insists that the death sentences were 'the result of popular consultation, and as one can read in Universal History, also occurred in certain European countries'.[31]

Forced marriage was a further repressive practice used by UNITA at Jamba. Amélia was forced into marrying a UNITA officer, although she was already married and had been separated from her husband at the time of being kidnapped. UNITA officials sought to justify this to her on the grounds that 'my husband had remained in the MPLA', a suggestion that a marriage contracted elsewhere had no legal or moral force in a society governed by UNITA. Forced marriage was also practised as punishment for a husband's perceived wrongdoing. Chiwale writes that in 1983, after he had been accused of plotting against Savimbi, been demoted and fallen from grace, he was summoned

[29] Chiwale, *Cruzei-me*, 261–264.
[30] Linda Heywood, 'Towards an Understanding of Modern Political Ideology in Africa: The Case of the Ovimbundu of Angola', *The Journal of Modern African Studies* 36.1 (1998), 166; Sousa Jamba, *Patriots* (New York, 1992), 201 and 265; Minter, *Apartheid's Contras*, 224–225.
[31] Chiwale, *Cruzei-me*, 270.

without prior knowledge to witness the marriage of his wife to another man.[32] When, at the beginning of 1986, Chiwale was called before Savimbi and told that he was to be rehabilitated since the accusations against him were still unproven, Savimbi concluded their meeting by saying, 'Also I would like to inform you that I know that your wives have abandoned you, but do not worry, I shall arrange you another.'[33] Women were to the UNITA leadership a commodity that could be withheld as punishment or granted as a reward.

Few interviewees spoke of the violence and repression of Jamba so fully. For the UNITA faithful, particularly those who had grown up there, Jamba was remembered as an embodiment of the ideas of personal freedom that were one strand among UNITA's sometimes self-contradictory official ideologies. Manuel, who had worked as a teacher at Jamba, insisted that 'in the days of UNITA the whole population had the right to talk, the right to expression, even if you only spoke Umbundu'.[34] According to Filomeno, 'in Jamba there was democracy because we were able to criticise – there we were able to ask for an audience with the president'.[35] Yet Filomeno had barely reached adulthood when UNITA abandoned Jamba. His adult life had spanned the last decade of the war when he had remained on the move with UNITA columns, and since 2002 he had lived in communities of long-time UNITA supporters. His idealised view of Jamba had been shaped by the shared memories of the communities in which he had lived. The impression of Jamba as a place of free political activity is unrecognisable as the place described by Amélia or by outsiders – or even by the doggedly loyal Chiwale.[36]

People who lived at Jamba contrast it not only with life under the MPLA but also with life in the more peripheral areas of UNITA's control, which lacked the schools, the electricity, and the imported food available at Jamba. One soldier from the generation that had joined UNITA in the mid-1970s recalled that 'at Jamba we no longer ate the people's food [farm produce], we had food from outside, things such as rice or pasta'.[37] For people who had lived most of their lives at the bases, the most basic manufactured items that could not be produced locally were salt and soap. People were aware that the closer

---

[32] Chiwale, *Cruzei-me*, 268.

[33] Chiwale, *Cruzei-me*, 272. Savimbi speaks of 'your wives' in the plural, though elsewhere in the text Chiwale does not mention having had more than one wife.

[34] Interviewee 62, Caála, June 2008.

[35] Interviewee 65, Caála, June 2008.

[36] Fred Bridgland, 'Savimbi et l'exercice du pouvoir: un témoignage', *Politique Africaine* 57 (1995), 94–102, which describes the violent and authoritarian manner in which power was exercised in Jamba, is striking for having been written by an author who had previously admired UNITA and Savimbi.

[37] Interviewee 72, Caála, July 2008.

they were to Jamba, the more likely they were to receive these essential items through supply lines from Jamba.

Comparisons between life under UNITA and life in MPLA-ruled Angola were a recurrent theme in interviews with people who remembered Jamba, particularly those who had grown up with UNITA and experienced life in government-controlled areas for the first time only after the peace settlement of 2002. These comparisons invariably favour the past over the present and as such must be read critically. Many of the interviewees who expressed these sentiments were people who still actively identified themselves with UNITA as a political party at the time of the interviews. All were living in poverty and felt, with some justification, that the social reintegration promised as part of the demobilisation process in 2002 had not been realised. They preferred to speak about UNITA rule as it was at times and in places when the organisation was better equipped to make a reality of the ideas it professed about the responsibilities of a political organisation. Their accounts suggest that this idealised vision of UNITA's relationship with the people under its control was the normal reality of life in UNITA-dominated areas. Even if they are not always historically accurate, the narratives of the past and the present are significant. First, we are able to discern in them something of the content of UNITA's official discourse as it was passed on through processes of political education to people who lived under UNITA's control. Second, the fact that interviewees chose to make comparisons between the past and the present is itself significant. The very fact that they made the comparison suggests an equivalence between UNITA's social order and the social order of the MPLA that formed the context in which I was interviewing them. Both were alternative possibilities of government, of which UNITA's was judged to have been more effective. Over and above the opportunities that Jamba presented for sustained political education, the very existence of Jamba was a symbol of UNITA's potential as a state.

MILITARY CONSCRIPTION

Men who had spent their childhood in UNITA-controlled areas, whether in Jamba or elsewhere, spoke of having been incorporated into UNITA's military forces at some point during their adolescence. Tiago said he had 'received education from first to seventh grade in Jamba, then I reached military age, so I joined the army, as was the duty of every citizen'.[38] Jorge, who had been kidnapped to Jamba and spent his childhood there, described his entry into army

---

[38] Interviewee 66, Caála, June 2008.

life as follows: 'When we arrived at Jamba we were selected for school. I stayed there for six years and was then nominated for battle.'[39] Young men and teenage boys were also conscripted from villages that were under the control of UNITA's rural bases. Whether they entered the army in Jamba or elsewhere, all those who had joined the army during the 1980s spoke of a process of political education as being part of their training in the forces.

People who had not undergone the process of politicisation that operated in UNITA's schools and armed forces describe UNITA's conscription methods as arbitrary and violent. Joana, a farmer from the north of Huambo province whose home area had fallen under UNITA control at the time of independence, spoke of UNITA recruiting people 'just by catching them. [...] They disappeared and I don't know if they were ever heard of again. Girls were also obliged to go to the bush and stay with them. A woman who had a husband who went, would go with him'.[40] Pedro, the catechist, also suggested that men did not join UNITA's forces by choice. Again, his position as someone who was able to maintain his autonomy from UNITA's politics while still part of the society controlled by UNITA allowed him a critical perspective. 'A teacher would go to a village and say 'study, study', then at age 15 or 16 they would be captured to the bases to become soldiers – not in the proper way.'[41] These accounts by Joana and Pedro not only reflect the more critical outsider perspectives of the speakers but also different experiences: experiences of a time and place when UNITA's control was mainly by force rather than being hegemonic. By contrast, the conscripts themselves, those who had grown up with UNITA and been educated in its schools, spoke of their incorporation into the army as though it were an extension of their education.

This was different from the perception of conscripts into the FAPLA who saw themselves as having been captured or, at best, having been subjected to an arbitrary process over which they had no control and which removed them from the society of which they felt a part. As noted in Chapter 3, the military was a present and visible part of life in MPLA government areas. Yet the popular discourse in government areas allowed a distinction between the military and the civilian realm in such a way that the movement between one and the other could be construed, at best, as 'conscription' or, at worst, as 'capture'. In UNITA zones, on the other hand, there was no possibility of imagining an alternative to joining the army. People who came from outside the UNITA space may have seen themselves as having been captured

---

[39]　Interviewee 75, Caála, July 2008.
[40]　Interviewee 17, Huambo, May 2008.
[41]　Interviewee 128, Chicomba, November 2008.

by UNITA, but within the UNITA space, the lack of distinction between the civilian and military spheres did not admit the concept either of 'conscription' or of 'capture'. For men who had grown up with UNITA, the process of entering the army did not represent any sort of rupture. The differences in how conscription was practised and spoken of between the UNITA space and the MPLA space is symptomatic of more general distinctions between the political strategies on both sides, distinctions that were shaped partly by political choices and partly by circumstance – in Messiant's words, the 'properly totalitarian' rule of UNITA versus the 'paradoxical dictatorship' of the MPLA.[42] I will return to this distinction at the end of this chapter.

FOREIGN CONNECTIONS AND IMPORTED IDEOLOGIES

So far I have suggested that UNITA ideology defined Angolan nationhood by situating UNITA as the guardian of the nation against hostile foreigners, specifically Cuba and the Soviet Union, whose proxy, according to UNITA, was the MPLA.[43] Savimbi's enthusiasm for Mao was primarily in methods of struggle and this interest faded as UNITA consolidated its connections with South Africa, as Chapter 2 made clear. Some existing literature on UNITA has emphasised its links at various times with China but more significantly in the post-independence period with the United States and South Africa. These links with foreign countries and the ideologies associated with them were of secondary importance in how UNITA presented itself inside Angola but are considered here in order to situate them within the overall pattern of UNITA discourse.

Muekalia recalls debates within UNITA among Marxists and Maoists and insists that 'UNITA was, and continues to be, a party ideologically of the left'.[44] Yet UNITA adherents consistently echoed Savimbi's fears of Soviet expansion, a theme voiced first at the 1977 Fourth Congress and repeated as Savimbi sought common cause with Western countries.[45] When he spoke to Western audiences, Savimbi would emphasise UNITA's democratic credentials, supporting this – as he had done in Huambo in November 1975 – with the

---

[42] Christine Messiant, 'Angola, les Voies de l'Ethnisation et de la Decomposition: I. De la Guerre à la Paix (1975–1991)', in Christine Messiant, *L'Angola Postcolonial: 1. Guerre et Paix Sans Democratisation* (Paris, 2008), 33–92. Originally published in *Lusotopie* I (1–2) (1994).

[43] Marcum, *Angolan Revolution II*, 195 describes UNITA's ideological themes in the early 1970s as 'consistent and persistent [...] nationalist and anti-imperialist – including anti-Soviet "social imperialism"'.

[44] Muekalia, *A Segunda Revolução*, 147–149.

[45] Chiwale, *Cruzei-me*, 246.

argument that the MPLA was avoiding multiparty elections. He would also call upon narratives of African authenticity:

> The people want to taste freedom in peace. For that they need a democratic government, elected and representing the three liberation movements, MPLA, FNLA and UNITA. The building of African socialism cannot be the same as the Castro model. We have our past, our customs.[46]

This statement to a French journalist suggests that Savimbi realised that 'socialism' was acceptable to a European audience, but the word was notably absent when he spoke to Americans. With them, he would call upon ideas of freedom, usually defined as opposition to communism. Talking to journalists in the US in 1979, he deployed a logic of African authenticity in order to reject the ideas of Marx, whom Savimbi characterised as 'a man of German origin, in an era dominated by French philosophy, living in Britain and dealing with the economic problems of Britain at that time'.[47] On another occasion, he told an American journalist who, thanks to a malfunctioning aircraft, found himself stranded in Jamba on 4 July 1981, 'We regret the circumstances in which you, Mr Richard Harwood, are celebrating this joyous day of yours, far away from your loved ones. But the values and ideals that have made your country the greatest on earth are the same values and ideals that bind us together – the struggle for freedom and liberty.'[48]

Jaka Jamba recalls Savimbi's ability to switch between different political idioms as one of his strengths:

> Dr Savimbi was very adept – he often told people what they wanted to hear. [...] He studied people's aspirations and concerns and within half an hour he could make people agree with him. He was a great mobiliser. But in terms of the context, at that time what were important were the concrete problems that existed: How to protect the population, feed the population, create the conditions for the population to feel they were able to govern.[49]

The MPLA and its sympathisers lost no opportunity to present UNITA's connection with the apartheid regime as evidence of UNITA's counter-revolutionary character, as noted in Chapter 3. The South African link also cost UNITA the sympathy of some European and most other African states.[50] Chiwale,

---

46 Interview with Dominique De Roux, quoted in Bridgland, *Jonas Savimbi*, 231.
47 Bridgland, *Jonas Savimbi*, 289–290.
48 Bridgland, *Jonas Savimbi*, 335.
49 Interview with Jaka Jamba, Luanda, September 2009.
50 David Birmingham, 'Angola', in Patrick Chabal et al. (eds.), *A History of Postcolonial Lusophone Africa* (London, 2002), 147.

like other UNITA officials, takes pains to emphasise that Savimbi opposed apartheid and justifies the decision to seek South African help as a matter of survival at a time when a substantial Cuban force was defending the MPLA.[51] But for the majority of UNITA's followers in Jamba, South Africa was not the liability that it represented in the eyes of the world outside. A present-day UNITA local official acknowledged that 'South African support was what made Jamba work'.[52] The fact that Jamba was positioned as a conduit for foreign assistance did not prevent people from invoking it as a symbol of UNITA's achievement. On the contrary, the fact that UNITA had foreign connections could be presented as evidence of the movement's capability and prestige. As former soldier Filomeno put it, 'We were politically connected worldwide – people could go from there to the United States or South Africa. We kept in touch with all the world: South Africa as the regional power and the US as the global power.'[53] Costa, another former combatant, recalled the presence of South Africans as 'a foreign element with technology, for Angolans to develop':[54] a resource that supported what UNITA saw as its own modernising project. A *soba* who had spent time at Jamba proudly recalled the visit by the then-South African foreign minister, Pik Botha. Outside the small circle of the UNITA leadership, its members knew nothing of the nature of the regime in Pretoria. South Africa was to them simply a distant but benevolent foreign power.

At the level of ideology, any links that existed between UNITA and its various foreign allies were a matter of convenience rather than of conviction. Ideas of freedom, democracy and African authenticity, which were central to UNITA's internal discourses, could be and were redeployed by Savimbi when he spoke to a non-Angolan audience, even if the meanings that these words had for his foreign interlocutors were different from the meanings that they had in Angola. Conversely, if UNITA's external links had any impact on its internal discourses, this impact came not so much from the ideological orientation of its allies as from the fact that international links could be evoked as a token of UNITA's legitimacy and potential.

---

[51] Chiwale, *Cruzei-me*, 237. These words are attributed to Savimbi. Chiwale also claims (251–252) that Savimbi used the opportunity of a meeting in 1978 with the then-foreign minister Pik Botha and defence minister Magnus Malan to call for the release from prison of Nelson Mandela.

[52] Interviewee 5, Huambo, May 2008.

[53] Interviewee 65, Caála, June 2008.

[54] Interviewee 63, Caála, June 2008.

CONCLUSION

Chapters 2 and 5 showed how UNITA's leaders, during their brief occupation of the towns and later in the bush of the Central Highlands, recognised the need to secure legitimacy through creating a state-like relationship with the people in the areas that they controlled. In the bush, this was based on a social contract in terms of which UNITA professed to offer security in exchange for agricultural produce. In the towns, however, UNITA, during its brief occupation in 1975 and 1976, placed a value on continuing the functions of the colonial state, the performance of the ritual manifestations of statehood as distinct from the creation of an organic relationship with society. But it was at Jamba that UNITA was better able to enact the rituals of statehood – the rituals, what is more, of a kind of statehood that had nothing to do with the reality over which UNITA was presiding. The need for a social contract was obviated by the ready supply of goods from South Africa. Instead, the rituals of state building that were enacted at Jamba, accompanied both by violence and by narratives about UNITA's role in liberating Angola from colonialism and defending it from the MPLA, served to create an image of UNITA that was both to be feared and to be respected.

To conclude this chapter, I consider two significant areas of difference in the ways the MPLA and UNITA operated in the areas they controlled, as noted in this and in the previous chapters. The first point has to do specifically with the ways in which each of the two parties used the forced movement of people as part of its military and political programmes. As we have seen in earlier chapters, both UNITA and the MPLA government habitually captured or removed people from areas controlled or influenced by the enemy and brought them into their own secure zone of control. This began with the exodus of teachers and other educated people from the towns with UNITA in 1976, some of whom were later brought back to the towns by the government; other professionals were captured by UNITA by trickery or during raids. Also starting in 1976, peasant farmers were forced by one or the other army to leave contested areas and go to an area in which one army was securely in control. With regard to professional people, the MPLA and UNITA had similar intentions: both needed their skills to provide the services on which their political legitimacy depended. However, where villagers were concerned, UNITA and the MPLA had different intentions. A priest who had experienced life on both sides of the conflict expressed it like this: 'UNITA needed young men for the military life, or to carry material. For the MPLA, it was about the security of the population. To know "they are not with UNITA"'.[55]

[55] Interviewee 105, Huambo, September 2008.

All the accounts by people who were kidnapped by UNITA or who voluntarily left government-controlled areas to live with UNITA emphasise how UNITA put people to work in service of its military and political project. By contrast, the peasant farmers who arrived voluntarily or involuntarily in the government's secure zones around the towns were seldom integrated into any kind of programme of productive activity. Sometimes they would receive assistance from the government or from donor organisations, but otherwise they would attempt to become self-sufficient. They were no great priority for the kind of state-building process envisioned by the MPLA, in which the welfare of town dwellers depended ultimately upon oil revenues rather than on agricultural production.[56] The government's policy of bringing them physically under its control appears to have been motivated not so much by a need to have them there as by a need to remove them from UNITA. UNITA in Jamba had a guaranteed income from South Africa just as the MPLA did from petroleum sales. External support could guarantee the delivery of food and therefore eliminate the need for a social contract with farmers, but it could not supply the Angolan cadres that were necessary for the social-service functions of state building. The MPLA already had its professional cadres in the towns. UNITA needed to bring cadres to Jamba, while in the Central Highlands, the relationship with peasant farmers was essential to UNITA's sustainability.

The second point has to do with the degree of social and political control exercised by UNITA at Jamba and by the MPLA in the towns. Messiant distinguishes between UNITA's 'properly totalitarian' dictatorship whose 'power was founded on force and on the display of force and on the adherence to a leader, and was exercised in a closed world, barely penetrable to the world outside and to foreigners' and the 'paradoxical dictatorship' on the side of the MPLA, which 'tolerated neither basic civil rights nor autonomous organisations nor associations' but which was nevertheless not quite totalitarian.[57] The analysis presented in this and the preceding chapters illustrates that there were indeed differences in the levels of social control that the MPLA and UNITA were able to exercise in their respective areas of influence, and it was certainly true that UNITA operated in an isolated and closed world. I would suggest, however, that inasmuch as UNITA's rule was more totalitarian than that of the MPLA, this cannot be separated either from the social environments in which the two movements sought to root themselves or from the history of their engagement with their societies. Both in the bush bases and at Jamba, UNITA's practices in relation to the people it controlled served to produce

---

[56] Christine Messiant, 'Deconstructing a nation', in Christine Messiant, *L'Angola Postcolonial: 2. Sociologie Politique d'une Oléocratie* (Paris, 2008), 232.

[57] Messiant, 'Angola, les Voies', 58.

a discourse in which UNITA as a military movement was coterminous with UNITA as a welfare movement and which conflated UNITA's political interests with local needs and interests. Chapter 2 described a merging of the political, economic and social spaces in government-controlled areas. However, the imbrication of these functions in the areas controlled by UNITA was of a different order. In government-controlled areas, the formal shops and supply networks were state controlled, but small-scale farmers were still able to participate in a cash economy through the people's markets, where they could sell their produce to urban dwellers. In UNITA areas, farmers were considered to be 'working for the party', and UNITA functionaries themselves effected the redistribution of food from farmers to soldiers and other officials. Similarly in the area of education, the MPLA promoted the idea of studying being a 'revolutionary duty' and teaching being a 'frontline activity', but this was not the same as the reality in UNITA areas, where bases that were primarily military in character were home to the teachers. When it came to military conscription, men conscripted into the FAPLA saw this as an imposition on their freedom, while for those who grew up in UNITA's political and military redoubt of Jamba, avoiding conscription was unimaginable.

The society governed by the MPLA in the cities was the heir to colonial society in its complexity, and social organisation under the MPLA involved greater differentiation of social categories – civil servant, worker, party activist, farmer, soldier, student – than was the case under UNITA, even if people could occupy more than one category. In the bush, the arrival of UNITA and its imposition of a completely new kind of socio-economic relationship upon the farmers created a social order that was differentiated only along the lines of the base and the villages, each with its inhabitants. At Jamba, the fact that the population comprised migrants, many of whom had lost families in the process of being captured or of voluntarily leaving the cities to live in Jamba, presented the opportunity for UNITA to create and to engineer social relationships to a greater extent than was possible for the MPLA, which operated in an urban social context that retained continuity with the past. UNITA's restructuring of social relationships amounted to a redefining of the political space, in a way that allowed UNITA to intervene directly in all aspects of social and economic life.

7

The War of the Cities

In the early months of 1993, following a failed demobilisation process and elections the previous year, UNITA took control of Angolan towns and cities for the first time since its retreat in 1976. This development inevitably marked a change in the character of a conflict that had previously been between an urban state and a rural guerrilla movement. Much of the writing that exists on the conflict in Angola suggests that 1992 was a moment of rupture, on the assumption that UNITA after 1992 abandoned its efforts to seek consensus among civilians and turned against the people of the Central Highlands who had once supported it. This chapter and the one that follows it suggest, however, that Angolans' experience of the years following 1992 varied widely and that the politics of this later phase of the war shows continuities with the understandings of political authority that had developed in Angola since the early 1970s. People's responses to the changes in the military situation that occurred during the 1990s were conditioned by the experiences and political loyalties of the past, which were related to their geographical location and prior experience of life under either or both political movements. This chapter considers the experience of civilians in the two main cities of the Central Highlands, Huambo and Kuito, during the period of conflict in 1993 and 1994. In Huambo, UNITA troops had been present from before the 1992 elections and remained in uniform and loyal to their UNITA commanders. UNITA took complete control of the city after fifty-five days of intense fighting during January to March 1993 and remained in command until the following year. Kuito, the capital of Bié province some 150 kilometres east of Huambo, is of particular interest as the only urban settlement in the Central Highlands that was not entirely occupied by UNITA during the war that followed the elections. It has entered official histories as a centre of popular resistance against UNITA.

The war of the early 1990s represented the failure of a peace process for which the impetus came initially from outside Angola and which was conducted according to the orthodoxy of the time: third-party mediation and peacekeeping directed towards a solution that would link peace to democratisation, with the former belligerents competing in elections.[1] The background to this attempt at settlement was the stalemate in the conflict between the MPLA government and UNITA as the Cold War drew to a close in the late 1980s. The battles around Cuito Cuanavale in 1987 and 1988 checked the advance of the South African Defence Force but did not allow the MPLA to advance further into the south-eastern extremity of the country, which remained UNITA's *terras consolidadas* (consolidated lands). Moves by the Angolan government and US moderates towards détente during the 1980s were held back both by the recalcitrance of US conservatives and by Cuba's rejection of any move that might entrench the position of the apartheid regime in South Africa. Against this backdrop, Cuba's strengthening of its military position in Angola made the prospect of negotiations more acceptable to Havana.[2] American interest in talks was driven by Washington's discomfort with South Africa's racial policies, alongside its confidence of its own imminent victory in the Cold War.[3] The New York Accord, signed by Angola, South Africa and Cuba in December 1988, set the terms for the independence of Namibia and the withdrawal of Cuban troops from Angola. UNITA survived the loss of its South African allies in Namibia, thanks to the continued support of the Zairean government. A summit at Gbadolite in June 1989 failed to reach a solution, apparently because the MPLA government would not at that stage countenance UNITA's participation in a future political settlement. However, the changing global political situation was such that the MPLA's and UNITA's foreign allies were now more inclined to apply pressure in favour of a peaceful solution to the conflict. Further talks between the government and UNITA led to the signing of the Bicesse Accords in Portugal in May 1991. These provided for the demobilisation of UNITA and government armies and the creation of a new 50,000-strong armed force, the Angolan Armed Forces (FAA), committed the government to organising multi-party elections and established a mandate

---

[1]   One of the most informed critiques of this approach was made by the then UN Special Representative in her memoir of the peace process and elections: Margaret Anstee, *Orphan of the Cold War: The Inside Story of the Collapse of the Angolan Peace Process, 1992–3* (Basingstoke, 1996).

[2]   Piero Gleijeses, *Visions of Freedom: Havana, Washington, Pretoria and the Struggle for Southern Africa* (Chapel Hill, NC, 2013).

[3]   Chester Crocker, *High Noon in Southern Africa: Making Peace in a Rough Neighborhood* (New York, 1992).

for the United Nations Angola Verification Mission (UNAVEM) to monitor compliance with the accords before and during the elections.

The implementation of the Bicesse agreement posed difficulties from the start. UNAVEM lacked personnel, funding and equipment, while UNITA and, to a lesser extent, the Angolan government failed to respect the disarmament process.[4] As the election dates of 29 and 30 September 1992 approached, only 41 per cent of the government and UNITA armies had been demobilised and the political and security situation had 'deteriorated significantly'.[5] Both FAPLA and UNITA soldiers retained their different uniforms and different loyalties. For the first time since 1976, there were UNITA soldiers visible in the cities of the Central Highlands.[6]

Both parties retained control of media outlets: UNITA its VORGAN radio station and the MPLA the whole of the state media, supported by Brazilian public-relations professionals. This enabled both parties to begin disseminating results soon after polling closed. As early results appeared to indicate a narrow victory for the MPLA, Savimbi began to hint that he would not accept an unfavourable result. On 3 October, he announced,

> We would like to draw the MPLA's attention to the fact that there are men and women in this country who are ready to give up their lives so that the country can redeem itself. As far as we are concerned, it will not depend on any international organization to say that the elections were free and fair.[7]

UNITA withdrew its generals from the FAA on 5 October, and the following day Savimbi flew from Luanda to Huambo and proceeded to set up his headquarters there. Results announced on 17 October gave 53.7 per cent of the vote to the MPLA and 34.1 per cent to UNITA in the parliamentary election and 49.57 per cent to Dos Santos and 40.07 per cent to Savimbi in the presidential election. The failure of either presidential candidate to secure 50 per cent of the vote required a second round, which never took place. The Interior Ministry 'began distributing arms to civilians in Luanda in an ultimately successful effort to revive *poder popular* [people's power] of 1975. In the countryside, UNITA was on the offensive, easily capturing towns and districts from poorly armed government forces'.[8] By the end of 1992, UNITA controlled 70 per cent of Angolan territory.[9] This was not entirely a process

---

4 Marrack Goulding, *Peacemonger* (London, 2002), 181–185.
5 Goulding, *Peacemonger*, 187.
6 This was confirmed by the interviewees who were in Huambo or Kuito at the time.
7 Karl Maier, *Angola: Promises and Lies* (London, 1997), 13.
8 Maier, *Angola*, 14.
9 Goulding, *Peacemonger*, 190.

of conquest, since much of rural Angola had never been under government control over the course of the war. Most significant, however, was the fact that for the first time since 1976, UNITA seized control of towns and exercised control over urban people.

Earlier chapters have demonstrated how the relationships that the rival political movements established with people were conditional on the circumstances in which they were working and the resources that they had at their disposal. At the same time, the idea of the city and the developmental possibilities that it represented were prominent in the political imaginations both of the MPLA and of UNITA. While the MPLA retained exclusive control of the main colonial-era urban settlements in Angola, for UNITA, the idea of Jamba being its own city, in the sense of an administrative centre and a nucleus of development, was central to UNITA's sense of itself as a potential alternative state. When UNITA took control of real towns, it failed to convince the townsfolk of its capabilities as an urban governing party. On the contrary: by the time UNITA retreated from the main cities in 1994, many of those who had quietly retained sympathy for the movement after 1976 had changed their opinion once they had experienced the way in which UNITA treated the towns and the people who lived in them in the early 1990s.

HUAMBO

Huambo's status as the principal city of the Central Highlands gave it a particular significance for UNITA. It had been UNITA's base at independence in 1975, and it was in Huambo that Savimbi once again based his operations after he lost confidence in the electoral process in October 1992. Before the 1992 election, there were already soldiers from both sides in the city, and the absence of an effective demobilisation process ensured that they retained their separate uniforms and lines of command. The rival armies at first made themselves known principally by means of roadblocks. In the weeks following the election, UNITA consolidated its position in the Cidade Baixa (downtown), São João and Benfica neighbourhoods. The former FAPLA soldiers controlled little more than the Cidade Alta (uptown) area, which contains the administrative quarter. Hence, although it is recorded that UNITA took control of Huambo in the course of a fierce fifty-five-day battle, it would be wrong to suggest that UNITA came from elsewhere and took the entire city by force. Before the heavy fighting happened, UNITA had already assumed effective control of part of the city, and the most intense conflict was in those parts of the city that the FAA sought to defend. The experience of violence, therefore, was not uniform across the city.

None the people who were interviewed about their experiences of life in Huambo under UNITA control in 1993 and 1994 said the population had bene-fited from UNITA's presence in any way: this contrasts with some interview-ees' nostalgic recollections of Jamba or of UNITA's other bases. Nevertheless, people's reactions to UNITA differed notably. These differences appear to be related to the various interviewees' relationship to the MPLA state, their prior political identities, and the circumstances of their encounter with UNITA. How they encountered UNITA during this period was in turn closely related to which part of the city they lived in. Those who spoke of UNITA's occupa-tion of Huambo in wholly negative terms were people who had spent their lives working within the MPLA state system. Their accounts of events linked UNITA's lack of legitimacy to the way in which its members behaved during the occupation, something that these city dwellers also associated with the fact that UNITA was from the 'bush'. Rui, a lawyer who had been a young man during the occupation, expressed it as follows:

> UNITA took control of the city by force of arms, and I had the misfortune to be there with them. It was a matter of running the city in a worse manner, with the habits of the bush. It was a dictatorship without precedent. That's normal, because they were coming from the bush. It's normal for someone coming out of the bush, this way of running things, but it was complicated for us because we were used to urban life and they weren't – this was part of the first big differences between us.[10]

Roberto, who had joined the MPLA as a young man at the time of inde-pendence, emphasised the killing of civilians and the atmosphere of fear that this created. The murder of Fernando Marcelino, director of the Chianga Agricultural Research Institute, along with his family was one of the most notorious acts of violence during the occupation.[11]

> In 1992 the situation started turning bad because the confrontations started in Luanda, just like in 1975. UNITA was driven out of Luanda. I don't know how it started. And after that, once it was positioned in the provinces, UNITA created situations where people would be fearful – that was easy. For example, killing an influential family, in their home [...] Chianga, the Agricultural Research Institute, was at the time the best research institute in Africa. Marcelino was the director at that time, a person very well known in intellectual circles [...] When he died and his wife died, and his sister who was a nun, it left everyone in a panic. After that, UNITA started to create reserve zones. It captured São João, it didn't allow anyone to go through

---

[10] Interviewee 9, Huambo, May 2008.
[11] See Victoria Brittain, *Death of Dignity: Angola's Civil War* (London, 1998), xiii–xv.

there, captured Benfica, didn't allow anyone to go through there. To the point where downtown and in São João there was only UNITA. The MPLA was only here [in the upper city]. [...] When the war broke out, the war was so fierce that regardless of whether you were with FAPLA or UNITA, wherever you were when the first shot was fired, you didn't leave there. It stayed like that for three months, and you didn't know who was on the other side. On that side you had to say you were with UNITA. The only lucky ones were the ones on the government side who managed to go with the government [when the FAA retreated] to Benguela.

UNITA killed, it didn't recruit anyone new. Because [...] they didn't have civilians. Old or young or whatever, everyone was a soldier. That was sufficient – not only sufficient, but more secure in terms of ideology, because ideologically they were strong. All those who were in UNITA were soldiers, not civilians. They were groups that had been in the bush. There were no farmers. Every farmer had a gun and a uniform. Agriculture wasn't a factor for them because they had great support from South Africa – they depended on the American Congress to give them a sufficient grant. I'm not saying they lived well, but they lived all right. In a guerrilla war, agriculture doesn't work well. Agriculture needs peace and stability.[12]

Roberto lived in the part of the city which was the last to be occupied by UNITA in 1993, which saw some of the heaviest fighting and which retained an identity as the MPLA part of Huambo. His experience of UNITA would therefore have been that of a force that attacked and then occupied where he lived. His narrative of UNITA's essentially military nature is linked to his view of UNITA as having no political legitimacy. Also significant is his statement that UNITA did not practice agriculture, an assertion that is precisely counter to UNITA officials' invocation of the movement's involvement in agriculture as a sign of its legitimacy. What he describes here is the antithesis of the indigenous, ideologically coherent and state-like organisation that UNITA claimed for itself.

According to Roberto, UNITA did not attempt military recruitment during this period in Huambo: its soldiers remained identifiably the group who had come from outside the city. Nevertheless, as in the past, people had to pretend that they had no links with the MPLA in order to avoid punishment by UNITA.

It was recruitment by fear – if they are here, this is their zone, and they didn't tolerate in their midst anyone who said 'I am from the other party'. You had to pretend to be with UNITA. That way they tolerated you.

___

[12]   Interviewee 3, Huambo, May 2008.

Others pointed to the minimal and inadequate nature of UNITA's attempts at governing the city. Mário, a schoolteacher who had served in the FAPLA and worked in the state education system since the early independence years, recalled:

> It was tough. Those of us who were used to earning salaries – it became very difficult for us. There was no employment. Employment was just with a hoe in a field. It was very tough.

Asked whether as a former FAPLA soldier he came under threat, Mário insisted that it was possible to remain politically neutral by not expressing support for the MPLA during the time that UNITA was in the city. His use of the word 'citizen', in the same way that other people used the word '*povo*', refers to a category of people who were not political actors but rather subject to whichever political movement was in control of the place where they were:

> I suffered no direct threat because I was a citizen – I identified neither with the MPLA nor with UNITA. But if someone made a complaint, if they denounced you… I stayed with my brother who was a priest. One day a woman arrived who was with UNITA's security, looking for a generator. When she found me there, she made it known that she knew who I was but, thank God, she took no action against me.

UNITA had a justice system of sorts, Mário said, but its workings were arcane.

> We didn't know where these structures were. But, for example, a person who was denounced was sent to be interrogated. But people didn't know for sure. My wife who at that stage was a teacher was working in the municipal education office – but it didn't function. She just stayed at home – to survive she worked in the field and sold things here and there.[13]

He concluded that with the violence and the breakdown in state services, 'the experience of this period turned people away from UNITA'.

All three men quoted here express their rejection of UNITA not only in terms of the suffering it caused but no less significantly in terms of the fact that authoritarian rule provided evidence that UNITA was nothing more than a guerrilla movement. This for them was in itself proof enough that UNITA had no place in the city. Nevertheless, as Mário pointed out, those who expressed no affection for either party could escape punishment. They could survive as long as they had land to cultivate and no expectations of state services.

---

[13] Interviewee 22, Huambo, May 2008.

Yet the violence and the deprivations of the period when UNITA controlled
Huambo ultimately served to change attitudes towards the organisation even
among those who had once supported it on ideological grounds. This emerges
clearly in an interview with a religious brother who had grown up in Huambo
in the 1980s. Although he and his family had suffered violence perpetrated
by both sides in the conflict during his childhood, he expressed support for
UNITA in the same terms used by the UNITA leadership, suggesting that the
organisation understood and promoted 'southern Angolan' values, which he
defined as follows:

> Values of solidarity – the concept of the extended family, as opposed to the
> Western family concept. Our life is very shared, we are very together. […]
> And hospitality. […] Before the Portuguese came we didn't write, but there
> was a wisdom in proverbs. In the *jango* [village meeting house], proverbs
> and history could be transmitted to new generations […] who could become
> adults within a culture, within a family. […] José Eduardo dos Santos doesn't
> speak Umbundu, he doesn't know the culture of this tribe. Savimbi could
> speak almost all the Angolan languages.

While he continued to assert the importance of such values, he recognised
that for most people in Huambo, anything that UNITA might have to offer
in terms of cultural solidarity was outweighed by the violence with which it
became associated after 1990.

> What destroyed UNITA's reputation was the problem of killing. The war
> manifested itself more and more fiercely, and they killed more each time.
> This created a contradiction. Some preferred to work with the MPLA. With
> the government, they felt more secure. But UNITA was the party that had
> grown out of a culture that we know.[14]

People's family political affiliations also had an impact on the kind of judgements that they made about UNITA while it was in Huambo. According to
Verónica, a schoolteacher whose family members had supported both UNITA
and the MPLA at different times:

> In 1993 many people I knew left Huambo. [Among those who remained]
> I knew people who would work in the hospital and then go to the fields
> [where they grew their food]. UNITA tried a system of management – but
> it was more by force of arms. I was asked to teach, but was not paid. No one
> could leave [the UNITA-controlled area] – you'd be punished if you were
> caught.

[14] Interviewee 2, Huambo, May 2008.

Asked whether her role as a government employee had caused her difficulty under UNITA, Verónica said:

> I wasn't punished as a civil servant, but those who were partisan were punished. It was the same under the MPLA – someone suspected of being on the other side was punished. My husband was imprisoned – he was accused of communicating with the MiGs [government aircraft], but it was just a personal grudge. He spent 28 days in prison. They just sent troops to fetch him. There was no trial. Military crimes were considered treason.[15]

Verónica talks openly about the injustices of life under UNITA without displaying any particular preference for the MPLA and, perhaps as a result of having had relatives on both sides of the conflict, is less judgmental than the other interviewees concerning the two movements' relative legitimacy as rulers.

While all the people quoted so far were professionals who were used to surviving on a cash income in an urban economy, those who had always depended on agriculture for their livelihood had less to lose with the arrival of UNITA in the city. Bárbara, a farmer at the time of the interview, described an early life similar to some of the farmers quoted in earlier chapters. She had grown up in a rural area of Huambo province that was contested by UNITA and the government after independence. She had seen villages burnt by the soldiers of both sides as they sought to purge the area of people who might support the enemy. After she eventually settled in a government area, she had worked for several years in a state-run shop but had lost her job when the business was privatised. After that she had made her living as a small farmer. At the time of the election, she was living in the São João area of Huambo and travelling regularly to the fields outside the city where she grew produce. São João was one of the first parts of Huambo where UNITA consolidated its control, and the near absence of government troops there meant that there was little resistance as UNITA took charge, and according to Bárbara, the local people saw minimal violence. After UNITA took control, manufactured items like salt and petrol were scarce, but people who had access to land and who were used to cultivating it did not suffer food shortages. Bárbara said that she and other farmers could journey freely to the lands east of Huambo which at that point were unchallenged UNITA territory. She said that UNITA had not sought revenge against the inhabitants of her neighbourhood because 'we are *povo* – they only punished those who were soldiers'. Nevertheless, denouncing a person as someone who 'works for the government' would condemn them to indefinite imprisonment. Bárbara insisted that people 'didn't choose

---

[15] Interviewee 108, Luanda, October 2008.

UNITA ... people accepted UNITA because they were occupying the area. If you didn't, they'd kill you'. Her account demonstrates that even in the violent period that followed the election, farmers in particular were able to avoid immediate harm by complying with UNITA's demands.[16]

Others in the farming communities on the city's periphery were more vocal about the lack of basic manufactured items – particularly salt and soap – as well as general food shortages during the UNITA occupation. This was particularly noticeable in those neighbourhoods that had served in the 1980s as resettlement areas for people who had been moved out of the countryside and been resettled on the edges of the city during counterinsurgency operations and who had been the most strongly influenced by the MPLA politicisation that accompanied the provision of land for resettlement and the management of aid from international donors. People in these areas also lived with the constant fear that came from denunciations: 'A person could say that someone had done this or that which they hadn't really done, and they would be killed. One could be accused of being a thief, or an MPLA sympathiser.'[17]

Urban people, whether MPLA loyalists or politically neutral, had adopted a definition of statehood based on the maintenance of peace and order and the creation of conditions for an adequate supply of food. Of course, such a definition is similar to the one invoked by UNITA in the bush, but two differences are noticeable in how it was understood and applied in MPLA-ruled cities as opposed to UNITA-dominated rural areas. Urban people, for example, expected salaries with which they could buy manufactured products. The pay packet retained a symbolic significance even after inflation eroded its value. People expected that state functions such as education and justice would be conducted according to norms and procedures that they had become accustomed to after a decade and a half of MPLA governance. The social service functions that UNITA had implemented at Jamba, and to a lesser extent at its guerrilla bases, were highly regulated, as we have seen in the previous chapter. But the UNITA that arrived in the towns of the Central Highlands around the time of the 1992 elections had neither the means nor the expertise to govern a city. It arrived as an organisation that was above all military in character and which was suspicious of an urban population that it judged to be hostile to it. In the relatively short period in which it remained in control of the city, it made few attempts to secure hegemony.

---

[16] Interviewee 115, near Huambo, October 2008.
[17] Interviewee 15, Huambo, May 2008.

KUITO

In a study of the Central Highlands during the early 1990s, Kuito is of interest as the only place within the region in which the MPLA state maintained a presence throughout the conflict. As UNITA took control of the surrounding countryside and the outer districts of the city after the return to war in early 1993, civilians participated in the FAA's efforts to defend the city centre against further UNITA incursions and suffered severe hunger as UNITA blocked food supplies from reaching the city. Kuito's peculiar history has given a particular political significance to the memory of events there. The memorialisation has been given substance in the years since the end of the war by the exhumation of the thousands of bodies that were buried in the city's public places and private yards and their reburial in a monumental memorial cemetery on the outskirts of town. The official history of the siege of Kuito appears in a slim book called *Esteve em Chamas o Kuito* (Kuito was in Flames) by a former army officer, Samuel Pequenino. The book speaks of Savimbi's 'senselessness' following 'the first free and fair elections held in 1992', which meant that 'the people of Angola and particularly of Bié saw themselves obliged to organise themselves to confront the new challenges that the moment made necessary'. In order to defend 'their fundamental rights, self-defence of their lives, their families, their goods, their way of life', the citizenry 'organised itself into sectors that defended themselves in almost all directions around the city'. As UNITA breached the city's defences on 16 March and intensified artillery shelling, youths grouped themselves into a 'Salvation Patrol' that later 'participated in the expulsion of the enemy from the martyred city, together with other civil defence forces from the Gabiconta [city centre] sector and the National Police'.[18]

The book also describes the efforts of the populace in keeping the city supplied with food through organising 'batidas', highly risky excursions outside the city to obtain produce from farmers in the UNITA-controlled countryside:

> As resources dried up and rejecting the enemy's call for us to survive by eating asphalt, the famous and very difficult '*Batidas*' were adopted.[19] *Batidas* were incursions made that crossed enemy lines and mine fields and travelled long distances in search of sustenance in areas controlled by the enemy. In this battle many compatriots remained in the ground [dead], the victims of attacks, ambushes, landmine detonations and weakness. In such

[18] Samuel Pequenino, *Esteve em Chamas o Kuito*, (Luanda, 2008), 51–52.
[19] *Batida*, generally meaning a hunting party or reconnaissance mission, is the term that was adopted for the expeditions that left Kuito to gather food across enemy lines.

situations there was no medical help, something that contributed to the unspeakable death of various compatriots. These *batidas* involved thousands of people: men, women and children.[20]

Interviews with people who lived through the siege confirm the suffering of the people in central Kuito and testify to the courage of those who took part in the *batidas*. But they also reveal that the choices that people made were informed by considerations more complex than the unremitting devotion to the MPLA that Pequenino's account suggests. Far from confirming the image of a population united in defence of the state against UNITA, their narratives tell of people motivated by pragmatic decisions and of political identities that were no less fluid than at any other time of the conflict. The people quoted here were teachers who were working in the state education system and all appeared to be firmly pro-MPLA in their political convictions. Their recollections of UNITA's soldiers' behaviour during the siege include accounts of violence and callousness towards human life even more extreme than what is described in Pequenino's book. But they also speak of violence and self-serving behaviour on the loyalist side. To explain the teachers' unequivocal loyalty to the MPLA in contrast to the ambivalence of their accounts of events during the siege, it is helpful to consider their narratives in the context of the discourses about political identity that had emerged around the time of independence and continued through the years of war preceding the elections.

One of the teachers, Adriana, recalled that when the *batidas* first began, 'the food was close by – we would come back the same day, even two or three times in a day, but later the food became ever more distant, to the point where it took fifteen days before we returned'.

> It was very risky. [...] UNITA, when they discovered that a group had passed that way would put down mines, when they realised that a route was being used. Sometimes a mine was a signal to know that someone had passed by – when they heard an explosion they knew there were people there and they would shoot. Many people died: shot dead, or from weakness. A person was already weak with hunger, and unprepared for such a journey. [...] A very hungry person who finds sugar cane and chews sugar cane is left with no strength – they have to stay there, and the others can't stop: 'you stay there'. Either you die of weakness, or if [UNITA] find you, you die.

While she recalled the dangers and hardships endured by the city dwellers during the *batidas*, Adriana also acknowledged that they were an act of

---

[20]   Pequenino, *Esteve em Chamas*, 55.

plunder. Peasants would flee as the raiding party, often accompanied by government soldiers, arrived and grabbed food from fields and granaries.

> Sometimes they found people. War turned them irrational. They would kill people. And if they found someone and the maize belonged to him, they would kill him as well. So, when people heard the *batida* was coming, they would run away. [Peasants] knew that if [the townspeople] found them, either they would give you a heavy load to carry, or else ... If one found a civilian in his field, or in his house, it was a case of grabbing a bag of maize that was then given to him to carry. The weight was such that sometimes the person didn't manage to pick it up – and if he didn't pick it up, he would be killed.[21]

Not everyone participated in the *batidas*. Another teacher, Elena, said that 'people had to go and do a sort of robbing of food in the villages', but she did not participate because she had children to care for. 'So I made liquor and bought food.' She said the ingredients to make alcohol came 'from the parachutes', referring to the airdrops that the Angolan Armed Forces made to the garrison in Kuito. Soldiers would sell items like sugar to civilians. Another survival strategy was to leave, though government soldiers initially tried to prevent this. Elena and her two daughters slipped out of Kuito during the night and walked to the Kunhinga district, thirty kilometres north of the city. There, in an agricultural area, there was no shortage of food. However, 'UNITA didn't like us because we hadn't lived there very long', Elena said. 'Their soldiers tried to rape my daughters who were aged 12 and 14'. Back in Kuito, she survived by growing what she could in her yard.[22]

Margarida, originally from a village in Andulo district, had moved to Kuito when she began her career in the 1970s. As hunger took hold of Kuito in 1993, she decided to return to the village where she had grown up. She believed the government had given its approval to people leaving the embattled town but she encountered terror at the hands of both armies as she passed through the checkpoints.

> The government soldiers took my clothes, ordered me to open my bag. Some who were carrying litres of cooking oil were killed. They showed the route that went to the place where there were people who killed them. If there were young men in civilian clothes this meant they were UNITA troops and they were killed as they left the city.

Having arrived in UNITA territory, Margarida and her companions were accused of being '*anti-motim*': literally 'riot police', this term was used by

---

[21] Interviewee 180, Kuito, August 2009.
[22] Interviewee 189, Kuito, August 2009.

UNITA to refer to the Rapid Intervention Police, the partisan force set up by the MPLA, and by association to any person whom UNITA viewed as an MPLA collaborator. In Andulo, 'UNITA ordered me to teach, without a salary. They said I must work as I had worked for the MPLA. Whoever didn't work didn't have the right to live'. Margarida resorted to taking the tiles from the roof of her family home and bartering them for grain in the villages.[23]

Many of the men who remained in the government-held enclave in Kuito participated in Civil Defence, an institution that had its roots in the People's Defence Committees of 1975. According to Alberto:

> As workers we took up arms in Civil Defence. There was no worker who didn't. I'd teach a class and then take up my gun. Everyone was obliged to do this. It was organised by the government for the protection of the people. The people in general participated. The government gave out the weapons and it was necessary for each one to protect himself.[24]

His colleague, João, also participated in Civil Defence before hunger drove him to leave the city in 1993 and to live in a village beyond the UNITA lines. His main complaint about life in the village was the unavailability of salt, which as we have seen was a common complaint from those who had experienced life under UNITA. But there were no UNITA soldiers stationed in the village. 'We worked in the fields, and were ignored by UNITA – whoever was in the village was *povo*, considered to be a peasant.' He compared this experience to what had happened eight years earlier, when as a government employee he had had to leave his home area and go to Kuito as UNITA advanced in the region. This earlier recollection, quoted in Chapter 4, clarifies how he views the political status of *povo*.

> Civil servants are controlled – *povo* are not. In 1985, we functionaries had to abandon the area and go to where there was protection. But the people stayed there. You know, the people weren't controlled. It doesn't matter whether UNITA appeared or the government. But functionaries, if you stayed you were captured.[25]

The possibility of the *povo* being apolitical was one that João could turn to his advantage when he went back to the village: like Mário in Huambo who felt he escaped punishment because he was a 'citizen', João recognised that by presenting himself as a farmer, he was improving his chances of survival. He knew that farmers were seen not as political actors but rather as people who

---

[23] Interviewee 188, Kuito, August 2009.
[24] Interviewee 190, Kuito, August 2009.
[25] Interviewee 191, Kuito, August 2009.

simply by their presence in an area belonged to the political movement that was in charge there. Similarly, when Margarida talks about '*povo da UNITA*' having helped her, she appears to acknowledge the fluidity of this designation. To her, they were '*povo da UNITA*' because that was how the official discourse defined people who were living in a UNITA-dominated area, yet she acknowledges solidarity between them and herself, a government employee.

Accounts of the siege suggest that UNITA's attitude towards civilians in Kuito was arbitrary and inconsistent and that in Kuito more than anywhere else, life or death could depend on an individual soldier's decision. In Huambo, UNITA was defending a precarious military victory throughout most of 1993, but during the same period in Kuito, UNITA remained on the offensive as it tried to drive the MPLA and the FAA out of the centre of the city. What is evident is that the most violent encounters took place at the boundaries of control between the two movements or when either government or UNITA soldiers made incursions into the territory of the other side. Soldiers of both armies used their guardianship of the frontlines as an opportunity for extortion, recruitment or sexual exploitation while expressing their authority in state-like terms of defence against an enemy, which rendered anyone coming from or going to the opposing side liable to violent punishment. Young men in particular were assumed to be enemy soldiers. Elena found herself and her family subjected to unbearable threats from UNITA, yet others found that UNITA could disregard the fact that they had previously worked for the MPLA: for Margarida, acceptance depended on working in UNITA's education structures, while for João, it was a matter of working as a peasant and concealing the fact that he had worked as a teacher. The discourses from the past on control and identity ensured that they could come to be seen as 'UNITA people' even if they were initially treated with suspicion as 'government people'.

The schoolteachers considered themselves affiliated to the MPLA regardless of whether they were in the MPLA-controlled city enclave or in the UNITA-controlled countryside. This contrasts with the situational shifts in political identity that have been noted in earlier chapters. Indeed, all of the teachers quoted in this chapter had experienced life under UNITA in the villages of Bié province after independence, before moving to the towns where they became self-identified government people and loyal to the MPLA. The choices that they made in 1992 and 1993 and how they spoke about these choices are best understood in terms of their earlier relationships with the two political movements, in the 1970s. Adriana's experience of living in a UNITA-controlled area and initially fearing 'capture' by MPLA forces is described in Chapter 4. Other interviewees of the same generation in Kuito spoke about how they had come to accept the MPLA and, indeed, to become actively involved in the process of state building that took place under the MPLA. All associated UNITA with their earlier lives in the villages and the MPLA with urban life and its opportunities for education, development and productivity within a modern, urban economy. In Alberto's words, 'There was one party in the bush, one in the city. Those in the city were of the city. Those from there [the bush] submitted themselves to that life.' Adriana recalled that after the FAPLA had brought her to the city, 'there we stayed, I began to study – we were living in war, with that insecurity, but it was enough to make some sort of a life – we in the cities were able to study'. Adriana's account of what happened next, the arrival of UNITA as a result of the Bicesse Accord and the subsequent siege, is rooted in the understandings of political legitimacy that had become current in the years between 1975 and 1990. As we have seen, she witnessed brutality on the part of FAA soldiers as well as UNITA. What preserved her loyalty to the MPLA was not only the fact that the FAA in this situation was less violent than UNITA's troops but also the fact that she believed the FAA was defending something that UNITA only threatened to destroy.

> I think that in Kuito, if the people hadn't been involved [in defence], UNITA would have taken the city. As the people had already suffered a lot from the war, and then that peace came along, people were excited that the war had ended. When they realised that the war was starting again, people organised themselves to fight against [war], so it wouldn't happen again.
>
> During the time when [the MPLA] lived together[26] with UNITA, it was evident that UNITA didn't like MPLA people. The intention was to limit everyone who was MPLA. So that only they [UNITA] would be left. Among the population that was with the MPLA, the feeling was to defend themselves so as not to fall into the hands of UNITA – it was known that if UNITA were to retake the city, everyone would die.

In an MPLA-ruled city such as Kuito, ideas of citizenship were constituted in a narrative of state building in which the MPLA was the only protagonist. According to this narrative, the main functions of the state were education and job provision and, crucially, defence against UNITA. Peace was a necessary condition for the social order that the MPLA had created, and people came to perceive UNITA as a threat to that peace. The interviewees acknowledge that in 1975 and 1976, they had lived with UNITA and accepted the understandings of power and legitimacy that UNITA offered but had readily accepted

---

[26] '*Durante o tempo quando conviveu com a UNITA …*' She refers to the pre-election period when both parties had representatives and troops in the city.

the MPLA's legitimacy once they were living under MPLA control. But a similar change of political affiliation was not possible in 1993. People had become accustomed to an urban order that was associated with the MPLA, and UNITA had come to represent the disruption of that same order. When, after the Bicesse Accord, UNITA appeared in Kuito in military form and tried to take control of the city by force, this was recounted as part of the same narratives that linked state building to the MPLA and to peace. Alberto's description of how the Civil Defence was constituted links the role of the state in organising employment to its role in organising defence and the duties of the citizen as a worker to the duties of the citizen as a defender. The involvement of the FAA in the *batidas* is a further example of the merging of the civil and military functions of the state.

The schoolteachers acknowledged the abusive behaviour of troops on both sides and the violence that was involved in the *batidas*. They justified the FAA's actions in terms of a legitimacy that was rooted in the government's position as the creator and defender of a society and an economy that UNITA threatened only to destroy. The fact that UNITA was presiding over productive agriculture a few kilometres outside the city allowed the urban population to see the UNITA areas as a short-term survival option but not as a longer-term political option. The narrative of heroic resistance referred to at the beginning of this section, which has come to dominate the official accounts of the siege, stems from the older official discourses that linked control and political identity. In order to construct a memory of an urban population united in purpose on the side of the MPLA, it was necessary to ignore the fact that some had taken the pragmatic decision to live with UNITA.

CONCLUSION

UNITA's presence in Huambo and Kuito in 1993 and 1994 represented for many town dwellers a period of violence, fear and material deprivation that served to decimate whatever support UNITA retained among the urban population during the 1980s. Nevertheless, the incidence of violence and the patterns of collaboration and resistance during the conflict in the Central Highlands towns are complex. The by now accepted idea of the MPLA as the urban party and UNITA as the party of the bush left UNITA's officers and soldiers deeply suspicious of people who lived in towns. Yet UNITA soldiers' behaviour towards town dwellers was shaped by military situations and varied depending whether they were on the attack, on the defensive or confidently in occupation. Town dwellers' responses were in turn conditioned by their particular experience of UNITA during the battle for the cities and also by their previous political views. These two factors were to an extent mutually reinforcing, since those who were most strongly opposed to UNITA to begin with were most likely to cast a harsh judgement on the excesses of its soldiers' behaviour. But all town dwellers, whatever their political opinions, had benefited from the security of life in the city and from the provision of services by the state. The UNITA occupation turned the previously safe cities into battle zones, and its presence was, manifestly, nothing but destructive.

Such reactions were contingent upon the specifically urban experience of life under the MPLA and the understandings of politics that had accompanied the MPLA's process of state building. As the following chapter will explore, the reaction of rural people to UNITA's presence in the 1990s was different from what was observed in the towns and was not uniform across the rural Central Highlands. In the countryside as in the cities, people's responses to UNITA depended on their particular history of politicisation by either or both of the political movements and on the pattern of military action and territorial occupation in the areas where they lived.

8

UNITA's Last Redoubts

The violence suffered by people in cities like Huambo and Kuito during 1993 and 1994 was not experienced in all parts of the Central Highlands. In the rural areas where UNITA's domination was not contested in the period after 1993, its behaviour towards local people and people's responses to the UNITA presence were quite different from its relationship with town dwellers in the same period. This chapter examines local politics in a rural part of the Central Highlands from the elections until the end of the war in 2002: Bailundo district, which forms the northernmost part of Huambo province.[1] In doing so, it demonstrates continuities in UNITA's relationship with rural people in the Central Highlands from the 1980s to the 1990s. However, as the government regained the military initiative in the later 1990s, a weakened UNITA was no longer able to sustain its civilian functions and struggled to keep control of people by force alone. In the process, it lost the trust of those who had once accepted its authority.

In Bailundo district, just as in other parts of the Central Highlands, the state's military and civilian apparatus were confined during the pre-1991 phase of the war to the administrative centres. These centres were thinly spread: the town of Bailundo lies 100 kilometres north-east of Huambo, and the district extends as far the provincial boundary, as much as 80 kilometres from the town of Bailundo itself. North of Bailundo, the next major town is Waku Kungo, more than 150 kilometres away in the neighbouring province of Kwanza Sul. UNITA had been the dominant military and political force in the district throughout the 1980s and retained soldiers there after the signing of the Bicesse Accord. One resident of the area recalled that 'UNITA troops entered Bailundo [town] in 1991, secretly, and lived among the population – they only let us know after the elections. Whoever was MPLA was killed.'[2]

---

[1]   I use 'district' for the Portuguese *município*.
[2]   Interviewee 133, Bailundo, November 2008.

However, the more distant rural parts of Bailundo district saw little violence in the post-election period, since – unlike in the towns – there were neither troops nor civilians present who were loyal to the MPLA. When Savimbi was expelled from Huambo in 1994, it was to Bailundo that he retreated, and he made the town his principal base.

By the end of 1994 UNITA was in a weak military position and eager to sign a ceasefire. The government, distrustful of UNITA's intentions and now confident that it could win the war by force, accepted ceasefire talks only as a result of diplomatic pressure. Talks in the Zambian capital led to the signing in November of the Lusaka Protocol, which among other provisions granted certain government positions to UNITA, provided for the integration of UNITA generals into the Angolan Armed Forces (FAA) and for the incorporation of UNITA soldiers into the National Police, and proscribed any other police forces: this last point was a response to UNITA's concerns about the partisan nature of the Rapid Intervention Police set up by the government before the 1992 election.[3]

A lack of mutual trust between the government and UNITA ensured that few of the provisions of Lusaka were implemented. In the last years of the 1990s, UNITA faced increasing difficulties. Following the end of the Cold War, the movement had enjoyed the continued support of Mobutu Sese Seko in Zaire and benefited from access to international diamond markets that allowed it to sell gems extracted from alluvial diamond fields. However, Mobutu was ousted in 1997. Meanwhile, the MPLA government had used the international legitimacy gained by its victory in the 1992 elections and by its increasing importance as a petroleum supplier to win diplomatic support that transcended the Cold War alignments of the past. The result of the new international consensus on the side of the MPLA government was the United Nations' declaration in 1998 of a ban on the purchase of diamonds from UNITA and a travel ban and financial sanctions against UNITA officials living outside Angola. Petroleum revenue also allowed the government to rearm the FAA. During the final years of the war, the FAA applied more systematically than ever before the counter-insurgency measures that its predecessor, FAPLA, had used from the earliest days of the civil conflict. In 1999, Bailundo and the town of Andulo in Bié province became the last Central Highlands towns to be captured by the FAA. Nevertheless, elements of UNITA remained active in the remoter parts of Bailundo district until Savimbi's death in 2002.

---

[3] Human Rights Watch, *Angola Unravels: The Rise and Fall of the Lusaka Peace Process* (New York, 1999), 1. Available online at http://www.hrw.org/reports/pdfs/a/angola/angl998.pdf, accessed 21 January 2015.

People interviewed in the district speak of having lived in peace under UNITA until the late 1990s but of spending the last years of the war on the move or in remote mountain areas as UNITA tried to prevent them from defecting to or being captured by government forces. As with all the interviews quoted in this book, the versions of history that people offered were entwined with their political beliefs and what they perceived to be the preferred versions of history put forward by those in power at different times.[4]

This chapter is based on interviews conducted in two areas within the district with distinct local histories. They reveal that rural people's interaction with UNITA was not uniform but varied according to people's earlier political views and their role as farmers or as skilled functionaries. The first group of interviewees was at a mission close to the provincial border. All of them had been born in the area and had been removed from it as part of the government's counter-insurgency operations in the 1980s but had returned at the start of the 1990s. The second group comprised people from villages farther south who had remained in the district throughout the conflict. Both locations were for many years beyond the reach of the MPLA state.

THE MISSION

The area surrounding the mission was contested between the MPLA and UNITA around the time of independence. In the early 1980s, the MPLA government evacuated most of the local population to Waku Kungo as part of the counterinsurgency strategies that it used in response to UNITA's growing military strength during that period. According to interviewees' accounts, the only people who did not go to Waku Kungo were those whom UNITA took to bases still farther from the main roads and towns. With the 1991 Bicesse accords, people thought the war was finished and returned from Waku Kungo to their lands around the mission. The MPLA state had not established itself in the rural areas during the brief peace after Bicesse. UNITA, however, had deployed soldiers there, and in the weeks after the 1992 election, they assumed control as they had done elsewhere in the province.

José was born near the mission in 1967 and began his education at the mission school before the government moved him and his family to Waku Kungo

---

4   The areas around Bailundo, before 1998, correspond in part to Richardson's characterisation of the 'core' UNITA zone and in part to the 'tax' zone: Anna Richardson, *Children Living with UNITA: A Report for UNICEF Angola* (Luanda, 2001). The period after 1998 saw the progressive destruction of the core and tax zones by the government's military advance. As UNITA's military position became more precarious, the zones it had occupied securely became more like 'pillage' zones.

in 1976, when he was nine years old. His description of events, presumably shaped by what his family had told him, suggests that neither the MPLA nor UNITA was endowed with greater legitimacy than the other in those early years of independence. 'We were taken from here by the MPLA's forces, FAPLA [while] others remained here under the control of UNITA.' Remembering his childhood in Waku Kungo, José said that people in the town saw the newcomers as 'displaced people' and suspected them of having UNITA links. When word went around that UNITA was trying to attack, 'the local people said to us: "your cousins are coming because of you" '.[5] José acknowledged that UNITA soldiers would indeed come into the peri-urban *bairros* of the town at night and talk to the resettled people. They would bring news about rural home areas, share information about common friends and even carry out clandestine propaganda with the help of sympathisers in the town. 'They would say "our war is for everyone to be the rulers of this fatherland – for people to cease suffering and to live in peace". They said our country's wealth was being taken away by others'.

Aged 15, José was in, his own words, 'captured' by FAPLA for military service but deserted and ran away to Luanda. He returned to the area of his birth shortly before the 1992 elections, only to find 'houses destroyed, bush where there had been villages' – and UNITA soldiers in control of the area. 'We were well received by UNITA, each of us was directed to an area [in which to live]. We then came to know we must abandon the politics of *there* and enter the politics of UNITA.' What he meant was the abandonment of loyalty to the government ('*there*', the other place) and the dedication of labour to the service of UNITA.

Because José had passed sixth grade, UNITA instructors trained him as a teacher, and he remained working in UNITA schools until the end of the war. 'There was a difference between UNITA's teaching and the government's teaching', José recalled. 'With the government it was just about passing grades. With UNITA, it was so that a person would know things.' His description of life with UNITA was one of an idealistic struggle to help the people amid straitened circumstances. There was no electricity, and schoolteachers wrote with charcoal in the absence of chalk. Under UNITA, 'each area had a health post, although medicine was not abundant', and the solution was to make remedies from roots and herbs. He described a hierarchical system of administration with officials at provincial, municipal and local level. He spoke of a justice system with trained magistrates, who would mete out punishments ranging from sentences in 'prisons' – underground pits – for serious offences

5   Interviewee 134, Bailundo, November 2008.

to extra work in the fields for minor offences. The well-organised systems that he had described started to break down, he said, as UNITA's army was put to flight by the government's offensives that began in 1998. With the end of the war in 2002, José proceeded to one of the quartering areas that had been set up in terms of the peace settlement for UNITA soldiers and adherents.

Another man in the same area, Ramos, had also been taken by the government with his peasant farmer family to Waku Kungo in 1976, when he was twelve. In contrast with José, Ramos in his recollections of life in Waku Kungo emphasised the assistance his family had received from the MPLA – food, clothes, free education, and employment on a collective farm. He remembered that 'all pupils joined OPA [the Organisation of Angolan Pioneers]', where they 'played sport, and cultivated fields for the school – wherever the MPLA was, OPA was there'. He described the town as a peaceful 'liberated zone', safe from the war that continued around it. Nevertheless, when he was 18, Ramos 'abandoned school because I was being chased to go to the troops'. FAPLA officers would regularly enlist school pupils, and Ramos reckoned that he would be safer in a village. Although only twenty kilometres from Waku Kungo, the village was undisturbed by either army until UNITA went on a new offensive on the eve of the Bicesse talks. At the time of the elections, 'UNITA and the MPLA were in Waku Kungo together', but as UNITA consolidated its control over the town, 'the government made efforts to make people abandon Waku Kungo'. Ramos, however, remained under the control of UNITA. During 1992 and 1993, UNITA trained him as a nurse, and when the MPLA returned and drove UNITA out, he left with UNITA. 'If the government found you had been living with UNITA, if you weren't lucky they could cut off your head.'

Ramos took a sceptical view of both parties' efforts to seek political support; 'there was no difference' between control by UNITA and by the MPLA. His acceptance of UNITA's presence was on the basis of its efforts at providing health and education services. He described a 'well-organised' hospital comprising adobe buildings, where it was possible to perform operations in sterile conditions with ketamine as a general anaesthetic. He said his son had studied to fifth grade under UNITA, with 'paper and pencils that the troops brought from the front, and exchanged for food'.

People who had been more closely integrated into the MPLA's political structures while in Waku Kungo in the 1980s made harsher judgements on life under UNITA in the 1990s, even though they also spent time working for UNITA. Francisco was born in 1950 and was thus already an adult when, upon independence, 'UNITA withdrew with its people to the bush', while he and his family, 'because we were close to the asphalt', were taken to Waku Kungo.

The government offered us education, and we had the right to food. I qualified as a teacher there. We had the right to a shop where we could buy things at a low price: soap, rice, manufactured goods. We had the right to a plot to cultivate. It was a normal life. The people from here are religious, and we were able to hold religious services. I was a member of the party. My role was to mobilise people, to know the flag and the party symbols.[6]

Like others at the mission, Francisco returned to his home area in 1991, only to find himself trapped there as UNITA assumed control. UNITA 'received' him as a teacher, but his work was in 'grass schools, or just lessons under the trees'. His duties as a teacher included disseminating UNITA propaganda, that UNITA would 'liberate the country' and eventually take Luanda. The curriculum also included the usual subjects like mathematics and Portuguese. 'Sometimes they would capture books from the government – they would tear off the MPLA flags or pictures of the president from the books.'

Paulo, some 20 years younger, had gone to Waku Kungo as a young child with his parents and had been an organiser in the MPLA Youth (JMPLA). 'My main task was to mobilise the youth to study, to train themselves in various professions, to improve the future of the country through health and education.' Like Francisco, Paulo's account of events suggested that his active involvement with the MPLA had an impact on how UNITA treated him and how he perceived UNITA once he found himself in an area controlled by UNITA forces.

For Paulo, UNITA had deceived people who returned to their rural homes before the 1992 elections:

Savimbi took advantage of the peace to promise free education, health and food. So people started returning to their areas of origin. When UNITA saw the area was full [of returnees] they started to close the access roads so the people could no longer go to the cities. They began to enslave the people, taking away everything that came from the people [i.e. agricultural produce]. Young men who had grown up in the MPLA were forced to join UNITA's troops. Anyone who had assets, such as a car, was killed. People had no right to possessions, nor to democracy. Everything a person had was taken away. It was against human rights. People were left without clothes or salt[7] – they walked naked.

Paulo's view of UNITA was also shaped by the experience of arrest on the road between Waku Kungo and the mission 'because I had FAPLA papers' and subsequent imprisonment for eighteen months in an underground pit jail. Upon

---

6   Interviewee 131, Bailundo, November 2008.
7   Note again the common complaint about the lack of salt in UNITA areas.

his release from the dungeon, Paulo was put to work at a UNITA hospital. He spoke of treating civilians and soldiers but emphasised that UNITA had no more than 'grass houses' and that 'whatever the government had organised, UNITA destroyed'. Similarly, while UNITA professed to organise schooling, 'the young people there just carried food for the troops – there wasn't much time for studying'. This was true for young people whose families were present and others who had been captured.

Later, Paulo was appointed second secretary of UNITA's party structures in the local *comuna*. He believed UNITA had moved him into a political role as a ruse to remove him from an area where he was too well integrated into the local community.

> It was just a matter of teaching the people to work for the party for free. Anyone who didn't do so would be killed. [...] Part of mobilisation was putting people to work [in agriculture] – one part [of the crop] for the family, the other for the soldiers. Those who were captured did not serve in [UNITA's] military forces: they were organised, politicised, put to work. The same with *povos encontrados*: if they produced 150 kilograms, then 100 kilograms would go to the troops. Those who were working for the party also had to grow food.

Paulo's more negative assessment of UNITA compared to other interviewees and his explicit endorsement of the MPLA was shaped by a series of encounters with the political structures of the two sides at different times during his life. In turn, his political attitudes and choices determined the ways in which he encountered the two movements. His early role in JMPLA made him accept conscription into FAPLA without complaint, and his service in FAPLA caused him to be treated as an enemy by UNITA. This suggests that UNITA sought to punish those who had served in FAPLA while tolerating those people who had lived under MPLA rule without working for it.[8] Even though he later worked in UNITA's medical services, in describing these, he emphasises the inadequacy of UNITA's health and education provision. Where others saw UNITA doing its best in difficult circumstances, he saw UNITA above all as a repressive force. In 2000, after the government had established a presence in Bailundo town, Paulo 'ran away' from the UNITA area to 'join the MPLA' in the town. This voluntary defection two years before the end of the war allowed him to present himself as an MPLA loyalist, and he was posted back to his home area as an MPLA representative when the war ended, an experience which, we may assume, would have further coloured the account that he gave of life under UNITA.

---

[8] Compare the discussion in Chapter 4 of how FAPLA soldiers were ordered to distinguish between enemy troops and '*povo*'.

The various people who were interviewed at the mission expressed differing views about UNITA, and their experience of UNITA varied over time. What they have in common, however, was that all had spent time in Waku Kungo, and all had at least basic professional training that caused them to be drafted to work in UNITA's institutions. Some of them saw this as a voluntary contribution to a worthwhile project by UNITA and others as involuntary labour on behalf of an oppressive occupying militia. As earlier chapters demonstrated, UNITA saw a distinction between the people who worked for UNITA in professional roles and those who tilled fields in areas under UNITA's control. This distinction continued during the 1990s. The people quoted so far in this chapter were among those deployed by UNITA as functionaries. The next section examines developments over the same period from the point of view of peasant farmers.

THE VILLAGES

People who came from the more isolated villages in Bailundo district were not attached to the mission, had not lived in Waku Kungo and did not have the skills that would have made them liable to be incorporated into UNITA's service organisations. This ensured that their perceptions of UNITA and the sort of relationship that UNITA strove to establish with them were quite different from what was reported by the people who worked near the mission. These perceptions and relationships varied according to individual experiences and also changed over time as the direct consequence of the changing relative military positions of UNITA and of the government.

Some of the villagers managed to avoid the demands of the warring parties, at least for the first few years of the 1990s. Horácio, born in 1947, had served in the colonial army from 1971 to 1975 and, after independence, had moved to Huambo to avoid being taken 'to the bush' by UNITA. In Huambo, he worked as a trader in the informal market, buying vegetables from farmers and selling them in town. With the prospect of peace, he returned to his home area in 1992, the period during which UNITA established bases in the area. Yet by his account, as a village dweller his experience of UNITA was minimal. 'We lived well, cultivated our fields, and went to Bailundo [town] to trade. I couldn't say whether the MPLA or UNITA was in control.'[9]

Eugênio said he had been 'captured' by UNITA in 1989 at the age of 20 and taken to a UNITA base in a remote mountain area. At the base, he received military training and also 'political education', of which the message was 'not to go back to the MPLA' and 'let's make an effort to stop [the government]

---

[9]   Interviewee 172, Bailundo, November 2008.

who is in Luanda'.[10] While still a soldier, Eugênio himself was put to work in a political role among the peasant farmers of the surrounding area.

> The soldiers went to the battlefront. The people had to grow food and take it to the front. My work was to talk to the people and tell them not to become demoralised. To work hard so the troops could eat. To speak to them with respect. The *soba* had to be a UNITA *soba*. The *povo* knew only UNITA. We taught people they mustn't go back.

Asked whether he believed in the message that he was communicating on behalf of UNITA, he replied:

> I believed the words that I said – obligatorily. You had to understand – otherwise you lost your life. And you had to battle with the hoe.[11]

He spoke of basic necessities being supplied by *'comércio da tropa'* (troops' commerce): 'If they went to attack somewhere, the things they would bring back – salt, soap, clothes – they would give to the people. People paid with maize.' UNITA teachers and nurses worked in the villages, and 'the nurses brought medicines from that place where Savimbi was'.

Carlos, a farmer who had never been involved in UNITA's political work, saw the relationship from a different perspective, but the facts of his account are essentially similar to those offered by Eugênio:

> It was bad on UNITA's side. We didn't have conditions, salt, clothes. We still exchanged goods with troops who went to get them. Whoever wasn't working for [UNITA] was [considered] enemy. Whoever wasn't working for them had to run away. The quotas [of food to be delivered to the troops] continued....There were political activities: [we were told to] battle with the hoe, so they could get into power. Many people accepted this – if you didn't accept, you would be dead. It was still obligatory. But some people still ran away, because there was so much suffering.[12]

FLIGHT AND SURRENDER

The interviews discussed so far in this chapter show that political identity in the 1990s continued to be associated with where people were situated, just as had happened in the 1980s. People were aware that the course of their lives over many years might be determined by sheer chance: by their proximity to government or to UNITA forces at a particular crucial moment. Efforts

---

[10] Interviewee 174, Bailundo, November 2008.
[11] *'Lutar com a enchada'*: a metaphor linking agricultural production to military progress.
[12] Interviewee 174b, Bailundo, November 2008.

by each side to move people into its territory were interpreted as a political strategy by the stronger movement to get people, politically as well as physically, onto its side. In José's words:

> 'Being with a party' means fleeing death, following so that life goes on. 'I am with UNITA or with the MPLA' means I have to follow what they say. If I say I am from UNITA, the MPLA will kill me. If I say I am from the MPLA, UNITA will kill me. They too knew that whoever had force, won the people.[13]

People realised that they had no choice when it came to expressing support for the dominant movement and, particularly in the case of UNITA, complying with its demands for labour and produce. When people spoke of making choices about going to live in territory controlled by one or other movement, this was usually motivated by the need for survival rather than by political preference, and the choice, such as it was, involved the risk of going to an area where the other movement was dominant. All were talking about a period when the MPLA had been in charge of the state for more than fifteen years, yet with the exception of those who been actively involved in MPLA politics while in Waku Kungo, they did not necessarily take for granted the legitimacy of the MPLA state.

The interviews reveal that political education continued to be important for UNITA during the years after 1990 as it had been in the 1980s and that UNITA still sought to present its view of its legitimacy in terms of nationalist struggle. Yet it also becomes clear that UNITA's political education during the 1990s was barely effective. The farmers who 'knew only UNITA' accepted the UNITA version of events because they knew no other. Those who had lived in the MPLA-controlled town before finding themselves under UNITA control after 1990 were sceptical towards UNITA's narratives or, in some cases, recognised the arbitrariness of political affiliation and believed that neither party was inherently more worthy of support than the other. Even some who, as teachers or political officials, were instrumental in propagating the UNITA political line recognised that they were doing no more than encouraging people to produce food for UNITA's benefit. Where people expressed approval or disapproval of political movements, this was expressed in terms of the movements' ability to organise society but even more importantly in terms of their capacity to provide certain goods and services. Even those most critical of UNITA acknowledged the structures that it created. They expressed their disapproval of UNITA in terms of the fact that, despite these structures, it

---

[13]   Interviewee 134, Bailundo, November 2008.

lacked the material basis to provide goods such as salt, soap and school books that urban dwellers were accustomed to having.

Such an understanding of how political identities were framed in the years following 1991 has a bearing on how we understand people's reaction to the events of the last three years of the war, when the FAA began to expel UNITA's forces from this part of Angola. As UNITA came under military pressure from the FAA, its response was to force people to move farther away from the government's military presence. The constant displacement destroyed agricultural livelihoods and put an end to the rudimentary services on which UNITA staked its political legitimacy. The Angolan military and civilian authorities turned this situation to the government's political advantage: 'After 1993 the war became more intense. FAPLA had more forces against UNITA, so the worst suffering was experienced by those people who were with UNITA.'[14]

Carlos, who had said that life under UNITA was always hard, said the situation of rural people in UNITA areas got progressively worse throughout the 1990s, and the arrival of the FAA (which he referred to by the pre-1991 name of FAPLA) caused further fear and alienation:

> There were many conflicts with the people because the people already knew UNITA. FAPLA seized animals, goats, chickens – the people's food. The people fled. The UNITA troops fled too. FAPLA surrounded the people to take us to the *comuna* to show us we were no longer with UNITA. The people accepted. If you fled with UNITA you were killed like an animal. Many UNITA troops also presented themselves to the government.

Once the government forces were in control, however, violence was replaced by political education.

> There was organisation [by the military] so we would not think about UNITA any more. To fall into line. They came and spoke to the *sobas*, for the people to go to the *comuna* and receive soap, salt and clothes so they would know well which party was in charge. They spoke with the *soba* to talk to the people not to run away any more and to know the MPLA.[15]

Even those people who had taken a positive view of UNITA's efforts at social organisation during the period of coexistence with the local people in the early 1990s acknowledged that this relationship broke down towards the end of the decade as UNITA came under pressure from the FAA. Although some stayed with UNITA until they received orders to gather in the quartering areas after Savimbi's death, others left UNITA earlier as their political loyalties were

---

[14] Interviewee 130, Bailundo, November 2008.
[15] Interviewee 174b, Bailundo, November 2008.

overridden by the need to survive. Miguel, a schoolteacher who had worked with UNITA, recalled,

> From 1998, with the war, we were running crazily. If anyone was caught [by the FAA] they would be sent to the city and if they weren't lucky they would die. Only at the end did we separate ourselves from the [UNITA] forces. The suffering was too much. For two years I didn't teach, because they weren't holding classes any more. With such suffering, some people went over to the government while others continued in the resistance – those who best understood UNITA's reasoning, and who believed that eventually there would be peace. It was necessary to go to the quartering area in order to receive food, and to begin life. [But] some people didn't accept to go to the quartering area – they thought the government would kill them.[16]

Nevertheless, there were some who remained far enough from the conflict that they never came into direct contact with the FAA, nor indeed with the civil authorities until after the war had finished. According to José:

> In 1998 the war started again. Not so much here, the war was more distant, closer to the town. It came closer to us in 2001. When the MPLA troops were coming the UNITA soldiers would advise us that we had to move. We went to live in the bush alongside the river. At night we would come out to gather maize from the fields. We continued to work in the fields, so there was plenty of food. The troops would bring things from the battlefront and trade them for food. [In February 2002] we heard Savimbi had died in Moxico. The troops were forbidden from saying he had died, but later they began saying he had died.[17]

As well as food, some of those who came from UNITA areas, if they had professional skills, were offered the opportunity of working in the government system.

> The situation got worse. It became a case of just working to save one's own life. Those who tried to run away to find the government were killed. [...] The people left UNITA in April 2002. Some went to the quartering areas – mostly those who had been soldiers, and some of the teachers – but not me. I went from the bush to the village, then went to the *sede da comuna* to be registered as a new teacher. The government had set up officials in the *comunas* so the people coming in from the bush could give their names. I had come from Waku Kungo [in 1991] with government documents but I had had to burn them, and this caused difficulties [when it came to re-registering].[18]

---

16 Interviewee 133, Bailundo, November 2008.
17 Interviewee 134, Bailundo, November 2008.
18 Interviewee 131, Bailundo, November 2008. The *sede* is where the local administration for the *comuna* is located.

Yet incorporation into the state system was, for some, only on condition of demonstrating an affiliation with the MPLA. Those few who were not prepared to accept the MPLA's conditions suffered for it.

> The MPLA ordered that all UNITA teachers must abandon UNITA and join the MPLA. When I didn't accept this they cut off my salary. Some accepted – those who didn't accept were persecuted. I wanted the truth. I could see the bad governance.[19]

Paulo said of the post-war era, 'Since 2002 there has been peace. People have been enjoying peace and the right to democracy.' Asked if there were still UNITA supporters in his community, he replied, 'People stopped supporting UNITA because of maltreatment. These days, the majority are with the MPLA. The only ones still with UNITA are those who resisted from 1976 until today. It was the MPLA who saved the people.'[20]

CONCLUSION

People's understandings of and responses to events in the last years of the war are shaped by two distinct yet related discourses on political identity and political legitimacy. In earlier chapters, I have discussed the ambivalence and ambiguity between these two discourses. The first assigns political identity to an individual on the basis of the political-military control of an area. The second discourse defines the legitimacy of a political movement in terms of its responsibilities towards the people under its control. These responsibilities might include the provision of health and education services and the guarantee of essential goods, particularly things such as salt, soap and clothing that cannot be produced in the peasant economy. The most minimal condition is the maintenance of a peaceful environment in which people may produce food.

What kept people in the UNITA-controlled areas of Bailundo in the 1990s was a combination of force and the fear of alternative possibilities. Few were motivated by a belief in UNITA's inherent superiority. Similarly, what compelled people to go to government-controlled areas was in most cases not political allegiance to the MPLA but rather the government's use of force of arms or the hope of relief from starvation. Yet the geographical displacement took on a political significance according to the discourse that linked control and political identity. An act of migration became an act of defection.

---

[19] Interviewee 133, Bailundo, November 2008.
[20] Interviewee 130, Bailundo, November 2008.

The government, by this stage of the war, appears to have realised that simply having people under its control was not enough and that by offering humanitarian assistance and, for some, the possibility of state employment, it would consolidate its gains.

Both this chapter and the previous one have shown how discourses on the relationship between political movements and people that had originated around the time of independence and developed during the war years of the 1970s and 1980s continued to shape how people understood and responded to the events of the 1990s. The changes in the discourses themselves and in the ways in which these related to political and military realities and to people's behaviour and choices must be understood in the context of the different terms on which power was contested in 1975 and in the 1990s. They must also be put in the context of the differing social, economic, military and political realities across urban and rural parts of the Central Highlands.

Five broad and interrelated factors influenced how people interpreted and responded to their experience of the contestation of power during the years that followed the 1992 elections. The first of these concerned people's prior ideological affiliation. Those people who had sympathised with UNITA in the past or at least had no strong links to the MPLA were more hesitant to condemn UNITA's presence even if they did not endorse the way it governed the territories under its control. The second factor that helped to determine how people responded to the events of the 1990s was their closeness to or involvement in the MPLA-led state-building process. This was not the same thing as a purely ideological preference for the MPLA, but it was related to it: in a situation where the state and the ruling party were so closely identified with each other, being involved in the work of the state as a teacher or civil servant often involved active participation in the political work of the party.

The third factor is related to the second. It concerns to what extent people were dependent on an urban economy – an economy, moreover, in which the MPLA state was the most important investor, employer and guarantor of livelihoods. Ideas about peasant farmers' economic autonomy and the implications of this for political mobilisation have been discussed in earlier chapters. Just as it was those people whose livelihoods depended on the MPLA's urban state who felt they had most to lose as UNITA assumed command of some areas, so it was farmers who had the least to lose from a change of political control, as long as they were still able to cultivate their land. There is a crucial difference here with the situation experienced in the late 1970s and early 1980s by those farmers who found themselves in contested areas and who consequently experienced both warring parties as a threat. The greater economic autonomy of rural people also explains how some of those people who left Waku Kungo for their home areas in the mission around 1990 had no strong objection to working for UNITA, even though they had been educated in an MPLA-controlled town and trained for roles in the MPLA state system. Unlike the people who remained in the cities and saw functioning urban social, political and economic formations threatened with destruction, these people had chosen to go back to a rural life, aware that this meant abandoning the amenities and the security of the city. Even if they had not necessarily expected to live in a UNITA-controlled countryside, in material terms it was of little consequence to them which party was in control. However, the different ways in which different people from the mission spoke about life under UNITA indicate that the political beliefs they had held prior to returning to the countryside also had an impact on how they interpreted subsequent events.

The fourth factor also concerns the dichotomy between town and countryside but in ideational rather than economic terms. Previous chapters have already considered how town and countryside assumed political meanings, the former being associated with the MPLA and the latter with UNITA. In the current chapter, such an association of meanings is present in the account of Francisco, who said that his peasant farming community fell under the control of the MPLA because it was 'close to the asphalt', and in Chapter 7, in Pequenino's recollection of the UNITA officers who told the citizens of Kuito to 'eat asphalt' during the siege, an insult laden with meaning about the superiority of UNITA's food-producing countryside over the MPLA's city. This discourse that linked political identity to geographical space merged with the discourse about the differences in style and capability between the MPLA and UNITA. In Chapter 7, we saw how MPLA-supporting town dwellers in Huambo and Kuito denigrated UNITA explicitly on the grounds that its ways were the ways of the bush and not of the city; the city represented an economy and a way of living that were coterminous with the geographical limitations of state-building efforts that were inseparably identified with the MPLA.

Fifth and last, the nature and circumstances of people's encounters with UNITA, and indeed with the MPLA, also emerge as important in shaping how they spoke of the political legitimacy of the two movements. The people of Huambo's Cidade Alta, which fell to UNITA only after a prolonged battle, and the people of central Kuito, which UNITA besieged and bombarded over months, came to associate UNITA with violence and destruction while downplaying acts of violence by government forces on the grounds that these were defensive. People from other parts of Huambo city and from rural zones, where UNITA took over by stealth rather than by force, were less inclined to speak of violent behaviour. The social geography of Huambo ensured that the central areas that suffered the worst of UNITA violence were also home to a substantial number of people in the higher echelons of the MPLA and the civil service. For them, the experience of UNITA violence confirmed long-held views about the nature of the rebel organisation. Nevertheless, the levels of deprivation and the constant threat of arbitrary violence or punishment experienced throughout the cities during the time of UNITA control were enough to change the views of people who had previously been inclined towards UNITA on ideological grounds. Even those people who expressed no strong political preference for the MPLA as a party and who might have voted for UNITA in the elections recognised the MPLA's capacity to maintain order within the urban enclaves it controlled and to guarantee the supply of at least basic goods to the cities. The UNITA that took control of the Central Highlands early in 1993 had no such capacity.

These five interrelated factors formed the basis on which people accounted for the events that surrounded them and for their political choices in the decade that followed the 1992 elections. Understandings about the relationship between territorial control and political identity that were the legacy of the earlier war years persisted. But more important in the 1990s was people's ability to make judgments based on a comparison between living conditions on the two sides of the conflict. In the 1970s, people's ideas about UNITA and the MPLA were based on the two parties' own ideological self-representations: UNITA's appeals to indigeneity and a mixture of Christian and 'African' values, the MPLA's promises of development led by a modernising and anti-tribal central state or the claims by both sides to be defending the nation against an external threat. By the early 1990s, however, many people had experienced life under both movements. Others had lived only under the control of the MPLA and had become accustomed to a way of living that they knew did not exist in areas dominated by UNITA. Those who initially were willing to accept the more basic conditions in UNITA zones found their acceptance of UNITA tested as the organisation found itself constrained by sanctions and military action. When interviewees spoke about questions of political legitimacy and affiliation after 1992, ideological considerations were almost entirely absent as people evaluated the MPLA and UNITA on the basis of the kind of living conditions over which each movement presided.

9

The Luena Agreement and Politics Today

When Jonas Savimbi died in battle in 2002 after a long war of attrition, the Angolan government took the opportunity to persuade UNITA's surviving leaders to accept peace on the MPLA's terms. The ensuing settlement served to dismantle what remained of UNITA's structures in rural Angola. People formerly attached to UNITA were resettled in areas administered by the state. The political logic inherited from wartime ensured that integration into state-administered communities was contingent on identifying oneself with the MPLA. The same logic underpins the politics of post-war reconstruction, which is presented as the gift of the MPLA. These factors can help us understand the collapse of UNITA's support in its former heartland in the 2008 election, a result that confounds ethnic or regionalist explanations of political loyalty.

The previous two chapters have shown that the events of the 1990s changed how people in the Central Highlands perceived the MPLA and UNITA. This was not because people's understanding of political authority had changed. On the contrary, people interpreted events in the 1990s in the same terms in which politics had been understood throughout the course of the war since before independence. Rather, it was the events themselves that were different. As UNITA battled to keep control of territory and people by force of arms, it lost all but its most loyal supporters. This chapter deals with the period after the end of the war. It situates political mobilisation since 2002 in the context of wartime politics and of the 2002 peace accord. Whereas the last two chapters dealt with how the last years of the war shaped political adherence in the Central Highlands, this chapter will begin by stepping back chronologically to consider government thinking and strategy after the 1992 elections and will then show how this determined the manner in which the conflict was brought to an end.

The Bicesse and Lusaka peace accords, as noted in the previous chapter, were the product of a particular conjuncture in international politics rather than of any initiative from within Angola. They were conducted according to norms that had been theorised and established during the final years of the Cold War: that the correct way to end a conflict was to transform armed adversaries into political parties and that international mediators should have a central role in the process. The failure of Bicesse and Lusaka ensured that by the end of the 1990s, Angolan political elites deeply distrusted international mediation as a way of bringing the war to an end. This distrust towards the international community was shared by the MPLA and by religious and civil society leaders, who by the end of the decade were beginning to constitute an independent and coherent voice in Angolan politics.

The government and the MPLA had always maintained that the government had kept its side of the Bicesse agreement and the MPLA had won the 1992 elections, while UNITA had betrayed its commitments by rearming and returning to war. According to this version of events, the international community had abandoned its responsibility for ensuring compliance with Bicesse and providing security for the transition. By 1998, the government had taken this position to its logical conclusion and resolved to defeat UNITA by force of arms. Arms purchases and the deployment of foreign mercenaries were made possible by oil revenue and by the diplomatic support for the MPLA that flowed both from Angola's increasing strategic significance as an oil producer and from the international community's acceptance that the MPLA had won a free and fair election. An important part of the government's military strategy was the counter-insurgency campaign, of which the consequences were described in the previous chapter. These military measures were accompanied by an increasingly assertive message from the government that UNITA was not a legitimate political actor. Part of the strategy involved persuading a group of UNITA parliamentarians to break from Savimbi to form the UNITA Renovation Committee, or UNITA-Renovada. On the grounds that the leader of this group was Eugênio Manuvakola, the one-time UNITA secretary general who had signed the Lusaka Protocol on Savimbi's behalf, the government recognised UNITA-Renovada as its interlocutor for the conclusion of outstanding business from the Lusaka agreement and, in so doing, wrote Savimbi out of the politics of the conflict. In the ensuing months, the UN Secretary General noted that President dos Santos saw no further need for contact with Savimbi and had asked the UN to support the government's approach: military action against Savimbi alongside negotiations with UNITA-Renovada.[1] State media were instructed not to refer to Savimbi as

[1]   Report of the Secretary-General on the UN Observer Mission in Angola S/1998/931, 8 October 1998; SG Report on the UN Observer Mission in Angola (MONUA) S/1998/1110, 23 November 1998.

the leader of UNITA and to label his forces 'armed bandits' or the 'forces of the criminal Savimbi'.[2]

The escalation of conflict after 1998 helped give coherence to an alternative understanding of the war that was articulated by a community of critical academics, clergy and civil society leaders in Luanda. They argued that international mediation was inappropriate to Angola's circumstances and had failed, but in all other respects their analysis brought them into direct opposition to government thinking. The members of this circle challenged the MPLA's claims that it enjoyed exclusive legitimacy on the basis of having won the election. Their critique, however, went further than the botched execution of the Bicesse and Lusaka agreements. They also argued that the accords were fundamentally flawed because they had been the initiative of international actors rather than Angolans and involved the participation of only the two belligerent leaderships with no input from wider Angolan society. Their insistence that 'peace is more than the silencing of guns' was couched in a language of 'positive peace' descended ultimately from the thinking of Johan Galtung.[3] The end of the war, it was argued, should be linked to moves to ensure greater political participation in Angola. The view of the war that they presented was not one of a conflict between two parties but rather one of two elites who together were waging war against the Angolan people. A peaceful termination of the conflict would represent a victory for the Angolan people. In this way, civil society and the churches asserted a new Angolan identity based around opposition to the war: a rethinking of Angolanness that challenged the attempts that the MPLA and UNITA had made throughout the war years to claim Angolan identity for their own. These ideas were developed and articulated at a series of public events between 1999 and 2002 under the auspices of a series of ad hoc groupings. The involvement of the churches, in particular the Catholic Church, allowed the message of a 2001 campaign – 'I'm for an Angola without war' – to reach parishes across Angola. Yet the paucity of independent social organisation at the time ensured that 'civil society' remained an elite form of organisation, albeit one that was not party political. 'Civil society' as understood in Luanda at the time came to be constituted by its opposition to the war. In the few years that this non-partisan approach to the war and to peace was gestated in Luanda, it made no significant impact outside of the main urban centres.

---

[2] Human Rights Watch, *Angola Unravels: The Rise and Fall of the Lusaka Peace Process* (New York, 1999), 88.

[3] Johan Galtung, 'Violence, Peace and Peace Research', *Journal of Peace Research* 6.3 (1969), 167–191.

The government barely acknowledged the initiatives, other than with some anonymous vitriolic comments in the pages of *Jornal de Angola*. The Sant'Egidio Community in Rome, a lay Catholic organisation that had contacted the government and UNITA in the hope of starting a new round of negotiations, revealed that Savimbi had indicated he was willing to begin negotiating but that the government had ruled out any kind of new talks with Savimbi.[4] The respective positions of the government and of Savimbi need to be seen in the context of the balance of military power at the time. Even if UNITA raids were still able to cause distress to people and embarrassment to the authorities, the government knew that it had the upper hand. Only after the end of the war would civilian society realise to what extent the counterinsurgency measures had weakened UNITA as a political and as a military force.

Savimbi's death in a fire fight with Angolan Armed Forces (FAA) soldiers on 22 February 2002 immediately changed the political context surrounding the war and the possibilities of ending it. The government assumed, correctly, that the removal of the man who had directed UNITA in an authoritarian manner for more than three decades would create a vacuum of authority. UNITA was further weakened by the absence of communication between its soldiers in the bush and its politicians in Luanda and in exile. This strengthened the government's negotiating position. The government's first approach to UNITA was to soldiers rather than to politicians. FAA officers were ordered to cease 'offensive movements' and mandated to make contact with their UNITA counterparts in preparation for a formal general ceasefire. Formal talks between the FAA and UNITA military leadership began on 20 March in Luena, the provincial town that had been the headquarters of the operation against UNITA in the east. By the end of the month, they had finalised a *Memorandum of Understanding*, which was signed in Luanda on 4 April by the commanders in chief of the FAA and of UNITA's armed forces.[5] UNITA politicians in Luanda and abroad had no direct contact with what was going on in Luena. These circumstances produced an agreement that consciously avoided politics. On political matters, all the Memorandum did was to reaffirm both sides' commitment to the Lusaka Protocol. It presented itself as a document to facilitate the implementation of

[4] Eric Morier-Genoud, 'Sant' Egidio, la Médiation & la Paix: Don Matteo Zuppi & Ricardo Cannelli', *Missions et Sciences Sociales* 13 (2003), 128.

[5] Government of Angola, *Memorando de Entendimento Complementar ao Protocolo de Lusaka para a Cessação das Hostilidades e Resolução de Demais Questões Militares Pendentes nos Termos do Protocolo de Lusaka* (2002), available online at http://www.usip.org/sites/default/files/file/resources/collections/peace_agreements/angola_04042002.pdf, accessed 20 September 2014.

the protocol. What was decided behind closed doors in Luena was a technical plan for the demobilisation and social reintegration of UNITA's armed forces. In this regard, the government's strategy in managing the talks with the UNITA officers was quite consistent with its assertion that the war was not a political matter but rather a problem of violence. Ending the war was therefore simply a matter of ending the violence: a notion diametrically opposed to civil society groups' insistence that 'peace is more than a silencing of arms'.

Central to the plan was the establishment of quartering areas where UNITA undertook to assemble its troops and their families and from where they were to be transported to their areas of origin following a process of disarmament and demobilisation. To understand the political consequences of this, we need to remember the basis of UNITA's political legitimacy during the war. In earlier chapters, I have shown how this rested on its capacity to provide and to maintain a perception of security and acceptable minimum conditions of life, which formed the basis of a social contract. This social contract was not only a matter of the provision of material goods. It also required the dissemination of an ideology in which the idea of the state linked together narratives about history and notions of mutual responsibilities between UNITA and the people under its control. For this ideology to become hegemonic required the maintenance of coherent UNITA communities in which no other world view was permitted and within which the UNITA narratives would take on the status of common sense. We have also seen how, during the years of the war, some people maintained their ideological convictions regardless of where they were, while others whose beliefs were less deep seated changed their beliefs as the result of passing from the control of one political movement to the other. Such an understanding of the identity politics of the civil war informed the government's strategy during and after the Luena talks, and being aware of this helps us to understand the reaction of people who had previously lived in UNITA areas.

During the year that followed the Luena accord, the people in the quartering areas retained a strong UNITA identity. They talked of themselves as part of a UNITA community and gave account of their own lives and actions in terms of UNITA narratives about its own history and its role in the liberation of Angola. During the same period, the government was insistent that the UNITA quartering areas were only a temporary measure and that their residents would be relocated to their home areas with all possible haste. Those included thousands who had been born in UNITA communities or at least lived in them since early childhood. Many of these would have known their 'home areas' only from the recollections of older family members. Those who had been kidnapped as children would most likely not know where their home areas were at all. The principle of return to home areas sounded like a compassionate one, but it was driven by the political logic of government strategy rather than by any clear wish on the part of the people in the quartering areas. Had the quartering areas remained and become permanent settlements, they would have been sizeable communities in which a UNITA ideology remained hegemonic. Such a scenario would have been irreconcilable with the logic of the politics that has come to dominate Angola since the end of the war.

Soares de Oliveira has used the term 'illiberal peacebuilding' to characterise post-war Angola: a process in which a powerful elite uses the post-war moment to extend and consolidate its control.[6] The term serves to highlight the contrast between the realities of the Angolan settlement and the liberal norms that were implicit in the demands of Angolan civil society in the late 1990s. Liberal peacemaking theory, with its emphasis on healing social divisions, assumes that conflict arises from an opposition of interests that pre-exists the conflict. The earlier chapters of this book have demonstrated that in Angola, by contrast, enmity between people was the consequence rather than the cause of conflict. On both sides of the civil war, each political elite worked to convince people that it represented their interests, and each elite enjoyed some success in doing so. The ending of the war has created the conditions for a single elite to make its control hegemonic. The remainder of this chapter will consider the logic of today's politics in Angola and show how it derives both from the logic of wartime politics and from the manner in which the Luena agreement was framed and implemented.

From the moment that the Luena accord was made public until the present day, the government discourse on the end of the war has been one of national reconciliation, but reconciliation on the government's preferred terms. The preamble to the *Memorandum of Understanding* considered 'the growing and pressing need to achieve peace and national reconciliation in Angola, expressed and felt daily by all Angolans'.[7] In the months after the Luena agreement, the Angolan government promoted a campaign to assist in the tracing of people who had gone missing during the war. Although much of the tracing work was done by the International Committee of the Red Cross and its Angolan affiliate, the state media carried emotionally charged reports each day of a process that they dubbed 'o reecontro da grande família angolana' (the reunion of the big Angolan family). The memorandum also committed the

---

6   Ricardo Soares de Oliveira, 'Illiberal Peacebuilding in Angola', *The Journal of Modern African Studies* 49.02 (June 2011), 287–314.
7   *Memorando*, 1.

government to passing an amnesty law 'in the interests of peace and national reconciliation' that would cover 'all crimes committed in the ambit of the armed conflict between UNITA Military Forces and the Government'.[8] This law attracted the criticism both of Luanda civil society and of the United Nations for the way in which it granted impunity to those responsible for crimes of war.

This apparently non-partisan discourse of reconciliation is at odds with other forceful statements made by government and MPLA officials and by the state media in the years that followed the Luena agreement. This other government discourse recalled the ideologies of the state that were established during the civil war: the identification of the state with a single party, the idea of the party-state as the nation's liberator from colonialism and defender against aggression and hence the rejection and even criminalisation of political opposition as being contrary to the interests of the nation. The discourse is rooted in the normative appeal of peace and is persuasive to the extent that it contrasts a peaceful present with the suffering of the wartime past. Yet far from constructing peace as a matter of reconciliation between adversaries, this discourse presents peace as the work of the MPLA and more specifically of President dos Santos. Such an interpretation of events was already evident in the way that the peace agreement was framed and presented to the public. In accordance with the government's position that the agreement was a military rather than a political matter, the *Memorandum of Understanding* was signed by the commander in chief of the FAA, Armando da Cruz Neto, and by General Geraldo Sachipengo Kamorteiro, the commander of UNITA's military forces. Dos Santos presided over the occasion in the manner of a chairman rather than one whose government had been a party to the conflict. General Paulo Lukamba Gato, who had succeeded Savimbi as UNITA's political leader, was relegated to a seat among the audience. General Cruz Neto praised dos Santos as 'the architect of peace', a formulation that the state media invoked repeatedly in the years that followed.

The idea of the MPLA as the creator of peace was put forward in an ever more strident way as the 2008 elections approached. The slogan '*MPLA trouxe a paz*' (MPLA brought peace) was seen on banners and placards, and its implicit message was carried in speeches as the MPLA prepared for the election. In the peri-urban *bairros* around Huambo, home to people who had been displaced during the 1980s, MPLA organisers spoke of suffering and deprivation during the time of the UNITA occupation of the city and contrasted this with the benefits of life under the MPLA in a time of peace. 'The government

---

[8] *Memorando*, 4.

supplied peace to people. With my money I can buy salt. In those days [with UNITA], even if you had money there was no salt, there wasn't anything'. At the same time, the campaigners presented a vote for the MPLA as an endorsement of the state services that the people were receiving, even though the *bairros* in which they were campaigning had seen little in the way of infrastructure development since the end of the war. The activists preached that 'it's our president who's helping us, who is teaching in the schools' and that their campaign was 'for our government to win the elections'.

In fact, for a decade after the end of the war, the MPLA was the only party able to operate publicly throughout much of the rural Central Highlands. The MPLA presented its role in a way that showed continuity with political understandings created in the course of the wartime contestation of power that has been described in the earlier chapters of this book, a narrative that served to justify the party's control over the resources of the state, while this same control allowed it to silence alternative interpretations. Accounts from rural Huambo province give an indication of how the roles and authority of the state and the party were understood. In one incident, tensions rose after the local administration installed a water pump in a village. When a group of people who identified with UNITA tried to draw water from the pump, MPLA members chased them away, saying that UNITA people had no right to use a pump that had been installed by an MPLA government. When a priest spoke out against the rivalry during Mass, MPLA members accused him of being a '*padre da UNITA*' (UNITA priest), and he eventually left the area after receiving death threats. In the same district, teachers who had previously worked for UNITA applied to work in the state education system and were told that in order to do so, they must receive MPLA membership cards. These cases illustrate how enjoyment of the rights of citizenship, whether as a beneficiary of state infrastructure or employment, could be made contingent on aligning oneself publicly with the MPLA. In this political climate, it is perhaps not surprising that in some villages that had been contested by the MPLA and UNITA during the civil war, there was no visible UNITA presence in the first decade of peace. In one village, I asked a group of elders whether parties other than the MPLA had representatives in the village. After they had discussed this question among themselves for several minutes, they responded, 'Here we have two committees, a church committee for spiritual matters and an MPLA committee for political matters. We have no need of any other committee.' People who formerly worked for UNITA could remain in these villages only on condition of denying any voluntary links to UNITA in the past. If they admitted to having spent time with UNITA, they would say that this was only because they were abducted and forced to work. People in the villages spoke of a fear that a vote for UNITA would mean a resumption of war but also a fear that the vote was not secret and that voting for the opposition would bring punishment.

The result of this strategy in the rural Central Highlands before the 2008 election was a dramatic reversal of UNITA's 1992 electoral success in the region. This needs to be understood in the context of the balance of military power during the two elections. The 1992 election had taken place at a time when UNITA retained military control over substantial areas and, through the propagation of its narratives of nationhood and identity, had ensured that its control was hegemonic. The nature of the Bicesse agreement did nothing to change the division of state-like power and its associated hegemony between the MPLA and UNITA, with the result that UNITA secured a majority of the vote in the Central Highlands, although it was defeated by the MPLA at the national level. In the 2008 elections, following the extension of the government's control over the whole national territory and the political processes described in this and the previous chapter, the MPLA won 82.05% of the vote to UNITA's 13.51% in Huambo province and 74.93% to UNITA's 18.25% in Bié.

The tight control over political discourse in rural villages was linked to the MPLA's incorporation of traditional authority structures into the party and civil administrative hierarchy. This was nothing new in Angola. The colonial government paid salaries and gave uniforms to traditional leaders. During the civil war, UNITA, as we have seen, approached *sobas* as its first point of contact with rural communities. The MPLA, initially suspicious of traditional authority on ideological grounds, had by the early 1980s realised the practical value of working through traditional leaders in those small parts of the countryside that fell under the control of the state during the war. As the FAA took back territory from UNITA in the 1990s, the *sobas* were the government's first point of contact as it sought a new political contract with rural communities that had previously been beyond its control. The soba occupies an ambiguous position in the Angolan political and administrative order, but this is an ambiguity that functions to the benefit of the ruling party. *Sobas* will typically describe their role as being one of 'the voice of the people' and the embodiment of the collective aspirations of the community. People who live in the village seldom challenge this conception of the *soba's* role. But when this conception is combined with a reality in which the *soba* receives a salary from a local administration that is for all practical purposes indistinguishable from the party, the result is the closure of any public discussion other than that approved by the party-state. Far from standing above politics, the figure of the *soba* embodies the collapse of the distinction between state and party.[9]

One *soba* who had worked with UNITA during the war told how after the war, because he refused to forswear his UNITA loyalty, the local administration had simply appointed a new incumbent to the role of *soba*. Since the authority of the *soba* rested on his capacity to control state patronage, there was little that he could do to resist his removal from office. He left his house and went to live with close family members outside the village. Another *soba* in a more remote district who refused to renounce UNITA retained the sympathy of his villagers, perhaps because his lands were too far from the administration to be of great concern to the MPLA. The administration nevertheless cut off the stipend that is regularly paid to traditional leaders. The incorporation of the *sobas* into the MPLA-dominated administration not only limited the possibilities of political discourse in rural villages but also served to legitimise violence against opponents of the MPLA. Most of the political violence that has taken place in the Central Highlands since the war has comprised attacks by government supporters against UNITA. These were noted first in the months before the 2008 elections and began again early in 2011. At least some of these attacks appear to have been prompted by memories of the war. In Londwimbali, for example, a group of a hundred MPLA supporters attacked a crowd that had gathered for a UNITA rally. A local journalist reported that the attackers had told him: 'We don't want UNITA, who made us suffer, we only want the government here – UNITA killed our families and destroyed our houses and fields.'[10] Early in 2012, again with elections on the horizon, there were further incidents of violence when UNITA members tried to hoist their party flag in two villages in the south of Huambo province. UNITA blamed the tensions on the fact that traditional leaders had been 'instrumentalised' by the MPLA, while the MPLA accused UNITA of trying to place its flag 'by force' in a community where the villagers did not want it.[11]

---

[9] See Aslak Orre, *Kalandula and the CACS: Voice or Accountability*, CMI Working Paper 2009:5 (Chr. Michelsen Institut 2009), 13, available online at http://www.cmi.no/publications/file/3 367-kalandu-and-the-cacs-voice-or-accountability.pdfa and Aslak Orre and Christian Larssen, '*How Can the Elections Help Us Quell Hunger': Final Report: A Mid-Term Review of Norwegian Support to UNDP's Trust Fund for Civic Education* (UNDP, 2008), 5, available online at http://www.cmi.no/publications/file/3149-how-can-the-elections-help-us-quell-hunger.pdf, accessed 22 January 2015.

[10] Interview with journalist, Huambo, August 2008.

[11] Club-K, 'Graves confrontos entre militantes da UNITA e do MPLA no Huambo' (29 February 2012), available online at http://www.club-k.net/index.php?option=com_content&view=artic le&id=10219%3Agraves-confrontos-entre-militantes-da-unita-e-do-mpla-no-huambo&catid=23 %3Apolitica&Itemid=123, accessed 25 January 2015.

People's attitudes towards political authority in the villages are the legacy of a particular historical experience. Many people had experienced conquest, removal or displacement that involved a change of military control. Those who had survived these changes knew that their survival was dependent on accepting the authority of whichever movement was in command at the time. This acceptance involved denying their previous acceptance of the other movement. The state's extension of its authority over the whole of Angola after 2002 was interpreted in exactly the same manner as the partisan contestation of power during the war. People in the villages continued to refer to the FAA as FAPLA. As we have seen, the state and the MPLA did nothing to dispel this; on the contrary, they positively encouraged it. *Sobas* were unaware of whether their role in the administration required them to be responsible to the local administration or to the local structures of the MPLA; since in most cases the same set of officials represented both the party and the state, the distinction had little practical significance. Similarly, villagers spoke of two campaigns before the 2008 elections: a registration campaign and an (MPLA) election campaign. The same officials visited the villages twice, first in their capacity as state functionaries to register voters and then in their capacity as party activists to tell people to vote for the MPLA. In the villages, then, the experience of conflict had caused the ideologies of the war to have a particular kind of impact on people's understanding of political authority, which persisted and continued to be instrumentalised in peacetime.

The villages of the Central Highlands are, clearly, not representative of Angola. Yet understandings of politics based on the experience of the war persist also in the ideologies that are articulated at the national level and in the cities, even if not in the same way as in the villages. Angola, after all, has a constitution guaranteeing multiparty democracy. In its towns, political parties maintain branches and conduct campaigns before elections. *Sobas* do not have the authority to stifle political discussion among urban populations. In the towns, the MPLA discourse is not the only discourse. Yet in the towns as much as in the villages, MPLA discourse asserts the party's legitimacy by drawing both upon the understandings of politics that were gestated in wartime and upon memories of the war and of events since the war ended.

At the level of national politics, the assertion of the MPLA's role in bringing peace to Angola is reinforced by an emphasis on the party's role in post-war reconstruction. This reconstruction discourse informed how and where money was spent on infrastructure, particularly in the period preceding the 2008 election campaign. The towns of the interior had seen little in the way of state-led reconstruction since 2002, but multiple projects were visible by 2007. Roads were resurfaced to connect the provincial capitals, a new hospital was built in Lubango and electrical generators were installed in Saurimo. The politically targeted nature of this reconstruction programme was confirmed when dos Santos, a man who previously had rarely travelled outside Luanda other than to take trips abroad, undertook daily visits to Angolan provincial capitals in the two weeks before the election in 2008 in order to unveil new projects. Although dos Santos had promised as head of state not to take part in the MPLA electoral campaign, his national tour acquired a partisan character. MPLA party banners, caps and t-shirts dominated the scene whenever he launched a new project. In Huambo, reconstruction was concentrated in the Cidade Alta, the neighbourhood that had remained longest under MPLA control during the war. The square that is home to the main provincial government offices were the first to be restored. Next came the restoration of a few blocks of nearby commercial buildings. The centrepiece of the redevelopment was a park, which was fitted out with illuminated fountains, a children's play area and concealed speakers through which music could be piped. Dos Santos officially launched the renovated Cidade Alta during the week before the election.[12] In an echo of the days of one-party rule, teachers and other state employees were told that they would face disciplinary action if they did not attend the rally.

The portrayal of the MPLA as peacemaker is complemented by a discourse that names UNITA as solely responsible for the war in the past and a continuing threat in the present. The reconciliatory words that accompanied the Luena peace agreement disappeared as the elections approached in 2008. In April that year, the minister of defence, Kundi Paihama, stated publicly and without foundation that UNITA was continuing to smuggle weapons into Angola and planned to return to war.[13] Later the same year, days before the election, state television included on the evening news an interview with a woman who was weeping as she recalled family members who had been killed in the war with UNITA and accused post-war UNITA leader Isaías Samakuva of lying by saying that his party had moved on from its military past. The obvious anti-UNITA message during the period before the election went alongside a more subtle set of messages that linked the government and the MPLA to stability and continuity and hinted at the possibility of a return to war.

Just as the MPLA during the civil war deployed a particular version of nationalist history to assert its sole claim to political legitimacy, so since the end of the war it has revived historical claims about its unique role in

---

[12] Huambo Digital, 'PR Desloca-se hoje ao Huambo' (26 August 2008), available online at http://huambodigital.com/pr-desloca-se-hoje-ao-huambo/, accessed 25 January 2015.

[13] AllAfrica.com, 'Angola: Africa Insight – Country's MPLA Hits the Campaign Trail Months to Elections' 12 February 2008, available online at http://allafrica.com/stories/200804101230.html, accessed 25 January 2015.

liberating Angola from colonial rule and in defending the nation against South African aggression. The twentieth anniversary in 2008 of the battle of Cuito Cuanavale showed how ideas about history remained as important to MPLA ideology as they had during the years of the civil war. It also illustrated how the MPLA view of history, rooted as it was in the contestation of civil war, sat uncomfortably with the ideas of reconciliation that were put forward in 2002 and with the notion of an inclusive multiparty democracy in which national identity might be free of partisan affiliation. Dos Santos stated that 'The battle, won by Angolan forces, gave rise to profound changes in Southern Africa, namely the application of UN Security Council Resolution 435/78, thus opening new perspectives for the fall of the apartheid regime in South Africa and the independence of Namibia.'[14] This rendering of the battle erases the fact that there were Angolans on both sides of the conflict at Cuito Cuanavale and the fact that Cuba's military backing for the MPLA was decisive.

The MPLA again evoked memories of anti-colonial struggle and civil war in its response to the street protests in Luanda against dos Santos's prolonged tenure that persisted throughout 2011. A counter-demonstration that the MPLA organised in March was promoted as a march in support of peace and development. The MPLA's provincial secretary for Luanda, Bento Bento, announced the march by insisting that 'the Angolan people crave only the consolidation of peace that will allow you to enjoy a planned development, as evidence of the fruits of nine years of peace and tranquillity' and appealed to Angolans to say no to 'disrespect, destruction, disorder and all that translates into an attack against democracy and stability in the country'.[15] Dos Santos delivered an address to the MPLA Central Committee that emphasised the party's role in revolutionary struggle against colonialism and contrasted it with how he interpreted the aims of anti-government activists.

> For these people, revolution means bringing people together and holding demonstrations, even when not authorised, to insult, to denigrate, to cause disturbance and confusion, with the intention of obliging the police to act and for them to be able to say there is no freedom of expression and no respect for rights.[16]

---

[14] *Seminário Angolense*, year 4, edition 256, 15 March 2008.

[15] Angop, 'MPLA realiza marcha patriótica em apoio à paz e ao desenvolvimento do país', (1 March 2011), available online at http://www.portalangop.co.ao/motix/pt_pt/noticias /politica/2011/2/9/MPLA-realiza-marcha-patriotica-apoio-paz-desenvolvimento-pais,08f5 1273-1147-4aad-bc08-b63ba36748bc.html, accessed 25 January 2015.

[16] Angop, 'Discurso do Presidente José Eduardo dos Santos na reunião do Comité Central', (15 April 2011), available online at http://www.portalangop.co.ao/motix/pt_pt /noticias/politica/2011/3/15/Discurso-Presidente-Jose-Eduardo-dos-Santos-reuniao -Comite-Central,e545cbc5-1a17-43e7-a00a-f7f3d1f3dbd4.html, accessed 25 January 2015.

The word '*confusão*' (confusion) was regularly used during the war as a euphemism for violence. With this history, '*confusão*' carries connotations more sinister than the English equivalent and provides a useful sleight of hand for a politician trying to erase the distinction between a lively protest and a threat to social and political order. Although the partisan violence seen in 2008 was less common in the run-up to the 2012 election, both Bento Bento and former Defence Minister Kundi Paihama revived specific accusations against UNITA, hinting that it was planning an insurrection along the lines of the uprisings earlier that year in north Africa – accusations that UNITA quickly denied.[17]

Previous chapters have shown how during the civil war, each political movement sought hegemonic control within the territory that it controlled by limiting public discourse and by propagating narratives about its own history and relationship with the Angolan nation. The result of this was to impose limits on the range of political expression that was possible on either side so that people came to express their identity as 'UNITA people' or 'government people'. Accepting these identities went together with articulating certain views about the legitimacy of each movement, views that were embedded in narratives about each movement's history and its effectiveness as a defender and as a provider. This chapter has shown how this process has continued in a post-war Angola dominated by a state that remains indistinguishable from the MPLA and which continues to assert its ownership of Angolan nationhood by branding its opponents as threats to a peaceful consensus that is the gift of the MPLA. The legacy of the war is evident not only in the persistence of a partisan notion of nationalism that links the national interest to the incumbency of a particular party. The selective memorialisation of the war and its consequences, from anti-colonial struggle through the civil war and its conclusion, also forms the basis of the MPLA's claims to legitimacy. This enforcing of a particular version of public memory is guaranteed by state domination of the media in the cities and by the MPLA's incorporation

---

[17] Angop, 'Bento Bento acusa UNITA de querer derrubar o Presidente José Eduardo dos Santos', (15 September 2011), available online at http://club-k.net/index.php?option=com _content&view=article&id=8836:bento-bento-acusa-unita-de-querer-derrubar-o-presid ente-jose-eduardo-dos-santos&catid=9:preto-e-branco&Itemid=143, accessed 25 January 2015. Voice of America Portuguese Service, 'Numa rejeita rumores de que pretende golpe de estado em Angola', (22 September 2011), available online at http://www.voaportugues .com/content/article-09-22-2011-kalamata-numa-130372013/1261223.html, accessed 25 January 2015. Club-K, 'UNITA considera inaceitáveis promessas de violência de Kundi Paihama', (8 August 2012), available online at http://club-k.net/index.php?option=com_content&vie w=article&id=12330:unita-considera-inaceitaveis-promessas-de-violencia-de-kundi-paihama -&catid=23:politica&Itemid=123, accessed 25 January 2015.

of traditional authority in the countryside. While the MPLA's post-war nationalist discourse, as Messiant notes, is a call to 'rally behind the banner of the MPLA' in the interests of national unity,[18] it also echoes the wartime nationalism that positioned UNITA as an alien threat. The idea of reconstruction, which positions the MPLA as the party whose role it is to repair the damage done by UNITA both to physical infrastructure and to national unity, serves to link state building to wartime legitimacy.

All this was made possible by the particular manner in which the war was brought to an end. The previous chapter showed how the counterinsurgency tactics of the last years of the war and the consequent movement of people from UNITA-held to government-held territory was a political as well as a military strategy. Given that political identity was so closely bound up with military control, the bringing of people into government-controlled areas made them '*povo do governo*'. Despite the counterinsurgency, many thousands of people were still living in areas dominated by UNITA when Savimbi was killed. Had these people remained where they were, or even if they had been resettled as intact communities in government-controlled areas, this would have allowed the survival of communities whose common understanding of their place in Angolan history had been inherited from what they had learnt from UNITA. The gathering of the last remaining people into quartering areas and their subsequent dispersal to towns and villages throughout Angola prevented such an outcome. It ensured that when people left the quartering areas, they had to resettle as an identifiable minority in communities where the hegemonic discourse was an MPLA one. At the national level, the ending of the conflict without any renegotiation of the political system guaranteed the MPLA's control over the resources of the state, which in turn allowed the party to consolidate voter support in the countryside through the incorporation of traditional leadership and to claim ownership of peace and reconstruction at the level of national politics.

---

[18] Christine Messiant, 'The Mutation of Hegemonic Domination', in Patrick Chabal and Nuno Vidal (eds.), *Angola: The Weight of History* (London, 2007), 120.

Conclusion

This book began with a problem about political identity: what did it mean to be a 'member' of UNITA or to be a 'government person' during the Angolan war? The subsequent chapters examined how political identity was understood at different moments in the conflict and the relationship between identity and changes in political control. This question has been overlooked or taken for granted in previous accounts of the politics of the Angolan conflict. One broad body of scholarship on Angola has examined the origins of Angola's rival political elites and the differences among them and within them based on historical experience or ethnolinguistic and class difference. While this body of work deals to an extent with political identity formation, its ambit does not extend much beyond independence.[1] Messiant's later writings chart the contestation of political legitimacy in independent Angola but largely at the elite level. Mabeko-Tali addresses the difficulties that the MPLA leadership confronted in securing hegemony in the immediate post-independence period. Heywood's work demonstrates the importance of ideology and identity in how UNITA asserted its legitimacy. In this book, I have built upon the insights of these scholars by examining political relationships on both sides of the conflict and how they changed over time.[2]

[1]   Jean-Michel Mabeko-Tali, *Dissidências e poder do estado: O MPLA perante si próprio* (1962–1977) (Luanda, 2001); John Marcum, *The Angolan Revolution, Volume I (The Anatomy of an Explosion, 1950–1962)* (Cambridge, MA, 1969); John Marcum, *The Angolan Revolution, Volume II (Exile Politics and Guerrilla Warfare, 1962–1976)* (Cambridge, MA, 1978); Christine Messiant, *1961: L'Angola Coloniale, Histoire et Société. Les Premises du Mouvement Nationaliste* (Basel, 2006).
[2]   Christine Messiant, *L'Angola Postcolonial: 1. Guerre et Paix sans Démocratisation* (Paris, 2008); Christine Messiant, *L'Angola Postcolonial: 2. Sociologie Politique d'une Oléocratie* (Paris, 2008); Linda Heywood, 'Unita and Ethnic Nationalism in Angola', *Journal of Modern African Studies* 27.1 (1989), 47–66; Linda Heywood, 'Towards an Understanding of Modern Political Ideology in Africa: the Case of the Ovimbundu of Angola', *The Journal of*

Accounts of the conflict that focus on the calculations of foreign actors and their consequences in Angola are interested primarily in the relationship between foreign governments and Angolan elites and tend to leave aside lower-level questions about the relationship between elites and other sections of Angolan society. The moral urgency of the struggle against apartheid in South Africa forms a normative master narrative for these studies, and this overshadows the internal complexities of Angolan politics.[3] Studies based in the political economy of mineral extraction provide a useful account of material incentives and of how conflict is paid for but are less concerned with processes of political mobilisation or the relationship between the elites and the adherents of a movement.[4] The material and ideational underpinnings of conflict are undeniably related, but in this respect, the testimonies presented in this book suggest the local distribution of everyday commodities such as salt, soap and foodstuffs was no less important than international trade in petroleum or diamonds.

By examining closely the discourses of power and authority in Angola and how these were articulated at different levels of society and how they changed over time, my findings demonstrate the contingent character of political adherence. They echo Kalyvas's suggestion that military control is the primary determinant of how civilians express their political adherence in civil war.[5] It would, however, be wrong to assume that such an explanation renders redundant the notion that people are motivated to support a political movement on ideological grounds or because they believe that the movement represents their interests. The interviews quoted in this book reveal that questions of ideology were indeed important, not only to elites but to the followers of political movements too, but that these ideological questions had only

Modern African Studies 36.1 (1998), 139–167; Linda Heywood, *Contested Power in Angola: 1840s to the Present* (Rochester, NY, 2002.)

3 William Minter, *Apartheid's Contras: An Inquiry into the Roots of War in Angola and Mozambique* (London, 1994); Piero Gleijeses, *Conflicting Missions: Havana, Washington, and Africa, 1959–1976* (Chapel Hill, NC, 2002); Piero Gleijeses, *Visions of Freedom: Havana, Washington, Pretoria and the Struggle for Southern Africa 1976–1991* (Chapel Hill, NC, 2013). Fernando Andresen Guimarães, *The Origins of the Angolan Civil War: Foreign Intervention and Domestic Political Conflict* (Basingstoke, 2001) has presented a considered account of the interaction between international and national concerns in creating the conditions for war in Angola.

4 Le Billon's outstanding political economy analysis acknowledges that material incentives are only one of many interrelated factors that must be considered in understanding conflict: Phillippe le Billon, 'Angola's Political Economy of War: The Role of Oil and Diamonds', *African Affairs* 100 (2001), 56–57. See also Jakkie Cilliers and Christian Dietrich (eds.), *Angola's War Economy: The Role of Oil and Diamonds* (Pretoria, 2000).

5 Stathis Kalyvas, *The Logic of Violence in Civil War* (Cambridge, 2006).

a tangential relationship to the global ideologies associated with the Cold War. The interviews show also that people who lived under the control of one movement came to believe that that movement was acting in their best interests, whether minimally as a guarantor of security or more positively as a provider of services. Such beliefs were nevertheless subject to change along with shifts in military and political control.

I have explained the relationship between political control and political adherence by offering a historical account of the interplay between the two and of the ideological strategies that the rival political leaders employed to make their rule hegemonic. During the months before independence in 1975, the MPLA, UNITA and the FNLA struggled to occupy the vacuum of authority left by Portugal as the colonial forces and administration left Angola. At this point, the Angolan movements competed for popular support on an equal footing. In the Central Highlands, UNITA initially gained the political advantage amid a military stalemate by presenting itself as indigenous to the region, while many town dwellers supported the MPLA on the basis of its ideological appeals. However, in the cities of the Central Highlands, UNITA's early advantage counted for little once the MPLA had secured Cuban military support and the South African soldiers backing UNITA had left. Those people who remained with UNITA were its own elite, plus the town dwellers who had fled the cities with UNITA and those among the rural population who had known only UNITA control. Even if people explained their political affiliations retrospectively in terms of choice on the basis of ideology, it is clear that for many of them, their adherence to one movement was conditioned first by fear of the other movement and that much of the political work of both movements consisted of cultivating fear of the adversary. In the years that followed, the MPLA made efforts to move people into the areas that it controlled. This had the effect of changing perceptions of the MPLA among people who had previously experienced only the control of UNITA. For some, this meant acceptance of the MPLA simply as the guarantor of their security. But others, more specifically those people whose skills allowed them to be productively employed in the structures of the MPLA state, very soon realised that life in government areas had advantages that life with UNITA could never hope to offer. Farmers were on the whole more sceptical than the town dwellers about the political movements, and if they spoke of adherence to either movement, it was expressed in terms of the need to avoid conflict rather than of any more positive expectations.

If we were to draw our conclusions only from the years following independence, we might infer that military control was the chief determinant of political identities and that identities shifted along with the conquest of territory. This, however, was not the case in 1993. On the contrary, UNITA's occupation of Huambo and much of Kuito during that year served only to breed antipathy towards UNITA in those cities. To understand this, we need to take into account the political advantage that the MPLA had acquired through its incumbency in the cities and towns of the Central Highlands in the decade and a half after independence. In 1975, both UNITA and the MPLA had appeared initially as civilian movements, and both had later taken up arms against each other and against people who were perceived as belonging to the opposing movement. In 1993 and 1994, the fiercest fighting was experienced in those areas where government control lasted longest. For those whose first encounter with UNITA was one of violence, the presence of UNITA was incompatible with notions of legitimacy based on criteria that included the ability to keep order. The people who lived in areas where UNITA took control in 1993 by means of violence also happened to be those whose connections with the MPLA state were closest. For them, UNITA's actions only served to confirm propaganda that the MPLA had disseminated about the nature of the enemy.

Conversely, UNITA was tolerated in the early 1990s or even accepted by those whose experience of UNITA control had not been primarily a violent one. In the rural areas discussed in Chapter 8, the interviewees' accounts confirm the conclusions of human rights investigators that people during this period endured forced labour and some of the worst violence of the entire war, but they also make clear that this violence was not uniform. UNITA's behaviour towards the rural population became more violent and predatory as its position became weaker. People who had been farming in UNITA areas were either forced to migrate with UNITA soldiers, or went, voluntarily or not, to government-held areas. In this process, people came to accept that going to a government zone and being counted among the '*povo do governo*' was a less bad option than staying with UNITA. This account emphasises the interplay between ideas of identity as lived and identity as imposed and the political functionality in the slippage of meaning between the two. It also demonstrates the continuities in understandings of politics, understandings that have their origins in anti-colonial struggle, throughout a succession of contingencies that ensured that these same understandings produced different political consequences at different times. The process of how, at the end of the war, people who had once been 'UNITA people' could in a short space of time come to see themselves as 'government people' is comprehensible only by examining the genealogy of the ideologies that defined political belonging.

The ideological claims that were made in the course of the Angolan conflict were varied. Frequently, such claims reflected an awareness of struggles that had gone before rather than the realities of the Angolan situation. The MPLA turned to Marxism-Leninism under the leadership of an 'administrative bourgeoisie',[6] while UNITA invoked Maoist ideas of peasant struggle in a war in which neither side sought to address the interests of peasants as a class. But the most consistent ideological claim, and one that was common to both protagonists in the conflict, was to be found in the ideas about political authority and legitimacy that were embodied in the practices of the two movements and which were articulated in the official discourses of both movements into an ideology that linked political legitimacy to normative ideas about the functions of a state. In understanding how the idea of the state functioned in the ideologies of the Angolan war, it is useful to recall the argument by Philip Abrams that the 'state idea' might be more significant than the 'state system' and that the state is above all 'an exercise in legitimation'.[7] The elites of the MPLA and of UNITA and the people who at various times had been associated with either or both parties shared a common basis for understanding the authority and legitimacy of a state or a state-like entity.

To recapitulate briefly the normative characteristics of the state that was constituted in the ideologies of the MPLA and UNITA: first, the state defined and embodied the nation. The association between nation building and state building was a historically contingent one, conditioned by the Angolan elites' knowledge of the international system in which they found themselves and more specifically of the experience of the states that had become independent in the twenty years before Angolan independence and which had envisaged their role as drivers of modernisation. This concern with modernisation brings us to the second characteristic of the state-like norm: that it bore responsibility for guaranteeing material needs. Political legitimacy depended on being seen to be doing things – on actions as much as on words. Third, the state exercised a prerogative of violence. This exercise consisted not only in bearing arms but also in defining which uses of violence were legitimate and which were illegitimate. Because legitimate violence was defensive violence, the discursive process of legitimating violence was intimately linked to the process of defining the common national interest. By definition, peace and order were where the

---

6   Mabeko-Tali, *Dissidências, II.ºVol.*, 153.

7   Philip Abrams, 'Notes on the Difficulty of Studying the State (1977)', *Journal of Historical Sociology* 1.1 (1988), 58–89. This perspective has subsequently been applied to questions of authority in postcolonial states: Akhil Gupta, 'Blurred Boundaries: The Discourse of Corruption, the Culture of Politics, and the Imagined State', *American Ethnologist* 22.2 (1995), 375–402; Thomas Blom Hansen and Finn Stepputat, *States of Imagination: Ethnographic Explorations of the Postcolonial State* (Durham, NC, 2001); Thomas Blom Hansen and Finn Stepputat (eds.), *Sovereign Bodies: Citizens, Migrants, and States in the Postcolonial World* (Princeton, NJ, 2005).

state was. Part of the idea of the state was the idea of peace. Recall here the remarks quoted in Chapter 2 by a civil servant who had dedicated his life to the service of the MPLA party and of the state that it constructed:

> [UNITA undertook] certain tasks ... in the midst of the conditions of war ... safeguarding certain health services, certain education services. These functioned, but not to the extent that people would have wished them to be in peacetime – they were services in a climate of war.[8]

What is important here is that he evokes peace itself as one of the criteria for the creation of state-like legitimacy. The idea that ownership of the idea of peace may endow a government with legitimacy emerged in many interviews, with barely educated rural people as well as with members of the urban intelligentsia. The later chapters have shown that by the end of the 1990s, life with UNITA was synonymous with life in a war zone, and this caused many thousands of one-time adherents to reject UNITA's legitimacy in the final years of the war.

In short, there was widespread agreement on the normative question of how and what the Angolan state should be. What was at stake was which elite was the rightful heir to the authority that was conferred by the idea of the state, a question that was elided with another question about which elite was better able to make a reality of the notional state. The changes in political adherence over the course of the war can best be understood as a response to changing circumstances and changing realities, alongside the persistence of a common commitment to norms throughout the years of the war. Although the control of territory passed back and forth between the MPLA and UNITA over the course of the war, in terms of political identity, the flow was largely unidirectional. People who started out with UNITA and were wooed by its promise of statehood were liable to change their views once they encountered the real state that was offered by the MPLA. In Chapter 6, I referred to Messiant's observation about the 'properly totalitarian' character of UNITA alongside an MPLA that was something less than totalitarian.[9] If UNITA's control of people was absolute, it was because it had the opportunity to create and to shape a society according to the military and political needs of UNITA itself. This 'totalitarian' control was possible precisely because UNITA was not presiding over a real state. Jamba was as close as UNITA came to realising its aspiration to statehood, and those who were impressed by Jamba's simulacrum

---

[8] Interviewee 31, Huambo, May 2008.
[9] Christine Messiant, 'Angola, Les Voies de l'Ethnisation et de la Decomposition: I. De la Guerre à la Paix (1975–1991)', in Christine Messiant, *L'Angola Postcolonial: 1. Guerre et Paix Sans Democratisation* (Paris, 2008), 33–92. Originally published in *Lusotopie* I (1–2) (1994).

of state building justified their admiration in terms of the supposedly superior standards of education and health care there that compensated for the
lack of concrete and asphalt. It is no coincidence that after the end of the
war, the people who continued most enthusiastically to defend UNITA's political worth were those who had spent time in Jamba. But for those who knew
UNITA only from its bases in the bush of the Central Highlands and who had
the skills that would allow them to make a useful contribution to an urban
society, the MPLA offered a role in a process of state building that UNITA
could only talk about. After the mid-1990s, the government's military superiority put an end to Jamba and to the political imaginaries that it sustained. It
also put an end to UNITA's efforts to sustain a consensual relationship with
the rural people of the Central Highlands.

The Angolan war was never a conflict between communities of people
defined on the basis of mutually incompatible prior interests. Rather, I have
demonstrated how the reality of conflict served to shape how people perceived
their own interests. The MPLA won the war through military might. But the
ending of the war was the culmination of a process whereby firepower, blood-
shed and starvation were employed to transform the possibilities of what was
imaginable. The conquest of territory and the relocation of people were less
significant in themselves than as the enabling conditions for a political process. Of course, the 2002 peace agreement did not signal the end of history for
Angola, and opposition parties and activists have since then continued to challenge not only what they see as the MPLA's policy failures but also the party's
implicit claims to be the sole representative of the Angolan people. The question of national identity, in other words, remains unresolved. Nevertheless,
the end of the war, on the terms that were determined by the MPLA leadership, represented the dismantling of the *povo da UNITA* in the sense of
an imagined community of people whose identity was defined by a political
entity that presented itself as a state and whose vision of its own legitimacy was
founded on the assumption of the illegitimacy of the MPLA.

Index

BOOKS IN THIS SERIES

Lightning Source UK Ltd.
Milton Keynes UK
UKHW040346150219
337300UK00001B/40/P

9 781108 468862